Integrating Serverless Architecture

Using Azure Functions, Cosmos DB, and SignalR Service

Rami Vemula

Apress®

Integrating Serverless Architecture: Using Azure Functions, Cosmos DB, and SignalR Service

Rami Vemula
Visakhapatnam, Andhra Pradesh, India

ISBN-13 (pbk): 978-1-4842-4488-3   ISBN-13 (electronic): 978-1-4842-4489-0
https://doi.org/10.1007/978-1-4842-4489-0

Managing Director, Apress Media LLC: Welmoed Spahr
Acquisitions Editor: Smriti Srivastava
Development Editor: Siddhi Chavan
Coordinating Editor: Shrikant Vishwakarma

Cover designed by eStudioCalamar

Cover image designed by Freepik (www.freepik.com)

Distributed to the book trade worldwide by Springer Science+Business Media New York, 233 Spring Street, 6th Floor, New York, NY 10013. Phone 1-800-SPRINGER, fax (201) 348-4505, e-mail orders-ny@springer-sbm.com, or visit www.springeronline.com. Apress Media, LLC is a California LLC and the sole member (owner) is Springer Science + Business Media Finance Inc (SSBM Finance Inc). SSBM Finance Inc is a **Delaware** corporation.

For information on translations, please e-mail rights@apress.com, or visit http://www.apress.com/rights-permissions.

Apress titles may be purchased in bulk for academic, corporate, or promotional use. eBook versions and licenses are also available for most titles. For more information, reference our Print and eBook Bulk Sales web page at http://www.apress.com/bulk-sales.

Any source code or other supplementary material referenced by the author in this book is available to readers on GitHub via the book's product page, located at www.apress.com/978-1-4842-4488-3. For more detailed information, please visit http://www.apress.com/source-code.

Printed on acid-free paper

Dedicated to my maternal grandmother Kanaka Maha Lakshmi and in (loving) memory of my grandparents: Rowgi (maternal grandfather), Venkaiah (paternal grandfather), and Raghavamma (paternal grandmother).

Table of Contents

About the Author

Rami Vemula is a technology consultant with more than eight years of experience in delivering scalable web and cloud solutions using Microsoft technologies and platforms, including ASP.NET MVC/Web API, .NET Core, ASP.NET Core, JQuery, C#, Entity Framework, SQL Server, and Azure.

He currently works for Microsoft India Global Delivery as a consultant. As part of his work, he architects, develops, and maintains technical solutions to various clients in public and private sectors.

Although web technology is his primary area of focus, Rami has also worked on big data analytics using HDInsight, Universal Windows Platform (UWP) apps, containerization using Docker, etc. He is also interested in providing streamlined DevOps integration flows through which development teams can achieve greater productivity. Nowadays he promotes open source technologies, platforms, and tools to build cross-platform solutions.

He is a Microsoft Certified ASP.Net and Azure Developer. He was a Microsoft Most Valuable Professional (MVP) in ASP.NET from 2011 to 2014 and an active trainer. In his free time, he enjoys answering technical questions at StackOverflow and forums.asp. net. He loves to share his technical experience through his blog at http://intstrings. com/ramivemula. Apart from technology, his other interests include movies, drama, and theater arts.

He holds a master's degree in Electrical Engineering from California State University, Long Beach. He is married and lives with his wife, children, and parents in Hyderabad, India.

You can reach Rami at rami.ramilu@gmail.com or https://twitter.com/RamiRamilu.

About the Technical Reviewer

Vrat Agarwal is a software architect, author, blogger, Microsoft MVP, C# Corner MVP, speaker, and mentor. He is also a TOGAF Certified Architect and a Certified Scrum Master (CSM). He currently works as a principal architect at T-Mobile Inc., USA. He started working with Microsoft .NET during its first beta release. He is passionate about people, process, and technology and loves to contribute to the .NET community. He lives in Redmond, WA with his wife Rupali, two daughters Pearly and Arshika, and a puppy named Angel. He blogs at http://www.MyPassionFor.Net and can be reached at vidya_mct@yahoo.com or on Twitter @dotnetauthor.

Acknowledgments

I would first like to thank my parents—Ramanaiah and RajaKumari—my wife Sneha, my three year old daughter Akshaya, and the rest of my family—my in-laws, aunts, uncles, cousins, and kids—for their valuable support. Without that support, I could not have achieved all the wonderful milestones and accomplishments in my life. Their consistent encouragement, patience, and guidance gave me the strength to overcome all the hurdles and kept me moving forward.

My serverless architecture endeavor would not have started without Ashwani Verma, Architect at Microsoft. He introduced me to the principles of software architecture and mentored me through the process of transforming complex technical challenges to reliable solutions.

I would like to thank Srikanth Pragada for introducing me to the world of .NET and for teaching me how to deliver technical solutions with the utmost discipline.

My heartfelt thanks to Vishwas Lele, Rajesh Agarwal, and Nasir Mirza of Applied Information Sciences (AIS) for introducing me to Microsoft Azure. The extensive training provided by Vishwas not only helped me provide cloud optimized solutions but also changed my thought process in architecting cloud solutions. Rajesh and Nasir always had confidence in me and motivated me to have a strong desire for excellence.

I will always be indebted to Mahadevu Durga Prasad for encouraging me to explore new opportunities and for helping me reach my full potential.

I would like to thank my friends at Microsoft—Jeeva, Srikanth, Ujjayini, Praveen, Mohit, Sachin, Hemanth P, Hemanth K, and Dinesh—for believing in and supporting me throughout my technical expeditions. Thanks also to my friends at Deloitte—Rohit, Manoj, Vaibhav, Mohana Krishna, Chaitanya, Ibrahim and Bibin—for always inspiring me with their passion for technology.

Thanks to Nikhil Karkal, Smriti Srivastava, Shrikant Vishwakarma, Matthew Moodie, Siddhi Chavan, and the other amazing people at Apress for this wonderful opportunity and for making this a memorable journey. Thanks also to Vrat Agarwal for providing his valuable technical review.

ACKNOWLEDGMENTS

I greatly appreciate the Microsoft communities for their prompt responses to technical queries. Their consistent effort in keeping the online documentation (`https://docs.microsoft.com/en-us/`) up to date is unprecedented.

Last but not least, I would like to thank all my readers for their time and effort spent reading this book. Feel free to share your feedback about this book. It will help me deliver better content in the future. I look forward to your comments and suggestions.

Introduction

The current decade of modern technology is not just encouraging businesses to undergo a technology shift, but is also providing innovative architectural solutions to serve their customers in a better way. The strategies like *cloud first, mobile first* from software giants like Microsoft are very promising. They provide new cloud architectures with greatest computational power at affordable prices. Gone are the days when developers needed to write thousands of lines of code to automate business workflows; the new cloud services provide numerous easy options to create and maintain business orchestrations. This opened doors for a whole new era of customer focused innovation and automation.

In the recent past, serverless computing gained significant momentum because of its built-in capabilities to abstract infrastructure and provide highly scalable solutions. Microsoft started its journey of serverless computing through Azure Functions. The streamlined development experience, event-driven approach, and ability to integrate with other solutions made the Azure Functions a favorite for projects where the Rapid Application Development model is followed. The overall ease of maintaining Azure Functions made them unique in serverless architectures.

Integrating Serverless Architecture Using Azure Functions, Cosmos DB, and SignalR Service provides a holistic approach to design and development of a Twitter Bot application by leveraging Azure Functions. The different types of Azure Functions narrated in this book will empower you to make the right decisions while adopting Azure Functions to specific business requirements. Azure's Cosmos DB is used as the backend for the Twitter Bot application. This book illustrates the basic concepts of Cosmos DB along with its change feed mechanism through multiple examples. ASP.Net Core is the latest open source web framework from Microsoft and is used in this book to build the Twitter Bot web application.

Overall, this book will provide deeper insights into the serverless architectures, which will empower you to build scalable cloud solutions. Additionally, this book dive deep into the following topics:

- Integrate Azure Functions with Azure SignalR Service to broadcast real-time messages.

- Store and retrieve secrets of Azure Functions from Azure Key Vault.

- Secure Azure Functions by enabling Twitter identity authentication using built-in app service authentication.

- Build Continuous Integration and Continuous Delivery pipelines for Azure Functions using Azure DevOps.

Chapter 1 introduces the Twitter Bot application that we are going to build in this book. Chapter 1 also illustrates the technology stack and the prerequisites of the Twitter Bot application along with its technical architecture. Chapter 2 introduces the world of Azure Functions, where we explore different features of the Azure Function app. In Chapter 2, we create a timer trigger-based Azure Function and integrate it with the custom dependency injection implementation. We also learn how to debug and publish an Azure Function from Visual Studio to the Azure environment.

In Chapter 3, we learn about the basics of the Azure Cosmos DB and its change feed mechanism. In the same chapter, we design a data model for the Twitter Bot application and create a C# repository pattern to perform data operations. At the end of Chapter 3, we create a Cosmos DB trigger-based Azure Function and integrate the repository pattern with existing functions.

In Chapter 4, we create and configure a service bus queue at Azure for our Twitter Bot application to decouple the dependencies between different functions. In this chapter, we integrate the Service Bus API with the existing Azure Functions and test the entire business workflow at an Azure environment. We integrate the Azure Key Vault service with Azure Functions in Chapter 5 to secure all the application secrets. In that same chapter, we learn how to implement logging and exception handling in Azure Functions.

Chapter 6 introduces the basic concepts of ASP.NET Core and material design techniques. In this chapter, we create the Twitter Bot web application and integrate it with ASP.NET Core Identity to enable customer authentication using the Twitter identity provider through the OAuth 2.0 protocol. In Chapter 7, we explore the new SignalR Service offering from Azure and integrate it with Azure Functions and the Twitter Bot web application. Chapter 8 details the security aspects of Azure Functions, where we integrate security flow from the Twitter Bot web app to Azure Functions using an authentication token.

Concepts related to Continuous Integration and Continuous Delivery (CI/CD) are discussed in Chapter 9. We create build and release definitions at Azure DevOps for the Twitter Bot application source code and automate the entire DevOps lifecycle.

As a last note, I encourage you to further explore Azure Function concepts like durable functions, function proxies, etc. As the digital world is transforming itself into microservices to serve a global audience, there is a need for technologies to collaborate and deliver high-performance, scalable solutions. Understanding and implementing the right technologies to enrich a business solution and building eminence around current-day technologies are the most common problems faced by software professionals and organizations in our fast-paced modern-day ecosystem. This book demonstrates an end-to-end application design through one of the latest serverless architecture paradigms and, in the process, attempts to build eminence around some of the latest technologies.

Let's get started...

CHAPTER 1

A New Era of Serverless Computing

Modern-day software engineering practices have evolved due to the fundamental improvements of automation techniques, computational speed, and operational strategies. The latest technologies and cloud platforms empowered software organizations and professionals to quickly adapt to new engineering practices without major technical and operational disruptions. The modernization of core software engineering practices like Agile development, customer focused testing, the Continuous Integration-Validation-Delivery cycle, predictive analytics, and more, have not only changed the process of building software but have also served as a foundation of a new software paradigm, *serverless computing*.

By leveraging the greatest computational power of cloud platforms, we can build highly scalable and reliable architectures with the help of serverless computing strategies. Software giants like Microsoft, Amazon, and Google deliver serverless computing capabilities by providing services through a pay-as-you-go subscription model. This model marked the last decade as the beginning of the serverless computing era. Serverless computing services are quickly emerging and maturing with new APIs, tools, monitoring, and debugging capabilities. Their cost-effective pricing models make them the first choice for many software organizations to incubate, develop, host, and maintain their products. Serverless architectures enables organizations and professionals to achieve fast-paced innovation through a rapid application development model.

In this chapter, we:

- Explore the fundamentals of serverless computing.

- Get introduced to the Twitter Bot application, which we build throughout this book.

- Define the scope of work for the Twitter Bot application.

1

© Rami Vemula 2019
R. Vemula, *Integrating Serverless Architecture*, https://doi.org/10.1007/978-1-4842-4489-0_1

- Learn about the logical and physical architectures of the Twitter Bot application.

- Set up the development environment on a local machine by installing the software prerequisites.

Introducing Serverless Computing

In this modern era of technology, businesses are not just focused on delivering great quality services to their customers but also strive to increase their footprint by breaking the geographical barriers through digital transformations. As business workflows, processes, and orchestrations became highly complex in order to achieve greater success through real-time customer-centric solutions, the traditional software design patterns and development strategies became equally complex to support extensive business requirements.

Cloud computing provides reliable, scalable, secured, cost-effective, sophisticated services and solutions to help businesses quickly adapt, upgrade, and modernize. Cloud computing not only provides great computational power but also solves typical hardware problems (from procurement to maintenance) that many software organizations have faced over the years. The latest trends in software engineering models and practices in cloud computing provide many different architectural paradigms to suit different requirements. *Serverless computing* is one the latest cloud-computing models that primarily focuses on abstracting the servers and low-level infrastructure management from software developers. Serverless computing helps developers focus on implementing mission-critical business logic in smaller units and scale it independently without worrying about hardware details.

Serverless computing has gained momentum during the current decade, especially after Amazon introduced its serverless computing offering called *AWS Lambda* in 2014. Microsoft introduced its serverless computing model called *Azure Functions* in 2016. Similarly, Google introduced *Google Cloud Functions* in 2016. Some of the other prominent serverless computing frameworks are Oracle's Fn and IBM's OpenWhisk. There are also popular open source serverless frameworks such as Serverless and Kubeless that are independent of cloud providers and can run in isolation on Docker and Kubernetes containers.

To better understand serverless computing, we need to understand the evolution of physical hardware and network topology strategies. In the 1990s, organizations used to procure and maintain their own hardware and build on-premises network topologies to host their applications. This strategy suited their immediate requirements but came with its own disadvantages in terms of cost, maintenance, and scalability issues. The advancement of cloud platforms solved most of the on-premises hardware problems by providing different layers of abstractions to the required hardware.

Infrastructure as a Service (IaaS) is the first cloud computing service to provide hardware requirements for organizations at different capacities. IaaS exposes virtual machines with different OS, memory, and storage options to serve small to large workloads. In IaaS, organizations manage operating systems, runtimes, and other middleware. Even the deployment of applications to IaaS is not developer intuitive, but IaaS offers great freedom to host and run customized applications.

Platform as a Service (PaaS) is the next cloud computing strategy. It provides greater abstraction to the hardware and operating systems and has much simpler application deployment options compared to IaaS. PaaS solutions are inherently highly available and scalable compared to IaaS-hosted solutions because, in PaaS solutions, all the hardware-related activities, including OS updates and security patches, are handled by the cloud provider.

Serverless computing is the latest strategy from cloud providers where application developers are fully isolated from hardware management. The term *serverless* doesn't mean zero servers; it means full abstraction with server management. Serverless computing services primarily started as *Backend as a Service (BaaS)* solutions and slowly transformed into *Function as a Service* (FaaS) solutions. BaaS is a completely online hosted service, such as Google's Firebase, Microsoft's Azure Mobile App service, etc., which provide a set of functionalities like data storage, authentication, notifications, etc. On the other hand, FaaS can execute a function designed by a developer using programming languages like C#, Python, etc. These functions are executed based on an event-driven model with the help of triggers.

Note   *Software as a Service (SaaS)* and *Container as a Service (CaaS)* are other types of cloud offerings. In SaaS, the cloud provider manages the application and the hardware. CaaS sits in between IaaS and PaaS, with the OS being managed by the cloud provider and the developer controlling the containers and their runtimes.

Function as a Service (FaaS) encourages developers to extract small functional blocks of multi-tiered large applications and host them as functions that can scale independently. This approach is cost effective because individual functions can be scaled based on their own load rather than scaling the entire application. FaaS is different from the traditional monolithic design, where the entire application is packaged as a single unit. Furthermore, FaaS goes one level deeper in breaking down the application into tiny functions when compared with a microservices architecture. Figure 1-1 shows the differences between monolithic, microservices, and FaaS architectures on a simple order management system.

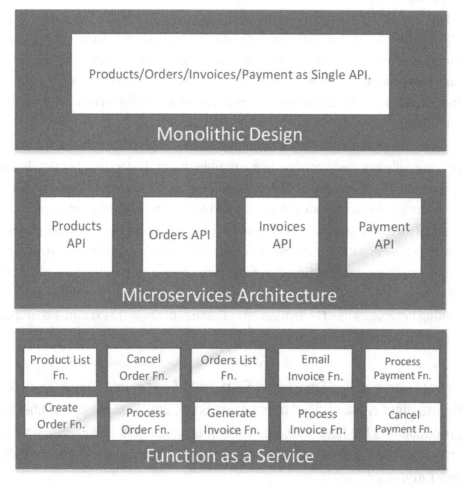

Figure 1-1. *Differences between monolithic, microservices, and FaaS models*

Microsoft Azure offers different services under different cloud strategies. Figure 1-2 shows some of the most prominent Azure Services.

Figure 1-2. *Microsoft cloud services*

Note   The primary motive of this book is to explore the serverless architecture by leveraging Azure Functions, which is a FaaS offering from Microsoft. In the process of developing an end-to-end application architecture, this book also covers the basics of other technologies, such as Cosmos DB and Azure SignalR Service.

Advantages and Limitations of Serverless Computing

Being relatively new to the software ecosystem, serverless computing has its own advantages and disadvantages (limitations, to be more specific). The following are some of the key points to remember while designing a serverless architecture.

Advantages:

- Superior auto-scaling during heavy loads
- No infrastructure maintenance
- Cost optimized, pay as you go
- Supports Agile and faster development cycles
- Low operational overheads
- Follows an easier deployment model
- Overall complexity of the application can be reduced

Limitations:

- At this moment, monitoring, logging, and debugging of functions are tricky as the tools for most of the providers are in the early stages.

- Cross-vendor incompatibility. Not all vendors support the same events, triggers, and development models. This risk can be mitigated by using open source independent serverless frameworks.

- Performance can be a bottleneck in certain scenarios where inter-function calls are required.

- Security systems should be strengthened. Multitenancy risk is persistent.

- State management should be centralized.

- Functions are not suitable for all requirements. For example, functions are not ideal for long-running tasks.

The fast pace at which serverless computing and its related technologies are maturing is proving it to be a tough competitor among its predecessors. It is considered the most reliable emerging software paradigm. Serverless computing's journey has just begun.

Introduction to the Twitter Bot Application

In this book, we study a near real-world business use case and deliver an end-to-end technical solution. I believe that this way of demonstration helps readers understand the concepts better because of the practical implementations. The step-by-step process of building the serverless architecture using Azure Functions will make the process of reconciliation easy at the end of each chapter.

The 21st Century is considered the golden age of digital technology, where the entire world has seen significant innovations in technologies and devices that helped to remove geographical barriers and communication boundaries. The Internet, considered a sparse resource in the 1990s, saw ground-breaking changes in the 2000s, where it was made available to the public. The combination of technology, devices, and Internet disrupted the traditional electronic media platforms and promoted free speech and its importance across the world. Gone are the days when one had to wait for newspapers and TV reports; now we can find anything over the Internet with a few clicks on a mobile phone.

Twitter, an online social networking and news platform, changed the way we communicate by allowing people to send short messages, called *tweets,* across the Internet. Twitter users use hashtags, which are typically keywords or phrases that describe the theme of the message. By using hashtags, Twitter users can find relevant content across the world. The popularity of a tweet can be estimated through the number of retweets (others sharing the same tweet) and favorites (others marking the tweet as their favorite). In this book, we leverage the Twitter platform to build a Twitter Bot application based on the serverless architecture.

The Twitter Bot application is an Internet-facing web application through which users can log in and save hashtags of their interest for tweet notifications. Once users subscribe to a set of hashtags, the Twitter Bot application will retrieve the latest and most popular information from the Twitter platform in periodic intervals and will notify users with the latest tweets. Users will receive a seamless experience on new tweets through push notifications on the web application. This application can be a one-stop shop for users to find curated lists of important information based on their interests.

Note   We call this application a *bot* because it looks out for new content on targeted platforms on a periodic basis and retrieves the information automatically. The same concept can be applied to any online social networking and media platform that provides a way to access data through different feeds and APIs. In fact, we could create an application that provided a feed of information from multiple social networking platforms.

By end of this book, you'll have a fully functional production-ready web application, as shown in Figure 1-3.

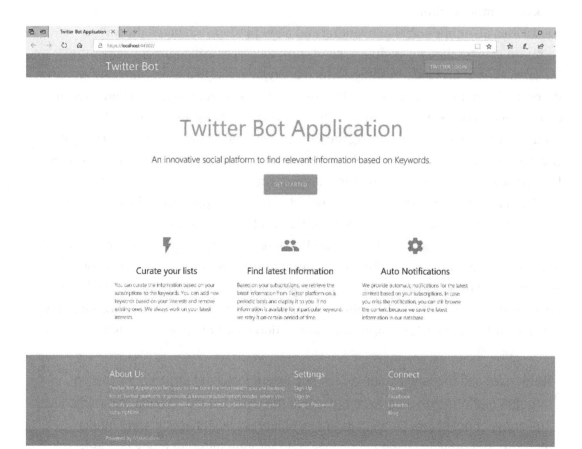

Figure 1-3. *The Twitter Bot web application*

Any business challenge—irrespective of whether it is simple or complex, small or big, good to have or mission critical—cannot be solved until we have a clear understanding of the functional requirements. Identifying the core features of the application is crucial for successful implementation. Table 1-1 details the requirements of the Twitter Bot application that are in the scope of this book.

Table 1-1. *Twitter Bot Application Scope*

Module	Functionality
Tweet Scheduler	1. A scheduler function should be developed to prioritize the hashtags from the database that are to be refreshed from Twitter. 2. The priority logic should be based on the last refresh time for a hashtag. Priority will be given for hashtags that are not processed in the last 10 minutes. 3. The prioritized hashtags should be placed in a queue. These hashtags will be picked up by subsequent levels for further processing.
Tweet Bot	1. This function should pick the prioritized hashtags from the Tweet Scheduler queue in a batch of five and process them using the Tweetinvi API to retrieve the latest popular tweets from Twitter. 2. The latest tweets should be saved to a database (tweets should not be duplicated) and the last refresh time for the hashtag should be updated.
Tweet Notifier	1. When the latest popular tweets are saved to the database, a notification should be sent to the users. 2. Relevant notifications should be sent to the users by correlating hashtag subscriptions and the latest tweets.
Tweet Web	1. Develop a web application through which users can log in using Twitter authentication. 2. Home page of the application should display the list of hashtags that the user subscribed to. 3. Create an option on the home page to enter a hashtag and subscribe to updates on it. 4. Create an option to remove a subscribed hashtag. 5. Create a page to display the feed of tweets based on subscribed hashtags.
Framework	1. All modules in the application should support information and error logging. 2. All application secrets should be stored in a secure location. 3. Enable Twitter authentication on public facing endpoints and functions.

Note I opted for limited scope while choosing the application requirements so that the application would be simple to understand, and it gives me the liberty to emphasize the technological concepts.

Technologies Used in Building the Twitter Bot Application

The foundational strength of the software industry comes from its technological diversity and its ability to provide great solutions by collaborating with different platforms and technologies. The rise of open source technologies and their fast-paced adaption by software organizations opened doors to new technological innovations. The diverse requirements of the Twitter Bot application demand a unique set of technologies and platforms. The implementations should also be orchestrated in a specific manner to achieve end goals. It is always a difficult task to pick up a technology for a particular requirement and it takes a lot of research and comparisons to pick the right technologies.

Note   In this book, I primarily emphasize Microsoft technologies. Having said that, the same requirements can be achieved in a different way using other cloud providers and technologies.

Microsoft open sourced its ASP.NET MVC, Web API, and Webpages frameworks under an Apache 2.0 license. Microsoft also introduced .NET Foundation as an independent organization to improve open source software development and collaboration around the .NET Framework. .NET Core is an open source development framework maintained by Microsoft at GitHub under the .NET Foundation. ASP.NET Core is the latest release of ASP.NET under .NET Foundation and it's capable of building cross-platform web and cloud solutions.

Azure Functions is the serverless computing service hosted on the Microsoft Azure public cloud. It is event-driven and can execute code on demand without provisioning the infrastructure. It can scale based on load and it is offered through a pay-as-you-go subscription model. It is open sourced under the MIT license. The Twitter Bot application leverages Azure Functions to build the serverless functions responsible to schedule, scan, and post the latest tweets from Twitter based on the hashtags. We use the C# programming language to develop Azure Functions. Azure Functions support the .NET Core and the .NET Framework. In this book, we use the .NET Core framework to develop different functions. Figure 1-4 shows the technologies used in the Twitter Bot application.

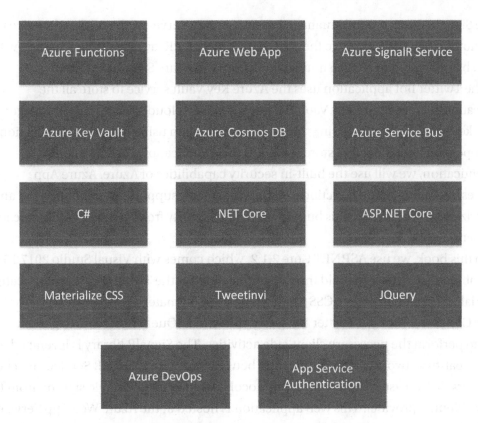

Figure 1-4. Technologies used in the Twitter Bot application

Tweetinvi is an open source .NET C# library used to access the Twitter REST API. It provides a wide range of API methods that facilitate easy access to the Twitter platform. Tweetinvi supports the .NET Core and the .NET Framework. The Twitter Bot application uses Tweetinvi to retrieve the latest popular tweets from Twitter.

Azure Cosmos DB is a globally distributed multimodel database service from Microsoft that can elastically and independently scale throughput and storage across any number of Azure's geographic regions. It supports document, key-value, graph, and columnar data models. We use the SQL API, which provides a schema-less JSON database engine with rich SQL querying capabilities. We rely on the Azure Service Bus to hold the prioritized hashtags for further processing by Azure Functions.

We use the ASP.NET Core SignalR library to enable real-time push notifications on the Twitter bot application. The SignalR library is open sourced under the .NET Foundation, which enables servers to push content to connected clients.

Azure SignalR Service, a fully managed Azure Service, serves as the backend service to send notifications. We leverage the ASP.NET Core SignalR JavaScript client at the Twitter Bot web application to receive notifications from the Azure SignalR Service.

The Twitter Bot application uses the Azure Key Vault service to store all the application secrets. Azure Key Vault is a fully managed cloud service that can safeguard secret keys like connection strings, passwords, etc. When using Key Vault, application developers no longer need to store secrets in their applications. When it comes to authentication, we will use the built-in security capabilities of Azure. Azure App Services, including Azure Functions, come with default support for authentication and authorization. We leverage this built-in federated identity from Twitter to authenticate our users.

In this book, we use ASP.NET Core 2.1.2, which comes with Visual Studio 2017 15.8.2, in combination with C# to build the web application for the Twitter Bot web application. Materialize is an open source CSS framework based on material design and it is used to create CSS themes for the Twitter Bot web application. JQuery is used throughout this book to perform the necessary client-side activities. The SignalR library is leveraged to enable real-time two-way communication between the Azure SignalR Service and clients (browsers in this case). The OAuth 2.0 protocol is used to enable single sign-on from the Twitter identity provider. This web application is hosted at the Azure Web App Service.

The Twitter Bot application's code is versioned using Azure DevOps, which is a distributed version control and source code management platform. As part of Continuous Integration and Continuous Delivery strategy, we create build definitions in Azure DevOps so that the source code will be compiled and deployed to the targeted hosting services.

Logical Architecture of the Twitter Bot Application

The logical architecture is a design specification in which we depict all the logical code components of the application and their interactions. The Twitter Bot application's logical architecture is shown in Figure 1-5.

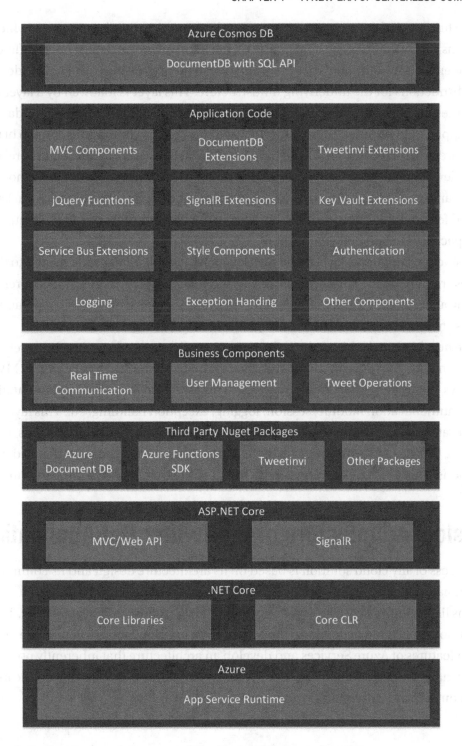

Figure 1-5. *Logical architecture of the Twitter Bot application*

The first layer of the architecture contains the Azure App Services runtime, which is responsible for running the application on the Azure platform. It also holds different components of virtualization, metering, and deployment strategies, which provide great abstractions for the underlying infrastructure. This layer is followed by a layer that constitutes the base frameworks and runtimes of the application. The base foundation of the application includes Microsoft .NET Core runtime and its libraries. On top of the .NET Core, we use the ASP.NET Core framework, which provides all the features related to web development. Microsoft designed the entire .NET Core ecosystem to be modular. That means everything is driven by Nuget packages and we can choose which packages we need for the application. So, the next layer in the hierarchy is to get all the required Nuget packages to build the application.

Business components layer is the next layer and it holds all the code related to the business requirements. This layer will have a modular design by segregating the relevant code through interfaces into multiple physical projects. For example, tweet operations, business functions, etc. are driven through the interface design.

The next layer in the hierarchy is the custom application code written by developers for web and function development. This layer contains all the artifacts related to MVC, like views, controllers, filters, stylesheets, etc. This layer also holds key implementations, like the authentication module, session, logging, exception handling, etc. This layer incorporated the extensions for Azure Key Vault, Cosmos DB, SignalR extensions, etc.

Azure Cosmos DB is the last layer of the hierarchy and it's responsible for all data operations. This API is a C# wrapper for SQL API of the DocumentDB infrastructure.

Physical Architecture of the Twitter Bot Application

The success of any cloud solution is based on its architecture design and its commitment to sustainable engineering practices. All architectures should follow basic design patterns like being loosely coupled, easily maintainable, effortlessly scalable, etc. The Twitter Bot application depends on the Microsoft Azure cloud infrastructure. We take the built-in features of Azure Services and develop an architecture that inherently possesses the advantages of high availability, security, disaster recovery, change feed notifications, scaling on demand, cost optimization, etc. See Figure 1-6.

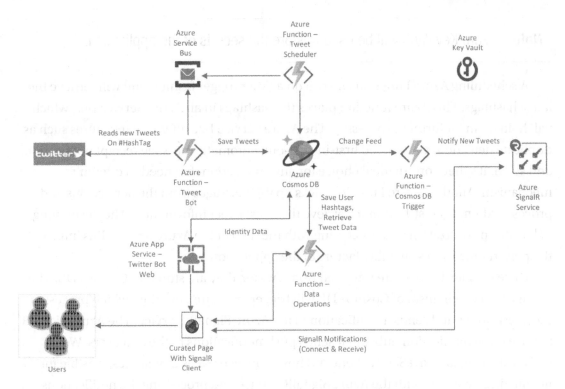

Figure 1-6. *Physical architecture of the Twitter Bot application*

The core architecture of the Twitter Bot application is built on top of Azure Functions, which are responsible for many operations like scheduling hashtags for processing, retrieving tweets from Twitter, handling data notifications from Cosmos DB, etc. We use Azure Cosmos DB powered by the SQL API of DocumentDB as the backend. We also leverage the change feed mechanism of Cosmos DB to get data updates to the subscribers through Azure Functions.

Users will interact with the Twitter Bot web application hosted in an Azure Web App Service. This app service is protected using a Twitter identity provider by using ASP. NET Core Identity, which will store the identity information at Azure Cosmos DB. Using this web application, users can save their hashtag preferences to Azure Cosmos DB. We will develop different HTTP event-driven Azure Functions to act as HTTP endpoints, which are responsible for transferring the data between the Azure web app and Cosmos DB. These endpoints not only save user's data to Cosmos DB, but also retrieve the list of tweets to display on the Azure web app.

Note   Azure Key Vault will be used to store the secrets of the application.

A scheduling Azure Function will run on a timer trigger fashion and will retrieve the latest hashtags. This Azure function places the hashtags in an Azure Service Bus, which will hold them for further processing. The Azure Service Bus offers great features such as duplicate detection, guaranteed first-in-first-out, automatic message receipt notification, and so on. It's therefore an ideal choice for any application that needs a queuing mechanism. Another Azure Function picks up the messages from the Service Bus and processes them against Twitter to retrieve the latest tweet information. The decoupling of hashtag prioritization and processing with the help of the Azure Service Bus improves the performance and scalability factors of the application.

Once the latest tweets are retrieved from Twitter, they are stored in Cosmos DB. The change feed mechanism of Cosmos DB will trigger an Azure Function, which processes the latest tweets and sends a notification to the Azure SignalR Service. The Azure SignalR Service is the notification hub and it sends push notifications to the end users. We will create a SignalR JavaScript client and host it on web pages that are responsible for negotiating a connect with the Azure SignalR Service and processing the notifications.

The architecture of the Twitter Bot application is robust, with the flexibility of individual components scaling based on their own loads. There are many other advantages of this architecture, which we explore throughout this book.

Software Prerequisites

Before we start the development process, we need to check all the software prerequisites and quickly set up the development machine.

This book is heavily dependent on Azure Services. I advise my readers to try the free Azure account or purchase an account. You will better understand the concepts and step-by-step application development narrated in this book if you practice it in a live environment. You can sign up for the free Azure account at `https://azure.microsoft.com/en-in/free/`. Azure offers a $200 credit within the first 30 days of signup and 12 months of popular free services (subject to change).

Note The software prerequisites we discuss in this section are the preliminary and basic software required to get started. I discuss in detail the required technologies and tools in their respective chapters. This way, every chapter is self-contained, which reduces the effort needed to search for relevant content throughout the book.

I use the Windows 10 Enterprise N (x64) Azure Virtual Machine, as shown in Figure 1-7, as my development machine. I use the Standard B-Series VM, specifically the B2ms general purpose VM with two VCPUS, 8GB RAM, four data disks, 16GB local SSD, and 4800 MAX IOPS.

Figure 1-7. *Create the Azure Virtual Machine*

Apart from providing the basic details, like the VM name and resource group during VM creation, we have to enable the RDP Port from the Select Inbound Public Ports option. This is required to remote desktop into the VM.

The created VM will be listed in the Virtual Machines section. Navigate to the VM and download the RDP file by clicking on the Connect button. We can access the development machine running on Azure by double-clicking the RDP file and providing the credentials (VM credentials used at the time of VM creation).

Note   Azure VMs might get a dynamic IP address upon shutdown and start. If the IP changes, we need to download the latest RDP file to connect to the VM.

It is not necessary to create an Azure VM for development. We can use our local machine for development. We must install the latest version of VS from `https://visualstudio.microsoft.com/downloads/`. Select the ASP.NET and Web Development, Azure Development, and .NET Core Cross-Platform Development workloads, as shown in Figure 1-8.

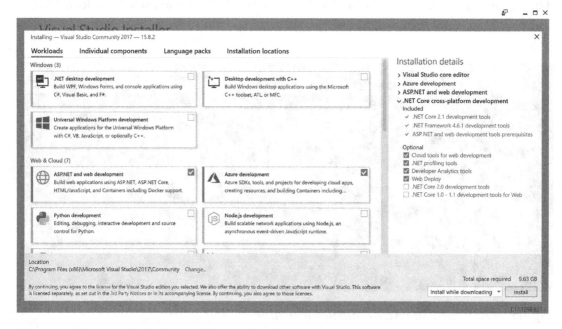

Figure 1-8.   *Install the latest Visual Studio version*

Once you're remotely connected, install Visual Studio 2017 Community, as shown in Figure 1-9. As an optional step, I suggest signing in to VS using a Microsoft account so that the VS community can be unblocked from the license information. Make sure to check that Visual Studio is up to date (as of this writing, it is in version 15.8.2), as shown in Figure 1-9. You can check by going to Help ➤ Check for Updates.

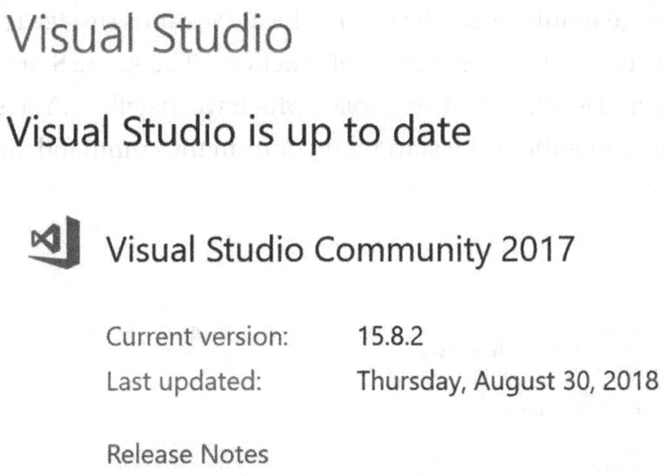

Visual Studio

Visual Studio is up to date

◁╱ Visual Studio Community 2017

Current version: 15.8.2

Last updated: Thursday, August 30, 2018

Release Notes

Figure 1-9. *Latest Visual Studio 2017 Community*

We need to make sure that we have the latest Azure Functions and Web Jobs Tools (choose Visual Studio ➤ Tools menu ➤ Extensions and Updates), as shown in Figure 1-10.

Figure 1-10. *Latest Azure Functions and Web Jobs Tools*

Note   Make sure the Visual Studio Community 2017 and Azure Functions and Web Jobs Tools are up to date. I faced some problems while debugging Azure Functions, especially the V2 Runtime version with old tools. After updating to the latest tools, I found the Azure Functions debugging experience in Visual Studio to be seamless.

The Azure Storage Emulator can be used as local Web Jobs storage for Azure Functions and it is required for some types of functions. The Azure Storage Emulator comes with the Azure Development workload (which we installed). You start the Azure Storage Emulator either from start menu or from the command line, as shown in Figure 1-11.

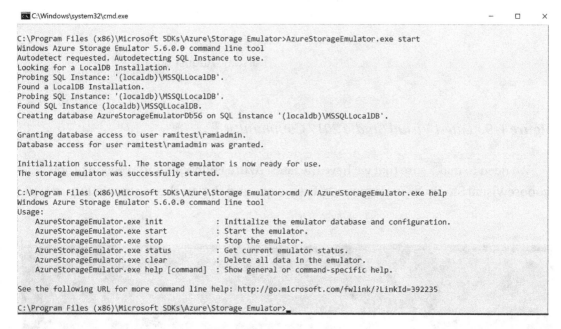

Figure 1-11. Starting the Azure Storage Emulator

Note   Sometimes the Azure Storage Emulator faces initialization problems with the error `Cannot Create Database 'AzureStorageEmulatorDb56'`. In this situation, there might be an existing DB in the `C:\Users\'Current Logged-in User'` folder (or the user who installed Azure Tools). Deleting the existing DB and running the Azure Storage Emulator will create the DB and then start the emulator without any issue.

We are using the .NET Core SDK 2.1.401 version, as shown in Figure 1-12.

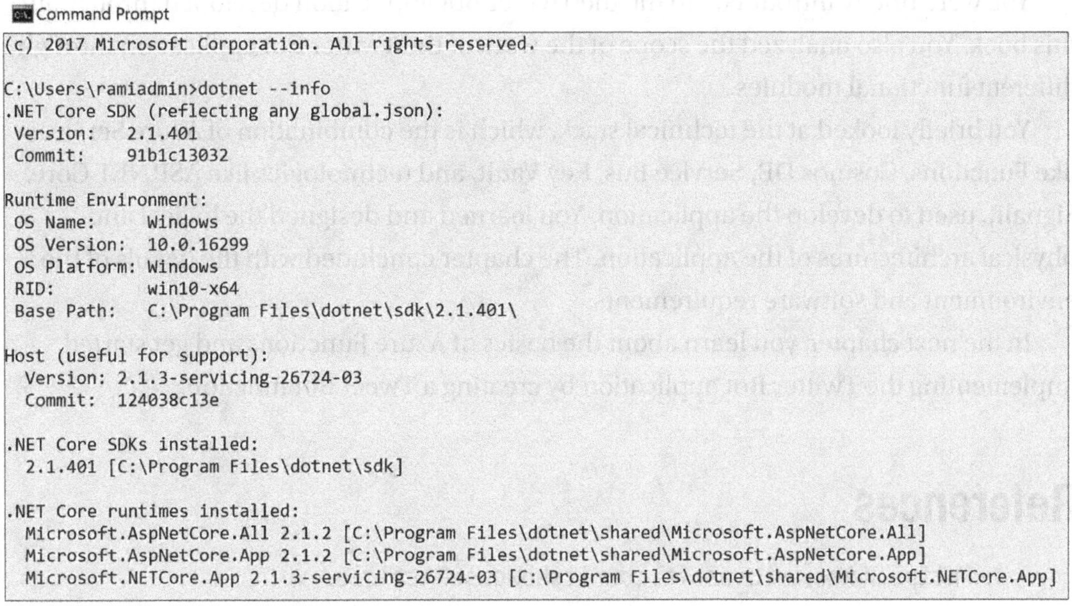

```
Command Prompt
(c) 2017 Microsoft Corporation. All rights reserved.

C:\Users\ramiadmin>dotnet --info
.NET Core SDK (reflecting any global.json):
 Version:   2.1.401
 Commit:    91b1c13032

Runtime Environment:
 OS Name:     Windows
 OS Version:  10.0.16299
 OS Platform: Windows
 RID:         win10-x64
 Base Path:   C:\Program Files\dotnet\sdk\2.1.401\

Host (useful for support):
  Version: 2.1.3-servicing-26724-03
  Commit:  124038c13e

.NET Core SDKs installed:
  2.1.401 [C:\Program Files\dotnet\sdk]

.NET Core runtimes installed:
  Microsoft.AspNetCore.All 2.1.2 [C:\Program Files\dotnet\shared\Microsoft.AspNetCore.All]
  Microsoft.AspNetCore.App 2.1.2 [C:\Program Files\dotnet\shared\Microsoft.AspNetCore.App]
  Microsoft.NETCore.App 2.1.3-servicing-26724-03 [C:\Program Files\dotnet\shared\Microsoft.NETCore.App]
```

Figure 1-12. *.NET Core SDK version*

Note   You can install the Azure Storage Explorer from `https://azure.microsoft.com/en-in/features/storage-explorer/`. This tool is extremely useful in exploring blob, tables, queues, etc. of the Storage emulator.

There are other tools required for development, such as the Azure Cosmos DB Emulator. These additional tools will be installed in the relevant chapters. The Continuous Integration and Continuous Delivery pipeline and its related workflows are discussed in later chapters.

Summary

In this chapter, you were introduced to serverless computing and its magnanimity in delivering scalable and flexible solutions. You also learned about the fundamental concepts of serverless computing and designing a serverless architecture by exploring different cloud strategies like IaaS, PaaS, CaaS, FaaS, and SaaS. You also understood the different offerings from Microsoft under each infrastructure abstraction strategy. The pros and cons of serverless computing discussed in this chapter will help you choose an architecture.

You were briefly introduced to the the Twitter Bot application developed throughout this book. You also analyzed the scope of the work of the Twitter Bot application through different functional modules.

You briefly looked at the technical stack, which is the combination of Azure Services like Functions, Cosmos DB, Service Bus, Key Vault, and technologies like ASP.NET Core, SignalR, used to develop the application. You learned and designed the logical and physical architectures of the application. The chapter concluded with the details of the environment and software requirements.

In the next chapter, you learn about the basics of Azure Functions and get started implementing the Twitter Bot application by creating a Tweet Bot function.

References

1. https://www.microsoft.com/itshowcase/Article/
   Content/730/Adopting-modern-engineering-processes-and-
   tools-at-Microsoft-IT

2. https://azure.microsoft.com/mediahandler/files/
   resourcefiles/17dfdca7-97b4-49dd-8b82-1c2f240334a7/EN-
   CNTNT-Whitepaper-ChoosingaCloudConnectedBackend.pdf

3. https://www.linkedin.com/pulse/brief-history-serverless-
   architecture-adam-roderick/

4. https://agileengine.com/serverless-architecture/

5. https://docs.microsoft.com/en-us/azure/azure-functions/
   functions-develop-vs

CHAPTER 2

Getting Started with Azure Functions

Over the last few decades, the process of innovation has changed drastically due to the advancements in technology. Microsoft's vision of Cloud First, Mobile First has triggered a massive avalanche of ideas from individuals by utilizing the power of the Microsoft Azure cloud. Azure's IaaS, PaaS, and SaaS offerings have shared their success with many researchers, inventors, and developers by supporting them in their mission-critical domain requirements.

In this competitive world, the success of an idea is directly proportional to the time it takes to reach the market. In short, the faster you take your idea to your customers, the greater chances of its success. This demand for speed and responsiveness in developing and delivering software products led to the search for new software patterns and designs that would fast-track the overall delivery process and provide other enhancements like scalable, cost-effective, flexible, robust, reliable, and developer-friendly environments. Serverless computing is one of the most discussed cloud computing strategies today. Azure Functions is Microsoft Azure's adaption of the serverless computing strategy delivered as a Functions-as-a-Service (FaaS) model.

In this chapter, we:

- Explore the fundamentals of Azure Functions and their pros and cons.

- Develop a tweet framework by using the Tweetinvi library to connect with the Twitter platform.

- Create a Tweet Bot Azure Function and integrate it with the tweet framework.

23

© Rami Vemula 2019
R. Vemula, *Integrating Serverless Architecture*, https://doi.org/10.1007/978-1-4842-4489-0_2

- Learn about the significance of different artifacts of an Azure Functions project.

- Debug and deploy the Tweet Bot Function to the Azure environment.

Understanding Azure Functions

Azure Functions is a Function-as-a-Service (FaaS) offering from Microsoft Azure with a clear vision of providing maximum infrastructure abstraction from developers. By leveraging Azure Functions, developers and architects can design small functional actions using different programming languages, which can be invoked via different triggers. In short, Azure Functions is an event driven, on-demand system that helps developers focus more on the functional aspects of the code rather than on planning infrastructure activities. Azure Functions can also react to events such as database notifications, timer schedules, HTTP calls, third-party integrations, etc. Microsoft open sourced the Azure Functions runtime and it is being enhanced in collaboration with the open source developer community.

The main features of Azure Functions are as follows:

- Developer friendly, with absolutely no infrastructure related activities.

- Wide range of language support, including C#, F#, JavaScript, and Java.

- Binding extensibility model helps in integrating third-party sources.

- Different input and output bindings can be used to operate on data from external sources, such as blob, queue, Cosmos DB, etc.

- Pay-per-use, which means you pay only for the time spent running the code.

- Integrated security with Azure Active Directory, Google, Twitter, Facebook, and Microsoft Account.

- Continuous Integration and Continuous Deployment support to various source version control providers like GitHub, Azure DevOps, etc.

- Support for different triggers such as HTTP, Timer, Cosmos DB, EventHub, Webhook, etc.

- Large APIs can be modularized into smaller units using Azure Function proxies.

- Azure Functions Runtime (preview) provide support to on-premises development and deployment.

- Stateful orchestration can be achieved using Durable Azure Functions.

Note   In this book, we focus on developing Azure Functions using Visual Studio 2017 and the C# programming language. Do not mistake C# with CSX, as CSX is a C# script that's primarily based on Azure WebJobs SDK. CSX-based Azure Functions can be used for quick development, but for large projects, C#-based functions are recommended.

Azure Functions have been released in two versions, V1 and V2. Table 2-1 details the major differences between V1 and V2.

Table 2-1. *Major Differences Between Azure Functions V1 and V2 Versions*

V1	V2
Supports only Windows (.NET Framework)	Supports several platforms (.NET Core)
Generally available	As of October 2018, it is in preview
Supports C#, F#, and JavaScript	Supports all V1 languages along with Java.
Support for basic bindings like HTTP, Cosmos DB, Blob storage, etc.	Support for additional bindings like Excel tables, Outlook, OneDrive, Dropbox, Twilio, etc.

Azure Functions can be hosted in two different plans—the Consumption plan and the App Service plan. In the Consumption plan, Azure Function instances are dynamically added and removed based on the incoming load. In this plan, we only pay for the time the functions are running. In the App Service plan, Azure Functions are hosted on dedicated VMs and they are always in the running state. In this plan, we typically pay the VM cost. Usually for resource- and time-intensive workloads, we go for the App Service plan; otherwise, we can opt for the Consumption plan.

By default, Azure Functions are used for stateless implementations, but there might be scenarios where we need to implement complex business requirements that will have multiple stages of data processing and business rules. Durable Azure Functions is an extension to Azure Functions and it can create an orchestration of Azure Functions to achieve complex business process. The most commonly used patterns with Durable Functions are: Function Chaining, Fan-In/Fan-Out, Long Pooling, Async HTTP API with Long Running Tasks, etc.

Note   Durable functions are not in the scope of this book.

Exploring the Azure Functions Architecture

In this section, we explore the high-level architecture of Azure Functions, as depicted in Figure 2-1. The bottom layer of the architecture holds the Azure app Service Runtime, which is responsible for hosting and deployment of functions. On top of that, we have Azure WebJobs SDK and Runtime, which are responsible for providing the programming model and execution context for functions. Language Runtime holds the language framework and executes the function code based on the targeted language. Azure Function's code and configuration together holds the top layer of the architecture.

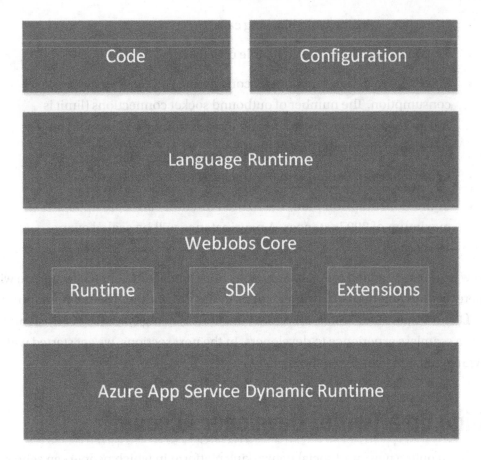

Figure 2-1. *Azure Functions architecture*

Microsoft recommends the following best practices when programming Azure Functions:

- Avoid long-running tasks, use smaller tasks.

- Try to process messages in batches.

- Break large functions that require a lot of dependencies into smaller functions.

- Design stateless functions. If a stateful nature is required, use Durable functions.

- Design functions to be resilient in failures. For example, a function failure should not impact downstream services or functions in the workflow.

27

- Use async code but avoid blocking calls.

- Configure host behaviors to handle concurrency.

- Make sure to design functions by considering CPU and memory consumption. The number of outbound socket connections (limit is 300 for the Consumption plan) and threads (limit is 512) should be considered during the design phase.

- Use Connection Pooling while connecting to external sources.

- In the Consumption plan, the Azure Function can scale up to a maximum of 200 instances. A new instance will be scaled every 10 seconds.

New features are added to Azure Functions from time to time. In the future, we will see more features and third-party integrations in the V2 runtime. The tooling support, both CLI and Visual Studio tools, for Azure Functions is being enhanced consistently to provide a seamless experience to developers. In the next sections, we get started with our first Azure Function—the Tweet Bot Function.

Setting Up a Twitter Developer Account

Twitter is an online news and social networking platform in which people can send short messages, called *tweets,* to others. Of late, it is considered one of the industry leaders in providing reliable and innovative social networking features. Currently there are around 335 million registered users who contribute 500 million tweets per day.

In this section, we sign up for a Twitter account and apply for Twitter Developer account with the Twitter Bot application details.

Note   A Twitter Developer account is required to access Twitter's REST API.

Let's get started by creating a Twitter account, as shown in Figure 2-2.

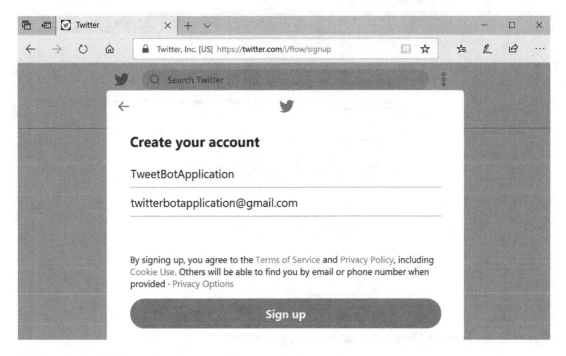

Figure 2-2. *Twitter signup*

Note   As part of the Twitter signup, we need to provide a valid password. We can ignore the personal preferences step. At the final step, we need to confirm email with which we have registered.

Now we will create a developer account at Twitter through which we can register an application and get access to the Twitter platform API. The step-by-step process of creating a developer account is as follows:

1. Navigate to `https://developer.twitter.com/en/apply/user`, as shown in Figure 2-3.

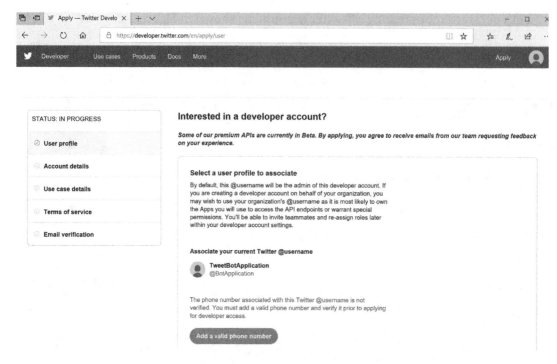

Figure 2-3. *Twitter Developer account registration*

Note   We need to add and validate our phone number before we proceed.

2. Provide the account details, as shown in Figure 2-4.

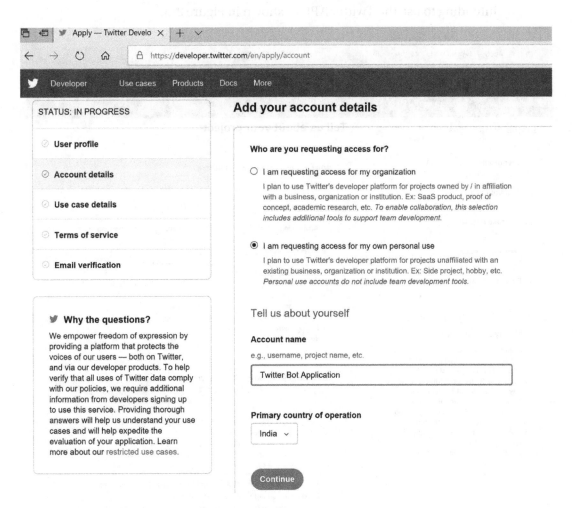

Figure 2-4. *Twitter Developer account details*

3. We now provide details about the project for which we are
    intending to use the Twitter API, as shown in Figure 2-5.

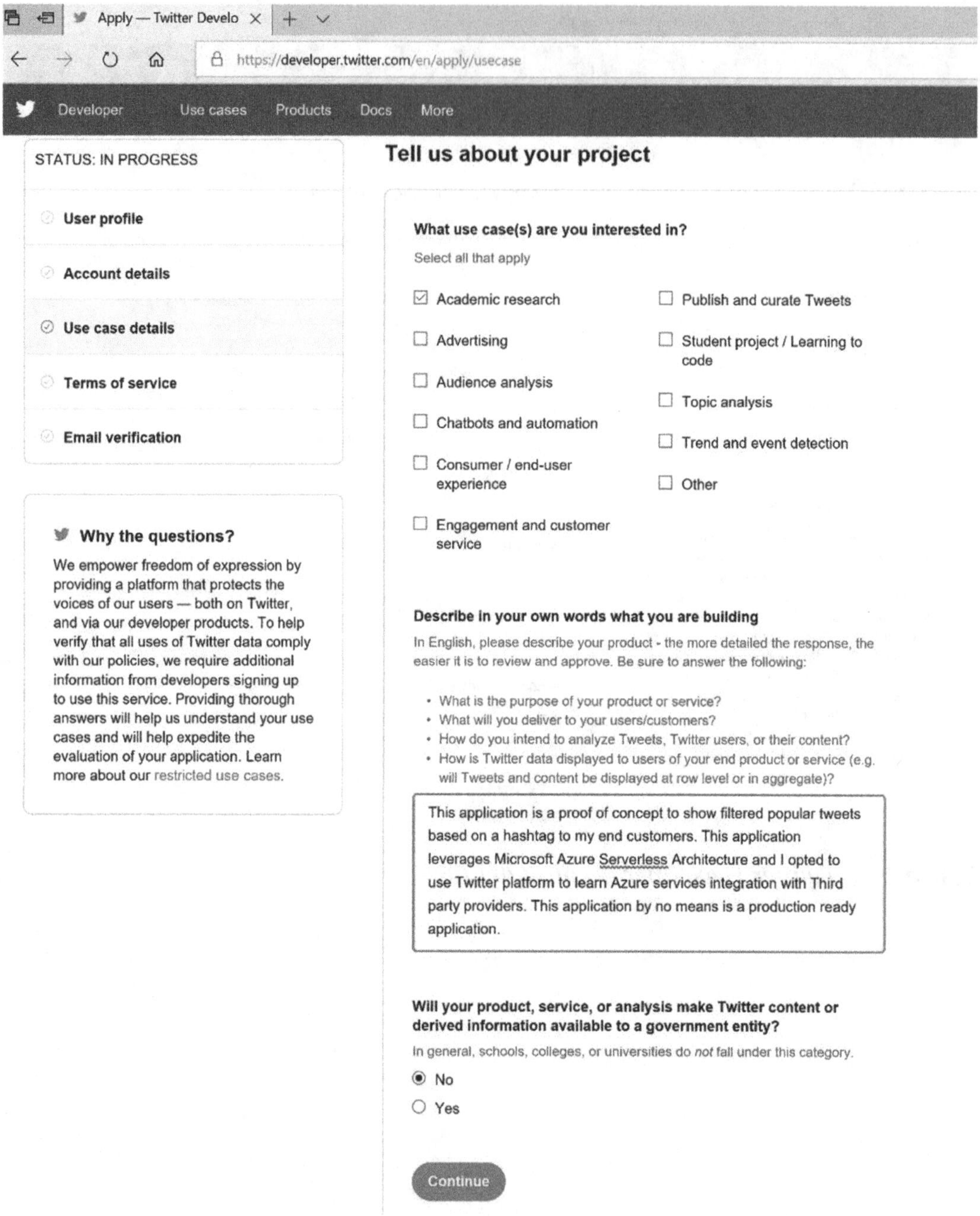

Figure 2-5. *Twitter Developer account project details*

4. Read the full agreement and click on Submit Application, as
    shown in Figure 2-6.

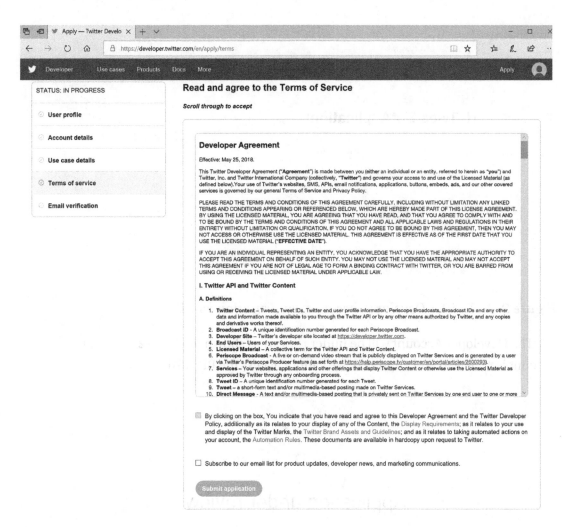

Figure 2-6. *Twitter Developer account agreement*

5. Confirm the email, which is sent to the registered email, as shown in Figure 2-7.

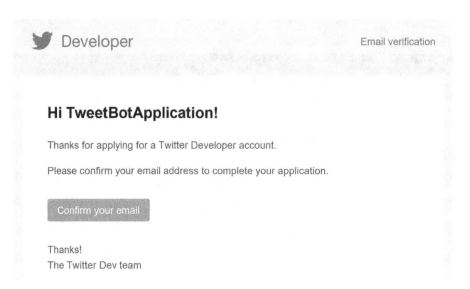

Figure 2-7. *Twitter Developer account confirmation email*

The Developer Account will be under review, as shown in Figure 2-8. Until the account is reviewed and approved, we cannot access the REST API.

Application under review.

Thanks! We've received your application and are reviewing it. We'll be in touch soon.

We review applications to ensure compliance with our Terms of Service and Developer policies. Learn more.

You'll receive an email when the review is complete. While you wait, check out our documentation, explore our tutorials, or check out our community forums.

Figure 2-8. *Twitter Developer account review*

Note   At this point, we just wait for Twitter's response. Twitter might get back to us via email seeking more information about our intended use of Twitter's API. We should include all required details in the reply email to Twitter.

Twitter will evaluate the application details and will decide whether to approve or deny the application. Finally, our TwitterBotApplication's developer account has been approved, as shown in Figure 2-9.

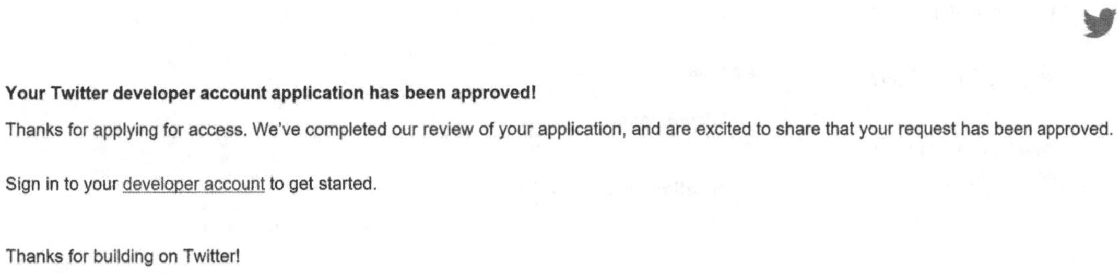

Your Twitter developer account application has been approved!

Thanks for applying for access. We've completed our review of your application, and are excited to share that your request has been approved.

Sign in to your developer account to get started.

Thanks for building on Twitter!

Figure 2-9. *Approval email of the Twitter developer account*

Log in to https://developer.twitter.com/. Navigate to the Apps section. Click Create an App.

Provide all the required information, such as Name, Description, Website URL (can be anything), and App Usage in App Details section, as shown in Figure 2-10. This application is not required to sign in using Twitter, so do not select the Enable Sign In with Twitter option. Click Create.

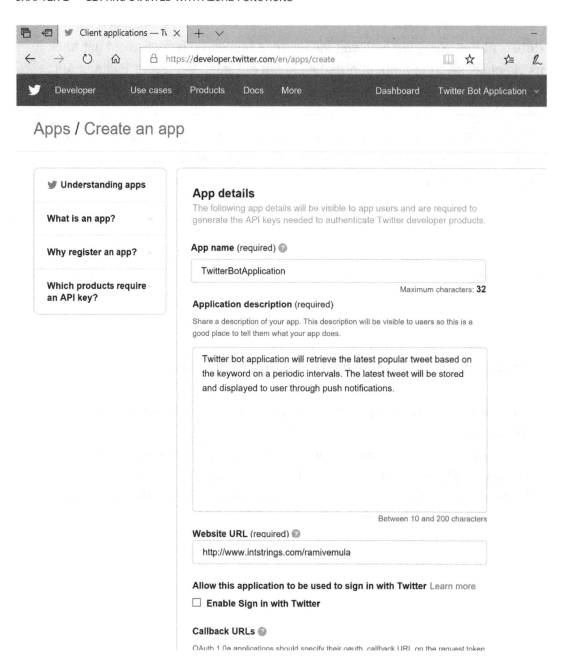

Figure 2-10. *Twitter app details*

The Twitter app will be created, as shown in Figure 2-11.

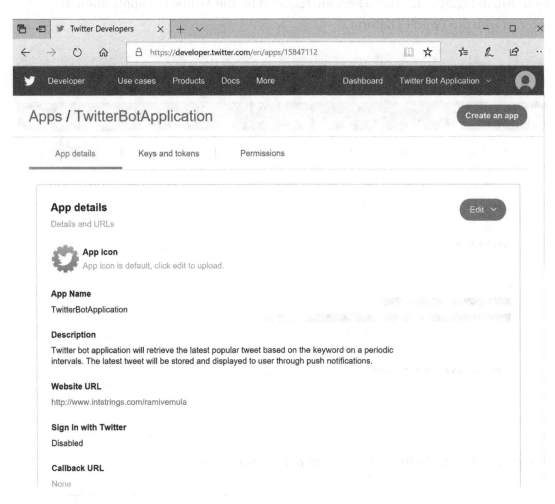

Figure 2-11. *Twitter app details*

The Application Secret Key and API key can be found in the Keys and Tokens section, as shown in Figure 2-12. These keys are required for the TwitterBot application to interact with the Twitter platform.

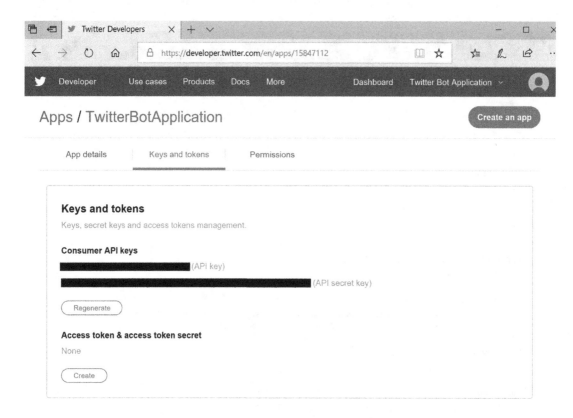

Figure 2-12.   *The Twitter App Keys and Tokens section*

Note   The Twitter application Secret Key and API Key should not be disclosed to any unauthorized source. Anybody who has access to these keys can access the Twitter platform on our behalf.

We are going to use these keys in the next section to develop a framework by leveraging the Tweetinvi library to interact with Twitter.

Creating a Tweet Operations Framework Using the Tweetinvi Library

The Twitter platform exposes REST API endpoints through which a registered application can interact with the Twitter platform and can perform certain sets of data operations in a secure way. Some of the operations include searching tweets, direct messaging, looking at account activity, finding trends, uploading media content, etc. The Twitter Bot application is going to rely on the Twitter REST API to retrieve the latest tweet information at periodic intervals.

Note   There are many technical ways to interact with the Twitter REST API. We can use C#'s `HttpClient` to build our own REST API wrapper. In this book, we are going to use the Tweetinvi library to interact with the Twitter REST API.

Tweetinvi is an open source .NET C# library used to access the Twitter REST API. It provides an intuitive API through which we can easily pull information from Twitter. Tweetinvi automates a lot of steps for us, which involves acquiring a bearer authentication token, formatting HTTP headers, constructing HTTP request messages, etc. Tweetinvi is a .NET Core and Portable Class Library that can be used for development on Windows, Xamarin Android, iOS, and Mac/Linux.

In this section, we create a C# .NET Core Class Library Wrapper, which will connect to Twitter and read the latest popular tweets based on a given hashtag.

Open Visual Studio and create a new solution called `TwitterBot` (choose File ➤ New ➤ Project ➤ Other Project Types ➤ Visual Studio Solutions and then select blank solution), as shown in Figure 2-13.

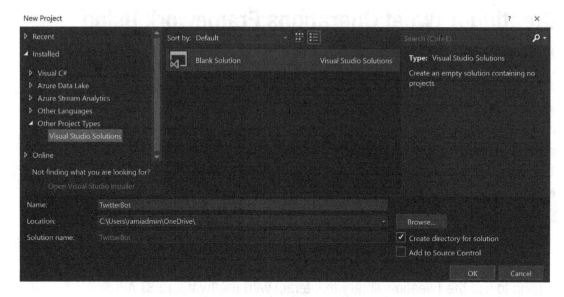

Figure 2-13. *Create the TwitterBot Visual Studio solution*

Create a new project under the TwitterBot solution called `TwitterBot.Framework`, as shown in Figure 2-14. Right-click on the TwitterBot solution and then choose Add ➤ New Project ➤ Visual C#. Then select Class Library (.NET Standard).

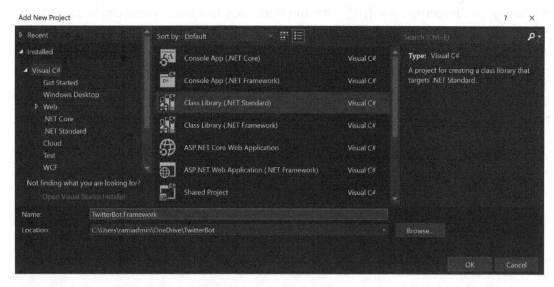

Figure 2-14. *Create the TwitterBot.Framework project*

Delete the default Class1 C# class file and create three folders—Contracts, BusinessLogic, and Types—as shown in Figure 2-15. In the Contracts folder, we are going to define interfaces for the core logic. In the BusinessLogic folder, we are going to have implementations of the interfaces. In the Types folder, we are going to create different types that will be shared across different projects.

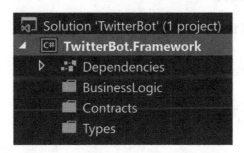

Figure 2-15. *New folders in the TwitterBot.Framework project*

We will first create a BaseType class in the Types folder, as shown in Listing 2-1. This BaseType will act as the base model for all framework entities. Typically, we add all common properties to the BaseType.

Listing 2-1. BaseType Class

```
using System;
namespace TwitterBot.Framework.Types
{
    public class BaseType
    {
        public string Id { get; set; }
        public DateTime CreatedOn { get; set; }
        public string CreatedBy { get; set; }
        public DateTime ModifiedOn { get; set; }
        public string ModifiedBy { get; set; }
        public bool IsDeleted { get; set; }
    }
}
```

Now we will create Hashtag and Tweet types in the Types folder, as shown in Listings 2-2 and 2-3. Both the types are inherited from BaseType to reuse the common properties. The Hashtag type represents the Twitter's hashtag and the Tweet type corresponds to the Twitter's tweet model.

Listing 2-2. Hashtag Class

```
namespace TwitterBot.Framework.Types
{
    public class Hashtag : BaseType
    {
        public string Text { get; set; }
    }
}
```

Listing 2-3. Tweet Class

```
namespace TwitterBot.Framework.Types
{
    public class Tweet : BaseType
    {
        public string FullText { get; set; }
        public int RetweetCount { get; set; }
        public int FavoriteCount { get; set; }
    }
}
```

Note   In this chapter, we will get started with the basic properties for now. In later chapters, we will add more properties to the types based on other requirements.

Now that we have types in place, we will create our first contract, ITweetOperations under the Contracts folder, as shown in Listing 2-4. This contract will have only one method for now—GetPopularTweetByHashtag—which will take a Hashtag parameter and return a Tweet.

Listing 2-4. ITweetOperations Interface

```
using TwitterBot.Framework.Types;
namespace TwitterBot.Framework.Contracts
{
    public interface ITweetOperations
    {
        Tweet GetPopularTweetByHashtag(Hashtag hashtag);
    }
}
```

Before we proceed to implement TweetOperations, we need to install the Tweetinvi nuget on the TwitterBot.Framework project. Right-click on the project and select the Manage Nuget Packages option. Browse for Tweetinvi, as shown in Figure 2-16. Click Install.

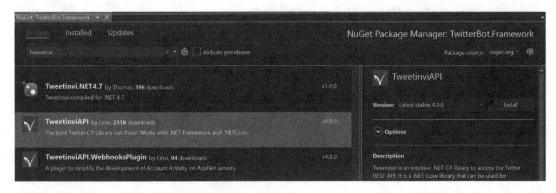

Figure 2-16. *Install the Tweetinvi nuget*

Add the TweetOperations class in the BusinessLogic folder, as shown in Listing 2-5. To get authenticated against Twitter, we use the Auth.SetApplicationOnlyCredentials method and pass the API Key and API Secret parameters (which we got from the previous section). The API Key and API Secret are injected through the constructor.

The search parameter is created by passing Hashtag.Text as input to the ISearchTweetsParameters instance. We do set the search type as Popular and the maximum number of results expected as one. Finally, we do a search by calling the Search.SearchTweets method with the ISearchTweetsParameters parameter. The result is then converted to the Tweet type and returned to the caller method.

Note   In subsequent chapters, we will leverage Azure Key Vault to store sensitive secret information and securely access it from code.

Listing 2-5. TweetOperations Class

```
using System.Linq;
using Tweetinvi;
using Tweetinvi.Models;
using Tweetinvi.Parameters;
using TwitterBot.Framework.Contracts;
using TwitterBot.Framework.Types;

namespace TwitterBot.Framework.BusinessLogic
{
    public class TweetOperations : ITweetOperations
    {
        private string _consumerKey;
        private string _consumerSecret;
        public TweetOperations(string consumerKey, string consumerSecret)
        {
            _consumerKey = consumerKey;
            _consumerSecret = consumerSecret;
        }

        public Types.Tweet GetPopularTweetByHashtag(Hashtag hashtag)
        {
            Auth.SetApplicationOnlyCredentials(_consumerKey,
            _consumerSecret, true);

            ISearchTweetsParameters searchParameter = Search.CreateTweetSea
            rchParameter(hashtag.Text);
            searchParameter.SearchType = SearchResultType.Popular;
            searchParameter.MaximumNumberOfResults = 1;
            var tweet = Search.SearchTweets(searchParameter);

            if(!tweet.Any())
```

```
    {
        return null;
    }

    var topTweet = tweet.FirstOrDefault();
    return new Types.Tweet { Id = topTweet.Id.ToString(),
    FullText = topTweet.FullText };
      }
   }
}
```

Now we will implement AutoMapper's mappings to convert the Tweetinvi.Model. ITweet type to TwitterBot.Framework.Types.Tweet. AutoMapper is an open source object to object mapper, which can solve complex mapping problems with very simple configurations. We are going to use AutoMapper to map different types in the TwitterBot.Framework project. Install the AutoMapper nuget on the TwitterBot.Framework project, as shown in Figure 2-17.

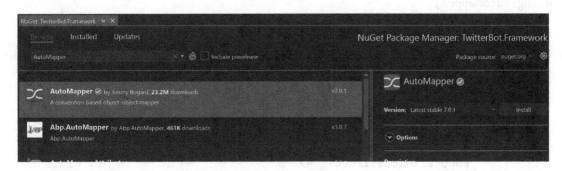

Figure 2-17. *Install the AutoMapper nuget*

Add a folder called Mappings to the TwitterBot.Framework project and add a class called MappingProfile, as shown in Figure 2-18.

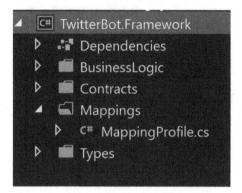

Figure 2-18. *The MappingProfile class*

Create the mapping between `Tweetinvi.Model.ITweet` to `TwitterBot.Framework.Types.Tweet`, as shown in Listing 2-6. The `Activate` static method will initialize the `AutoMapper` mappings configuration.

Listing 2-6. AutoMapper MappingProfile Class

```
using AutoMapper;

namespace TwitterBot.Framework.Mappings
{
    public class MappingProfile : Profile
    {
        public static void Activate()
        {
            Mapper.Initialize(cfg =>
            {
                cfg.CreateMap<Tweetinvi.Models.ITweet, Types.Tweet>();
            });
        }
    }
}
```

Note In Listing 2-6, we directly mapped the types without specifying which source property mapped to which destination property. If the property names are the same, there is no need to explicitly specify the property mappings.

Update the `GetPopularTweetByHashtag` method of the `TweetOperations` class, as shown in Listing 2-7. We include an `AutoMapper` namespace and use the `Mapper.Map()` method of `AutoMapper` to convert the `Tweetinvi.Models.ITweet` result to `TwitterBot.Framework.Types.Tweet`.

Listing 2-7. Updated GetPopularTweetByHashtag Method with Mapper.Map() Usage

```
using AutoMapper;
/*****Code Removed for brevity****/

namespace TwitterBot.Framework.BusinessLogic
{
/*****Code Removed for brevity****/

        public Types.Tweet GetPopularTweetByHashtag(Hashtag hashtag)
        {
            /*****Code Removed for brevity****/

            var topTweet = tweet.FirstOrDefault();
            return Mapper.Map<Types.Tweet>(topTweet);
        }
    }
}
```

We can quickly create a console application (.NET Core) and test the `GetPopularTweetByHashtag` method. We need to add the `TwitterBot.Framework` project reference to the console application. Install the `AutoMapper` and `Tweetinvi` nuget packages on the console application. Listing 2-8 shows the code to test the `GetPopularTweetByHashtag` method in a console app. We first load the `AutoMapper` mapping configuration by calling the `MappingProfile.Activate` method. Next, we invoke the `GetPopularTweetByHashtag` method of the `TweetOperations` instance by passing a hashtag `#justsaying`. Finally, we display the tweet that was retrieved from Twitter.

Listing 2-8. Console Application Code

```
using System;
using TwitterBot.Framework.BusinessLogic;
using TwitterBot.Framework.Mappings;
using TwitterBot.Framework.Types;

namespace ConsoleApp1
{
    class Program
    {
        static void Main(string[] args)
        {
            MappingProfile.Activate();

            var tweetOps = new TweetOperations("API Key", "API Secret");
            var result = tweetOps.GetPopularTweetByHashtag(new Hashtag {
            Text = "#justsaying" });
            if (result != null)
            {
                Console.WriteLine(result.FullText);
            }

            Console.ReadLine();
        }
    }
}
```

Note   The console application is merely to test the code. It has no relevance in the Twitter Bot application's business requirements.

Creating and Understanding the Basics of the Tweet Bot Azure Function

In this section, we develop our first Azure Function—TweetBotFunction—and learn about the basic artifacts of an Azure Function. We integrate TweetBotFunction with the Tweet Operations framework, which we built in the previous section to fetch the latest tweet information from Twitter.

Let's get started by adding a new Azure Function project called TwitterBot. AzureFunctions to the TwitterBot solution, as shown in Figure 2-19. Right-click the TwitterBot solution and select Add ➤ New Project ➤ Visual C# ➤ Cloud Template ➤ Azure Functions. Choose a name and click OK.

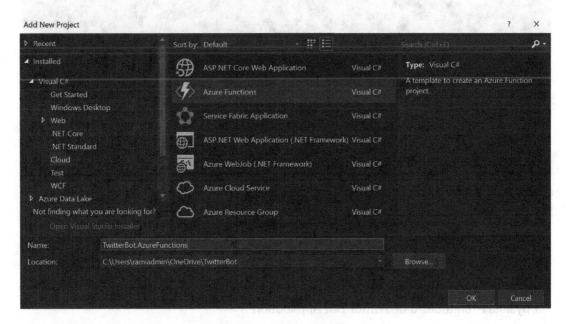

Figure 2-19. *The TwitterBot.AzureFunctions project*

Now we need to select which type of function trigger we need for TweetBotFunction. Select Azure Functions V2 (.NET Standard) as the Azure Function Runtime, which supports cross-platform development. Select Timer Trigger as the Trigger Type, as shown in Figure 2-20.

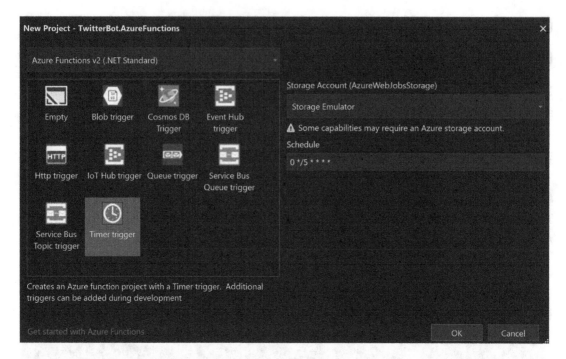

Figure 2-20. *Configure a trigger for the TwitterBot.AzureFunctions project*

Leave the Storage Emulator as the default option for the Storage Account; this is required for all types of functions except HTTP triggered based functions. The default schedule of a Timer Trigger function is 0 */5 * * * *, which triggers the function every five minutes.

Note   Before reading the rest of this section, refresh your memory about the Twitter Bot application's physical architecture from Chapter 1's section entitled "Physical Architecture of Twitter Bot Application".

We should be cautious in selecting the trigger type for an Azure Function, especially for TweetBotFunction, which will scan the Twitter platform for the latest popular tweet updates based on a hashtag. We primarily have two options to design the TweetBotFunction—a Timer Trigger, which will be invoked at periodic intervals, and a Service Bus Trigger, which will respond to messages on a Service Bus Queue.

For the Twitter Bot application, we will go with a Timer Trigger because of the following reason. Let's do quick math—assume we have a user base of 10,000 with a unique hashtag subscription average of 1.0, which means we will have 10,000 unique hashtags to be scanned for popular tweets. Assume we scan the hashtags every five minutes, which gives us 288 scans per day. The total scans for 10,000 hashtags would be 2.88 million function executions.

Given these numbers, if we go with the Service Bus Trigger Azure Function, we can expect all 2.88 million function invocations. But if we process the hashtags in batches of 10 by a Timer Trigger Azure Function with an interval of three seconds, we would need 10 instances of Timer Trigger instances with a total of 0.28 million function executions.

As the Azure Functions pricing is primarily based on the number of function executions and resource consumption in GB/s (Gigabytes seconds), the Timer Trigger function has an edge over Service Bus Trigger function in execution cycles. Both trigger types will have nearly the same resource consumption. It is always recommended to have periodic processing of data in batches through Timer Triggers for applications where a higher load is expected consistently on every day. On the contrary, if the load fluctuates from day to day with some days being heavier and other days being lighter, then on-demand processing of data would be more efficient.

Additionally, we can achieve cost optimization during the first few weeks in production of the Twitter Bot application because of the flexibility of executing fewer instances of the Timer Trigger function with larger intervals. As load increases, we can scale the timer functions with smaller execution frequencies.

The functional requirements should also be considered while opting for a choice between the trigger types. Currently, the Service Bus Queue Trigger based Azure Functions don't support session-based queue messages, which is a major issue for applications that expect First-In, First-Out (FIFO) order of messages. The Twitter Bot application leverages FIFO order to ensure hashtags are synchronized based on priority. Because of this technical limitation of the Service Bus Queue Trigger and being a little flexible in the functional requirements of the Twitter Bot application, we will implement a Timer Trigger for `TweetBotFunction`.

Note   In Chapter 4, we will implement an alternate version of `TweetBotFunction` using a Service Bus Queue Trigger (with sessionless queue messages).

Click OK to create the `TwitterBot.AzureFunctions` project. A default function is created. Rename the `Function1` class and class file to `TweetBotFunction`.

Note   Clean the `Bin` and `Obj` folders from the `Project` directory. This will remove unwanted references of the `Function1` name.

Let's look at the Azure Function's artifacts, which are shown in Figure 2-21.

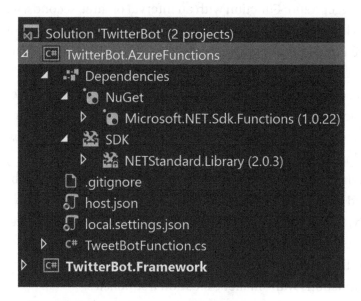

Figure 2-21.   *The TwitterBot.AzureFunctions project artifacts*

Note   Update the `Microsoft.NET.Sdk.Functions` nuget package to the latest version, not less than 1.0.19. This is required to support Dependency Injection implementation, which will be discussed in later sections.

- Dependencies: Dependencies of the project include `Microsoft. NET.Sdk.Functions`, which serves as the base framework for all the Azure Functions. The project also references the `NETStandard. Library` metapackage, which will reference a set of nuget packages that are defined in the .NET Standard library on which the function is dependent.

- `.gitignore`: This file is required to specify the Visual Studio temporary files and other project related files that are to be ignored from source version control.

- `TweetBotFunction.cs`: This file holds the C# code of the Azure function.

- `local.settings.json`: This file stores app settings and connection strings that are used when executing the function locally, as shown in Listing 2-9. The `IsEncrypted` value, when set to `true`, encrypts all the values using the local machine key. In the Values section, we can define all the key value pairs of application settings. We can also define the ConnectionStrings section to hold all the connection strings. A Host section is used to configure the function's host process, especially settings related to HTTP port where the functions should run and configuration related to Cross-Origin Resource Sharing (CORS) requests.

Listing 2-9. The local.settings.json File

```
{
    "IsEncrypted": false,
    "Values": {
        "AzureWebJobsStorage": "UseDevelopmentStorage=true",
        "AzureWebJobsDashboard": "UseDevelopmentStorage=true",
        "FUNCTIONS_WORKER_RUNTIME": "dotnet"
    }
}
```

- `host.json`: This file stores the configuration settings that affect all the functions in the project when running locally or in Azure.

- The following are some of the important configuration settings that can be configured in `host.json`.

  - **HTTP:** This section can define the route prefix for incoming HTTP calls, maximum concurrent requests, maximum number of outstanding requests, dynamic throttle value to enable request rejection in case of high CPU/memory, etc.

  - **Function Timeout:** Defines a timeout value, which functions will use to timeout.

  - **Logger & Tracer:** Defines logging and trace settings.

- **Id:** The unique ID for a job host. ID can be a lowercase GUID with dashes removed. ID plays a crucial role when scaling timer triggered functions. If two function apps share the same ID then only one timer instance will be shared across them.

- **Application Insights & Aggregator:** Configure sampling and max telemetry items to be sampled per second. Aggregator settings defines how the runtime should aggregate the function invocations.

- **Health Monitor:** Holds the settings to enable the health of host, health check interval, and its associated threshold values.

- **Singleton:** This setting will ensure only one function execution at a time.

- The Host.json file also has configuration settings for queues, the Service Bus, and event hubs.

Now we look at the C# code of the TweetBotFunction, as shown in Listing 2-10. Functions are identified by the static methods that have a FunctionName attribute. The FunctionName attribute marks the method as a function entry point. The name must be unique within a project. It should start with a letter and can only contain letters, numbers, _ and -, up to 128 characters in length. The trigger type of a function can be identified by the Trigger attribute. For example, in TweetBotFunction, the TimerTrigger attribute indicates that this function runs on a timer basis.

Listing 2-10. The TweetBotFunction Class

```
using System;
using Microsoft.Azure.WebJobs;
using Microsoft.Extensions.Logging;

namespace TwitterBot.AzureFunctions
{
    public static class TweetBotFunction
    {
        [FunctionName("TweetBotFunction")]
        public static void Run([TimerTrigger("0 */5 * * * *")]TimerInfo
        myTimer, ILogger log)
```

```
    {
        log.LogInformation($"C# Timer trigger function executed at:
        {DateTime.Now}");
    }
  }
}
```

The Function method signature can contain the following parameters:

- Input and output bindings.

- An `ILogger` or `TraceWriter`

- `CancellationToken`

- Binding expressions

Input and output bindings are used to take input and return the output from the functions. For example, a queue-triggered function can be configured to get a queue message as input. It processes the message and writes it back to a Service Bus. There are many kinds of output bindings that are supported, such as Cosmos DB, Blob Storage, Notification Hubs, Twilio, etc.

`ILogger` and `TraceWriter` are used for logging. `CancellationToken` is used to handle the terminate events of functions. We can check for the `CancellationToken.IsCancellationRequested` property from within the function code to see if a cancellation is requested and thereby execute specific code that gracefully handles the termination.

Binding expressions are used to resolve the values at the runtime from difference sources. For example, the app settings values should be specific to an environment in which function is running, so it is always advisable to use `%appSettingsKey%` to use an app setting from configuration. In a similar way, we can get the additional metadata from the trigger source, especially from queues. We can also extract the information from JSON payloads using binding expressions.

Note   Implementation of triggers, bindings, and binding expressions is subjective to requirements. We may not be able to cover them all in the context of this book. Refer to `https://docs.microsoft.com/en-us/azure/azure-functions/functions-triggers-bindings` for more details on triggers and bindings.

The TweetBotFunction trigger uses TimerTrigger, which takes the Scheduler CRON expression {second} {minute} {hour} {day} {month} {day-of-week}. The expression 0 */5 * * * * translates to a timer function executed every five minutes. Other variants of the CRON expression are shown in Table 2-2.

Table 2-2. *CRON Expressions*

Expression	When Triggered
0 0 * * * *	Occurs every hour.
5,8,10 * * * * *	Occurs at fifth, eighth, and tenth second of every minute.
0 5 * * * *	Occurs at fifth minute of every hour.
0 0 */2 * * *	Occurs for every two hours.
0 0 9-17 * * *	Occurs at every hour from 9 AM to 5 PM.
0 30 9 * * *	Occurs at 9:30 AM every day.
0 30 9 * * 1-5	Occurs at 9:30 AM every weekday.
0 30 9 * Jan Mon	Occurs at 9:30 AM every Monday in January.

Note   UTC is the default time zone of timer functions. If we want to specific a different time zone, we should add the WEBSITE_TIME_ZONE app setting with a value, such as India Standard Time.

A complete list of available time zones can be found at https://docs. microsoft.com/en-us/previous-versions/windows/it-pro/windows-vista/cc749073(v=ws.10).

If the functions are hosted in the Azure App Service, they also support TimeSpan executions, where we can specify the time interval between each function execution.

The ILogger parameter is used to log the information to the Application Insights in a structured way, where the formatted string along with the passed objects are stored for rich analytics support.

Integrating the Tweet Bot Function with the Tweet Operations Framework

In this section, we integrate the Tweet Operations framework that we created earlier with the newly created TweetBotFunction. Let's get started by adding the TwitterBot. Framework project reference to the TwitterBot.AzureFunctions project, as shown in Figure 2-22. Right-click on Dependencies from the TwitterBot.AzureFunctions project and then choose Add Reference ➤ Project. Select the TwitterBot.Framework project and click OK.

Figure 2-22. *The TwitterBot.Framework reference in the TwitterBot. AzureFunctions project*

Once the reference has been added, we can update the TweetBotFunction to integrate with the TweetOperations class, as shown in Listing 2-11. We added the using namespaces for TwitterBot.Framework.Types, TwitterBot.Framework.Mappings, and TwitterBot.Framework.BusinessLogic. The static constructor will initiate AutoMapper's mappings.

Within the Run method, we have created a new instance of the TweetOperations class and invoked its GetPopularTweetByHashtag method by passing a hardcoded #justsaying hashtag. The result of the method is logged in to the console using the ILogger's LogInformation method.

Listing 2-11. TweetBotFunction Integrated with Tweet Operations

```csharp
using Microsoft.Azure.WebJobs;
using Microsoft.Extensions.Logging;
using TwitterBot.Framework.BusinessLogic;
using TwitterBot.Framework.Mappings;
using TwitterBot.Framework.Types;

namespace TwitterBot.AzureFunctions
{
    public static class TweetBotFunction
    {
        static TweetBotFunction()
        {
            MappingProfile.Activate();
        }

        [FunctionName("TweetBotFunction")]
        public static void Run([TimerTrigger("0 */5 * * * *")]TimerInfo
        myTimer, ILogger log)
        {
            var tweetOperations = new TweetOperations("API Key", "API
            Secret");
            var tweet = tweetOperations.GetPopularTweetByHashtag(new
            Hashtag { Text = "#justsaying" });
            if (tweet != null)
            {
                log.LogInformation($"Latest popular tweet for #justsaying :
                { tweet.FullText }");
            }
        }
    }
}
```

> **Note**   1. The hardcoding of `#justsaying` in Listing 2-11 will be removed in later chapters, when we integrate the `TweetBotFunction` with the Azure Cosmos DB.
>
> 2. Furthermore, directly initiating `TweetOperations` instance is not a recommended practice. The next section in this chapter will introduce the Dependency Injection concept through which dependencies are injected into the function at runtime.

Dependency Injection in Azure Functions

Dependency *Injection* (DI) is a software pattern through which an application can achieve loosely coupled layers. Instead of directly creating objects of various classes at different layers of the application, Dependency Injection will inject the dependent objects at runtime through different techniques (for example, constructor injection or property injection). This pattern uses abstractions (usually interfaces) and containers (it's essentially a factory that is responsible for providing instances of types) to resolve dependencies at runtime.

> **Note**   Currently Azure Functions doesn't have built-in support for Dependency Injection. There is an active feedback from community supporting Dependency Injection feature for Azure Functions: `https://feedback.azure.com/forums/355860-azure-functions/suggestions/15642447-enable-dependency-injection-in-c-functions`.
>
> Dependency Injection is planned in V3 of Azure Functions.

In this section, we focus on Dependency Injection in Azure Functions V2 (.NET Core). Open Source Community developers previously developed a nice implementation of Dependency Injection using `Inject` binding and `ExtensionConfigContext`. With the recent extension model changes in Microsoft.Net.Sdk.Functions 1.0.19, the previous implementations of DI are obsolete.

The new extension model allows us to have a `Startup` class with an
`[assembly:WebJobsStartup]` attribute, which implements `IWebJobsStartup`. In the
`Startup` class, we can define our own custom extensions by adding binding rules
between custom attributes and binding providers. Using the custom attribute, we can
inject the dependency into the function at runtime.

Note   Credit goes to `Dibran Mulder` (`https://github.com/
DibranMulder`) for implementing a DI solution using `IWebJobsStartup`
(`https://github.com/DibranMulder/azure-functions-v2-
dependency-injection`).

We are going to use his version of DI for our Tweet Bot application.

Creating a Custom Dependency Injection Framework

In this section, we create a custom Dependency Injection framework for
`TwitterBot.AzureFunctions`. Let's get started by adding the `Microsoft.Azure.WebJobs`
nuget package to the `TwitterBot.Framework` project, as shown in Figure 2-23.

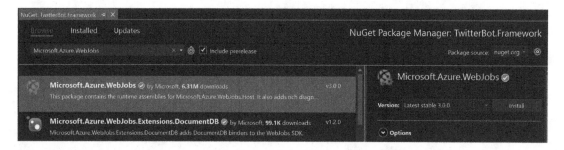

Figure 2-23.   *Install the Microsoft.Azure.WebJobs nuget*

Create a folder called `DependencyInjection` in the `TwitterBot.Framework` project.
Create a new attribute called `Inject` in the `DependencyInjection` folder, as shown in
Listing 2-12. This attribute is used to provide the binding information.

Listing 2-12. Inject Attribute

```
using Microsoft.Azure.WebJobs.Description;
using System;

namespace TwitterBot.Framework.DependencyInjection
{
    [Binding]
    [AttributeUsage(AttributeTargets.Parameter, AllowMultiple = false)]
    public class InjectAttribute : Attribute
    {
    }
}
```

We need to create IBinding and IBindingProvider classes in the DependencyInjection folder, as shown in Listings 2-13 and 2-14. The IBinding class holds the information of the binding. The binding provider is used to create bindings. IBindingProvider's TryCreateAsync method will be called for each instance of the Inject attribute to create an IBinding instance. IBindingProvider passes IServiceProvider and Type (from InjectAttribute) information to IBinding. Whenever a binding is resolved, IBinding's BindAsync method will be called with the Type information and the instance of the type and is returned as an IValueProvider (InjectValueProvider) instance.

Listing 2-13. InjectBinding Class

```
using Microsoft.Azure.WebJobs.Host.Bindings;
using Microsoft.Azure.WebJobs.Host.Protocols;
using Microsoft.Extensions.DependencyInjection;
using System;
using System.Threading.Tasks;

namespace TwitterBot.Framework.DependencyInjection
{
    internal class InjectBinding : IBinding
    {
        private readonly Type _type;
        private readonly IServiceProvider _serviceProvider;
```

```csharp
        internal InjectBinding(IServiceProvider serviceProvider, Type type)
        {
            _type = type;
            _serviceProvider = serviceProvider;
        }

        public bool FromAttribute => true;

        public Task<IValueProvider> BindAsync(object value,
        ValueBindingContext context) => Task.FromResult((IValueProvider)new
        InjectValueProvider(value));

        public async Task<IValueProvider> BindAsync(BindingContext context)
        {
            await Task.Yield();
            var value = _serviceProvider.GetRequiredService(_type);
            return await BindAsync(value, context.ValueContext);
        }

        public ParameterDescriptor ToParameterDescriptor() => new
        ParameterDescriptor();

        private class InjectValueProvider : IValueProvider
        {
            private readonly object _value;

            public InjectValueProvider(object value) => _value = value;
            public Type Type => _value.GetType();
            public Task<object> GetValueAsync() => Task.FromResult(_value);
            public string ToInvokeString() => _value.ToString();
        }
    }
}
```

Listing 2-14. InjectBindingProvider Class

```csharp
using Microsoft.Azure.WebJobs.Host.Bindings;
using System;
using System.Threading.Tasks;
```

```
namespace TwitterBot.Framework.DependencyInjection
{
    public class InjectBindingProvider : IBindingProvider
    {
        private IServiceProvider _serviceProvider;

        public InjectBindingProvider(IServiceProvider serviceProvider)
        {
            _serviceProvider = serviceProvider;
        }

        public Task<IBinding> TryCreateAsync(BindingProviderContext context)
        {
            IBinding binding = new InjectBinding(_serviceProvider,
            context.Parameter.ParameterType);
            return Task.FromResult(binding);
        }
    }
}
```

Now we will set up the configuration between IBindingProvider and
InjectAttribute by creating an implementation of IExtensionConfigProvider through
InjectConfiguration, as shown in Listing 2-15. The initialize method adds a rule on
ExtensionConfigContext to bind the Inject attribute with the binding provider.

Listing 2-15. InjectConfiguration Class

```
using Microsoft.Azure.WebJobs.Host.Config;

namespace TwitterBot.Framework.DependencyInjection
{
    public class InjectConfiguration : IExtensionConfigProvider
    {
        private InjectBindingProvider _injectBindingProvider;

        public InjectConfiguration(InjectBindingProvider
        injectBindingProvider)
```

```
    {
        _injectBindingProvider = injectBindingProvider;
    }

    public void Initialize(ExtensionConfigContext context)
    {
        var rule = context
                    .AddBindingRule<InjectAttribute>()
                    .Bind(_injectBindingProvider);
    }
  }
}
```

Configuring Azure Functions with a Custom Dependency Injection Framework

In this section, we configure Azure Functions with the custom Dependency Injection framework by creating a WebJobs Startup class and registering InjectConfiguration as an extension. Create a class called WebJobsExtensionStartup in TwitterBot. AzureFunctions, as shown in Listing 2-16. The [assembly: WebJobsStartup] attribute and IWebJobsStartup interface will make the class a startup for the TwitterBot. AzureFunctions project. In the Configure method, we configure ITweetOperations to resolve as the TweetOperations class instance. We will also register the InjectBindingProvider type and add the InjectConfiguration as an extension.

Note   As shown in Listing 2-16, the MappingProfile.Activate() invocation is moved to the Configure method of the WebJobsExtensionStartup class (from the static constructor of the TweetBotFunction class) to achieve one-time configuration of mappings in the TwitterBot.AzureFunctions project. Remove the static constructor along with MappingProfile.Activate() from the TweetBotFunction class.

Listing 2-16. WebJobsExtensionStartup Class

```
using Microsoft.Azure.WebJobs;
using Microsoft.Azure.WebJobs.Hosting;
using Microsoft.Extensions.DependencyInjection;
using TwitterBot.AzureFunctions;
using TwitterBot.Framework.BusinessLogic;
using TwitterBot.Framework.Contracts;
using TwitterBot.Framework.DependencyInjection;
using TwitterBot.Framework.Mappings;

[assembly: WebJobsStartup(typeof(WebJobsExtensionStartup), "TwitterBot
Extensions Startup")]
namespace TwitterBot.AzureFunctions
{
    public class WebJobsExtensionStartup : IWebJobsStartup
    {
        public void Configure(IWebJobsBuilder builder)
        {
            MappingProfile.Activate();
            builder.Services.AddSingleton<ITweetOperations>(new
            TweetOperations("API Key", "API Secret"));
            builder.Services.AddSingleton<InjectBindingProvider>();
            builder.AddExtension<InjectConfiguration>();
        }
    }
}
```

Once we build the Azure Function project in Visual Studio, it will generate an extensions.json file in the bin\Debug\netstandard2.0\bin folder of the TwitterBot.AzureFunctions project, which will hold all the configuration related to custom extensions, as shown in Listing 2-17. The Azure Functions runtime will depend on this file to load all the extensions at runtime. By default, only some extensions—like HTTP and Timer—are loaded by default by the runtime. The other extensions should be mentioned in the extensions.json file or the runtime will not load them.

Listing 2-17. The extensions.json file

```
{
  "extensions":[
    { "name": "TwitterBot Extensions Startup", "typeName":"TwitterBot.
    AzureFunctions.WebJobsExtensionStartup, TwitterBot.AzureFunctions,
    Version=1.0.0.0, Culture=neutral, PublicKeyToken=null"}
  ]
}
```

Finally, update the TweetBotFunction with the Inject attribute for ITweetOperations, as shown in Listing 2-18. The ITweetOperations instance is used to invoke the GetPopularTweetByHashtag method.

Listing 2-18. ITweetOperations Injection into the TweetBotFunction Class

```
using Microsoft.Azure.WebJobs;
using Microsoft.Extensions.Logging;
using TwitterBot.Framework.Contracts;
using TwitterBot.Framework.DependencyInjection;
using TwitterBot.Framework.Mappings;
using TwitterBot.Framework.Types;

namespace TwitterBot.AzureFunctions
{
    public static class TweetBotFunction
    {
        [FunctionName("TweetBotFunction")]
        public static void Run([TimerTrigger("0 */5 * * * *")]TimerInfo
        myTimer, ILogger log, [Inject]ITweetOperations tweetOperations)
        {
            var tweet = tweetOperations.GetPopularTweetByHashtag(new
            Hashtag { Text = "#justsaying" });
            if (tweet != null)
            {
```

```
                log.LogInformation($"Latest popular tweet for #justsaying :
                { tweet.FullText }");
            }
        }
    }
}
```

Note   At this point, there is an open issue with executing Azure Functions on the Azure Function App Services with Dependency Injection through custom extensions. The `extensions.json` file, which will hold the custom extensions configuration, is not holding the configuration during the publish activity from Visual Studio. Details of this issue can be found at `https://github.com/ Azure/azure-functions-host/issues/3386`.

To mitigate this issue, as mentioned in the link, we will create a `Directory. Build.targets` file in the `TwitterBot.AzureFunctions` project and place the configuration as shown in Listing 2-19. This build target will copy the `extensions.json` file (which has all the configuration) from the `build` directory to the `publish` directory.

Listing 2-19. The Directory.Build.targets File

```
<Project>
  <PropertyGroup>
    <_IsFunctionsSdkBuild Condition="$(_FunctionsTaskFramework) != "">
    true</_IsFunctionsSdkBuild>
    <_FunctionsExtensionsDir>$(TargetDir)</_FunctionsExtensionsDir>
    <_FunctionsExtensionsDir Condition="$(_IsFunctionsSdkBuild) ==
    'true'">$(_FunctionsExtensionsDir)bin</_FunctionsExtensionsDir>
  </PropertyGroup>

  <Target Name="CopyExtensionsJson" AfterTargets="_
GenerateFunctionsAndCopyContentFiles">
    <Message Importance="High" Text="Overwriting extensions.json file with
    one from build." />
```

```
<Copy Condition="$(_IsFunctionsSdkBuild) == 'true' AND Exists
('$(_FunctionsExtensionsDir)\extensions.json')"
      SourceFiles="$(_FunctionsExtensionsDir)\extensions.json"
      DestinationFiles="$(PublishDir)bin\extensions.json"
      OverwriteReadOnlyFiles="true"
      ContinueOnError="true"/>
  </Target>
</Project>
```

In this section, we have successfully implemented Dependency Injection in TweetBotFunction. In subsequent sections, we will run the TweetBotFunction and learn about the basics of Azure Function debugging.

Note   The Dependency Injection approach detailed in this section might change with future releases of Azure Functions SDK.

Debugging the Tweet Bot Function

In this section, we will run the TweetBotFunction in a local development environment and review the overall execution process. To execute an Azure Function from Visual Studio, we simply need to set that Azure Function project as the startup project (right-click the project and choose Set as Startup Project) and then press thee F5 key (the Start Debugging option from the Visual Studio Debug menu).

Note   Visual Studio may sometimes prompt you to download the latest version of the Azure Functions CLI tools, which are required to run the Azure Function locally. Allow it to proceed and download the latest version. In my development environment, Visual Studio prompted and downloaded Azure Functions CLI 2.8.1 tools.

Visual Studio will compile the source code and create function.json in the bin\Debug\%targetRuntime%\%FunctionName% folder (in this case, it is bin\Debug\ netstandard2.0\TweetBotFunction). The function.json file defines the function bindings and other configuration settings, as shown in Listing 2-20.

Listing 2-20. The function.json File

```json
{
  "generatedBy": "Microsoft.NET.Sdk.Functions-1.0.22",
  "configurationSource": "attributes",
  "bindings": [
    {
      "type": "timerTrigger",
      "schedule": "0 */5 * * * *",
      "useMonitor": true,
      "runOnStartup": false,
      "name": "myTimer"
    }
  ],
  "disabled": false,
  "scriptFile": "../bin/TwitterBot.AzureFunctions.dll",
  "entryPoint": "TwitterBot.AzureFunctions.TweetBotFunction.Run"
}
```

Note   It is not advisable to edit the `function.json` file manually.

The Azure Functions Runtime uses this file to determine the triggers and bindings of the function from the execution context. The following are some of the important settings:

- `disabled`: Can be set to `true` to prevent the function from being executed.

- `scriptFile`: Points to the function compiled assembly.

- `entryPoint`: Specifies the starting point of the function.

- `configurationSource`: If set to `config`, the Azure Functions Runtime gets the bindings and triggers information from the `function.json` file. If set to `attributes`, the runtime will get the bindings and triggers from the assembly. The `Function.json` file cannot be edited if `configurationSource` is set to `attributes`, because the same file is used for scaling the function.

- generatedBy: Specifies the SDK version that generated the file.

- bindings:

  - type: Conveys the type of trigger.

  - schedule: CRON expression representing the timer schedule.

  - useMonitor: When true, Schedule monitoring persists the occurrences to ensure the schedule is maintained correctly even when the function app instances restart.

  - runOnStartup: If true, the function is invoked when the runtime starts.

  - name: The name of the variable that represents the timer object in the function code.

Note   The full schema supported by function.json can be found at http://json.schemastore.org/function.

The Bindings section will be different for different types of triggers, for example the httpTrigger binding will have a route property to define HTTP route template.

There can be non-trigger input/output bindings that can be set to in/out using the direction property of the binding.

The compiled folder in the netstandard2.0 folder is shown in Figure 2-24. We have host.json and local.settings.json (discussed in previous section). The TwitterBot.AzureFunctions.deps.json file holds the references of runtime and all the dependencies. The TweetBotFunction folder holds the function.json. The Bin folder will contain all the assemblies along with runtimes.

TwitterBot › TwitterBot.AzureFunctions › bin › Debug › netstandard2.0 ›

	Name	Status	Date modified	Type	Size
☐	bin	⟳	9/28/2018 10:05 A...	File folder	
	TweetBotFunction	⟳	9/28/2018 10:05 A...	File folder	
	host	⟳	9/28/2018 9:07 AM	JSON File	1 KB
	local.settings	⟳	9/28/2018 9:07 AM	JSON File	1 KB
	TwitterBot.AzureFunctions.deps	⟳	9/28/2018 10:05 A...	JSON File	122 KB

Figure 2-24. *Compiled folder of TweetBotFunction*

Visual Studio uses the Azure Functions Core Tools to run the Functions projects, as shown in Figure 2-25. The Core Tools is a command-line interface for the Functions runtime. Visual Studio will launch `func.exe` from the Azure Function Core tools with the context of `TwitterBot.AzureFunctions`. The `Func.exe` will load the configuration from the JSON files and initialize and start the host process. It then publishes the schedule of function runs, displays the host listening port information, and finally executes the function on schedule.

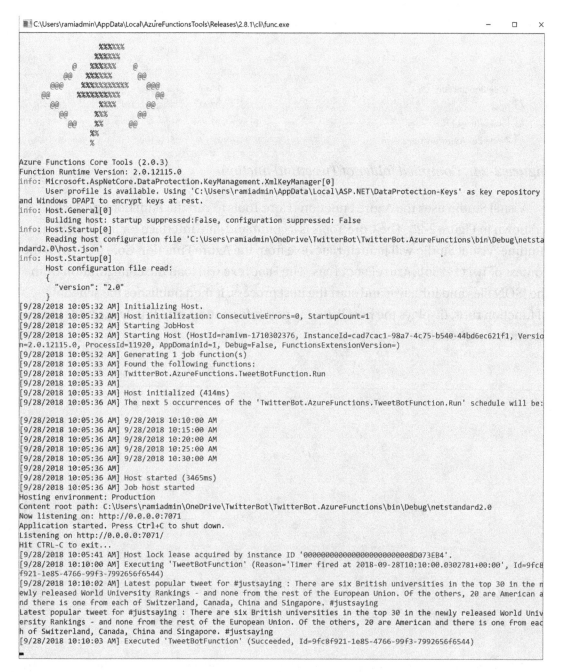

Figure 2-25. *Azure CLI execution of TwitterBot.AzureFunctions*

The host storage lock acquired by the instance is used by the timer trigger to ensure that there will be only one timer instance when a function app scales out to multiple instances.

Debugging a timer trigger function is very simple. We can set the breakpoints in the code and run the function locally. When the runtime executes the function, the breakpoint will get hit and we can inspect all the execution context in Visual Studio.

Note Similarly, we can debug other trigger types as described here.

`HttpTrigger`: Can be invoked directly from the localhost endpoint.

`QueueTrigger`, `BlobTrigger`: Using Azure Storage explorer, we can insert data into blobs and queues in the local storage emulator, which will invoke respective functions.

`ServiceBusTrigger`: There is no local emulator for ServiceBus, so we can create a new Service Bus instance on Azure and connect to it from the local debugging session.

Third-party triggers: Third-party triggers like GitHub and Webhook need proper connections from respective platforms to test the functions locally.

Cosmos DB Trigger: We discuss this type of trigger in the next chapter.

Deploying the Tweet Bot Function to an Azure Function App

In this section, we will look at the process of publishing an Azure Function to Azure Function App Services. We will deploy the `TweetBotFunction` to Azure Services.

Note The focus of this section is to introduce the deployment concepts of an Azure Function. The detailed Continuous Integration and Continuous Delivery strategy for the Twitter Bot application is discussed in later chapters.

The step-by-step process of creating a Function app in the Azure portal is described as follows:

1. Log in to the Azure portal and navigate to App Services, as shown in Figure 2-26. Click on +Add.

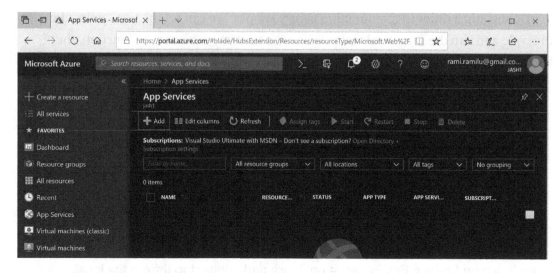

Figure 2-26. *Azure App Services*

2.   Select Function App, as shown in Figure 2-27, and click Create.

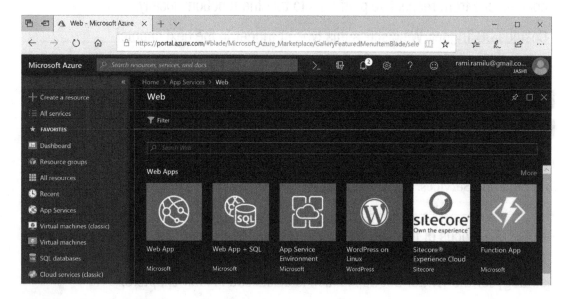

Figure 2-27. *Add a Function app*

3.   Provide the details of the Function app, as shown in Figure 2-28.
     Click Create.

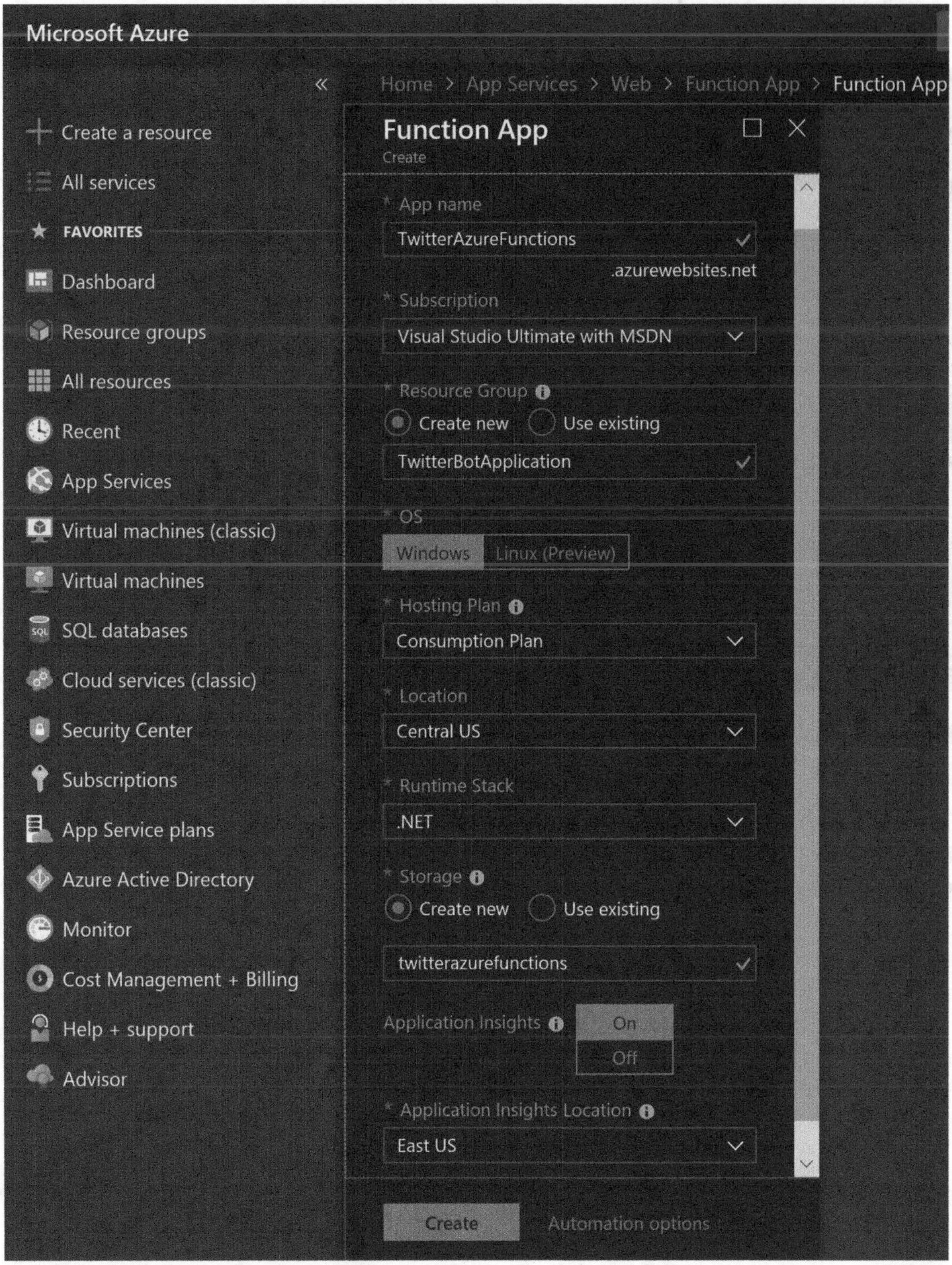

Microsoft Azure

+ Create a resource

≣ All services

★ **FAVORITES**

🔲 Dashboard

🔘 Resource groups

▦ All resources

🕐 Recent

🔵 App Services

🖥 Virtual machines (classic)

🖥 Virtual machines

🗄 SQL databases

☁ Cloud services (classic)

🛡 Security Center

🔑 Subscriptions

📇 App Service plans

◈ Azure Active Directory

🌐 Monitor

🔵 Cost Management + Billing

🗨 Help + support

☁ Advisor

Function App ☐ ✕
Create

* App name

TwitterAzureFunctions ✓

.azurewebsites.net

* Subscription

Visual Studio Ultimate with MSDN ∨

* Resource Group ❶

◉ Create new ⚪ Use existing

TwitterBotApplication ✓

* OS

Windows   Linux (Preview)

* Hosting Plan ❶

Consumption Plan ∨

* Location

Central US ∨

* Runtime Stack

.NET ∨

* Storage ❶

◉ Create new ⚪ Use existing

twitterazurefunctions ✓

Application Insights ❶ | On |
| Off |

* Application Insights Location ❶

East US ∨

Create   Automation options

Figure 2-28. Function app service details

4.   The new Azure App Function is shown in Figure 2-29.

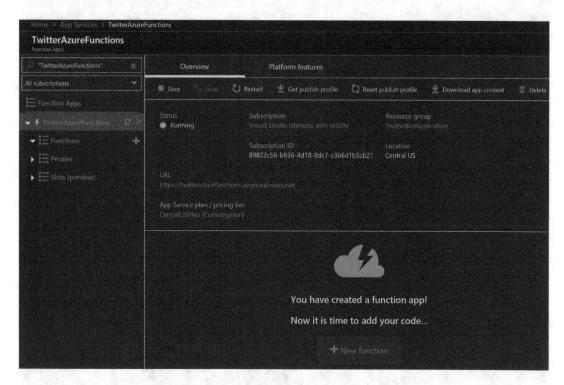

Figure 2-29.   *New TwitterAzureFunctions Function app*

Now that we have the function app created in Azure, we will publish the
TweetBotFunction from Visual Studio, as shown in Figure 2-30. Right-click on the
TwitterBot.AzureFunctions project and select the Publish option.

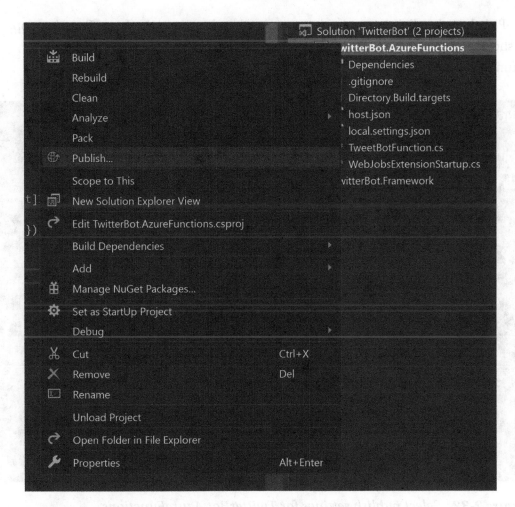

Figure 2-30. Publish TwitterBot.AzureFunctions from Visual Studio

Click Start on the Publish wizard, as shown in Figure 2-31.

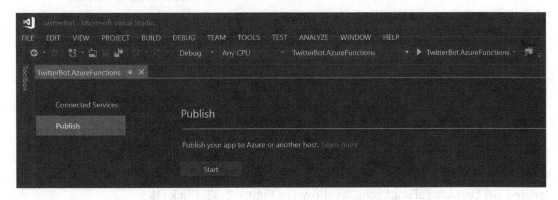

Figure 2-31. The Publish wizard

Pick the Select Existing option because we already created the Azure Function app, as shown in Figure 2-32. Check the Run from ZIP option, as it is the recommended setting. Click on Publish.

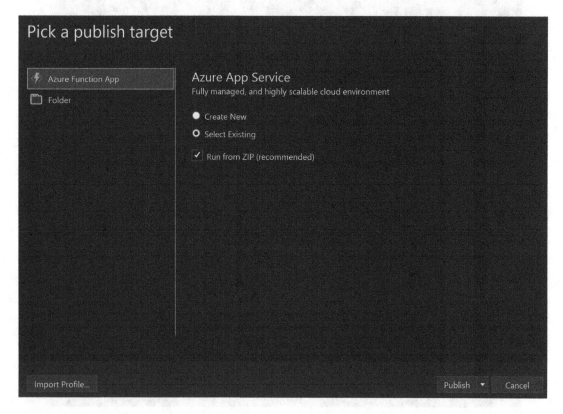

Figure 2-32. *Select publish settings for TwitterBot.AzureFunctions*

Note   The Run from ZIP option will enable the Azure Function app to run the function directly from the deployment package. In normal deployment options, all the files are copied to the wwwroot folder of the App Service. But with the Run from ZIP option, files are not copied to the wwwroot folder. The ZIP file itself is mounted on wwwroot as a read-only filesystem.

Based on the Azure subscription that we used to log in to Visual Studio, the Publish wizard will display the list of Azure Functions available from that subscription. We can select any Azure Function and can deploy our TweetBotFunction to it. Select the already created TwitterAzureFunctions, as shown in Figure 2-33. Click OK.

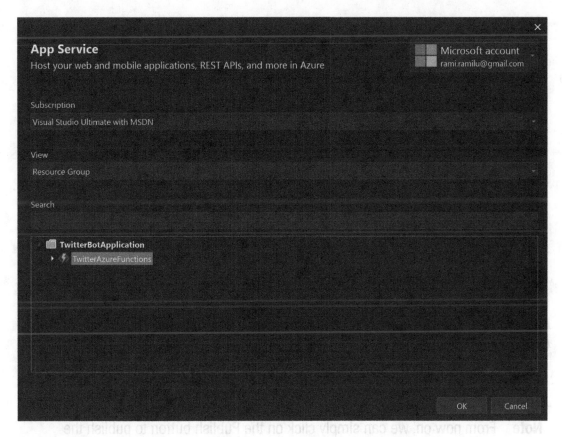

Figure 2-33. *Select the TwitterAzureFunctions Azure function app*

Visual Studio might prompt you to update the Azure Functions Runtime version at the remote app, as shown in Figure 2-34. Click Yes to initiate the publish.

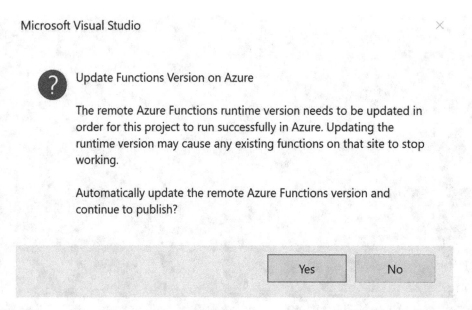

Figure 2-34. *Update prompt for the Azure Functions Runtime in the Azure Function app*

TweetBotFunction will be published to the Azure Function app.

Note   From now on, we can simply click on the Publish button to publish the latest changes to the Azure Function app.

Features of an Azure Function App

In the last section, we published the TwitterBot.AzureFunctions project to the Azure Function app. In this section, we learn about the features of the Azure Function app. We can navigate to TweetBotFunction in the App Services of the Azure portal, as shown in Figure 2-35. We can see the function.json file.

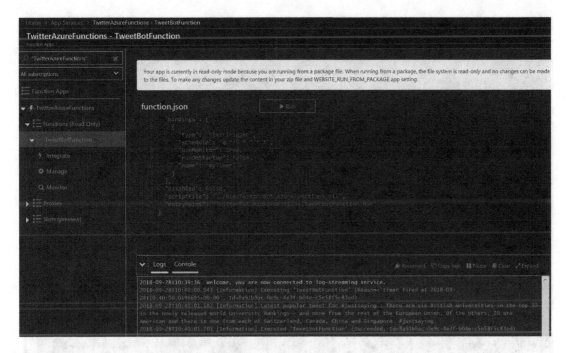

Figure 2-35. *Deployed TweetBotFunction in the Azure Function app*

After a few minutes, we can see the first execution of the function in the Logs
window, as shown in Figure 2-36. We can use the console window to run the commands
on the hosted wwwroot folder.

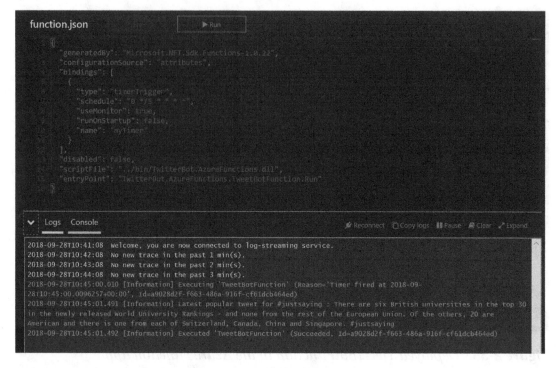

Figure 2-36. *Execution details of TweetBotFunction*

We can configure the Function settings, Application settings, Deployment options, etc., from the Platform Features tab of the Azure Function, as shown in Figure 2-37. Some of the important features supported by the Platform features are mentioned here:

- **Function Settings:** Includes host.json configuration, runtime version, app edit mode (readonly/read-write), deployment slots, daily usage quota in GB/sec, etc.

- **Application Settings:** Includes HTTP and platform (32/64-bit) configuration, app settings, ConnectionStrings, virtual application and directory mappings, handler mappings, FTP access, remote debugging, etc.

- **Monitoring:** Turn on/off diagnostic logging at application and web server level, configure request tracing and detailed error messages, live streaming logs, details of worker processes, metrics, etc.

- **Deployment:** Configure deployment options, credentials, Continuous deployment, etc.

- **Development Tools:** The App service editor can be used to quickly edit function artifacts, console window to access the function directory, Kudu access to troubleshoot environment, debug console and analyze process dumps. There are options to Access Azure resource group resources, install third-party extensions, create logic apps, etc.

- **Networking:** Configure SSL, certificates and custom domains, configure authentication and authorization, register with Azure Active Directory, Enable mobile push notifications, configure Azure CDN and IP address restrictions.

- **Others:** Configure CORS, check app service plan, quotas and scale up, generate swagger API definition, etc.

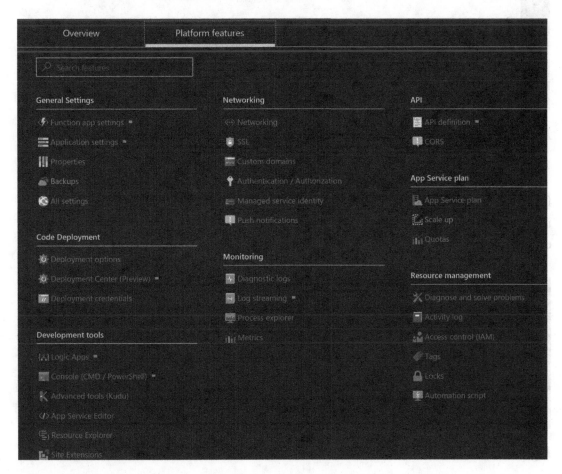

Figure 2-37.   Platform features of the Azure Function app

We can explore the Azure Function artifacts using the App Service Editor of the Platform features, as shown in Figure 2-38. We can edit the files using the App Editor.

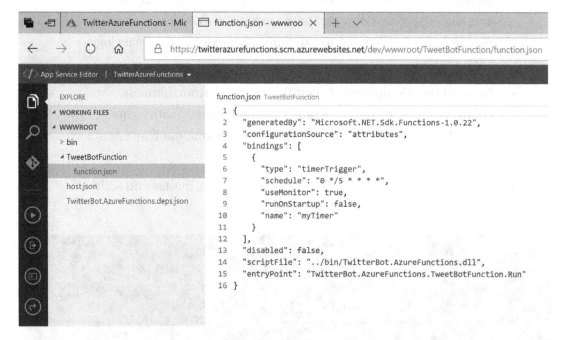

Figure 2-38. *Exploring Azure Function artifacts using the App Editor*

We can monitor the function execution by navigating to the Monitor tab of a function, as shown in Figure 2-39. Monitor will display success and error counts. We can navigate to Application Insights, where we can get more detailed information through different logs.

DATE (UTC) ⌄	SUCCESS ⌄	RESULT CODE ⌄	DURATION (MS) ⌄	OPERATION ID ⌄
2018-09-28 10:45:00.009	✓	0	1481.9947	4EpVVWUzv3U=
2018-09-28 10:40:00.021	✓	0	1680.4496	Qpp3ebmqaSA=

Figure 2-39. *Monitor Azure Function executions*

Using the Manage tab, we can enable/disable a function from execution and configure the host keys that are common for all functions, as shown in Figure 2-40. These host keys are primarily used to authenticate and authorize webhooks and HTTP-triggered functions. The _master key provides administrative access to the runtime API, which we can use to access other function specific keys and host keys. The default key is used by default for webhook communication. When the keys have the same names, function-specific keys will take precedence over host keys.

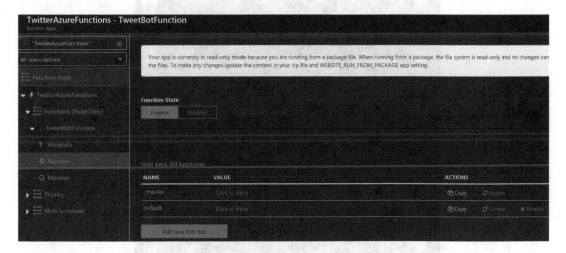

Figure 2-40.   *The Manage tab of a Azure Function*

To understand the next set of features, create a new Azure Function App Service called NewTempFunction, as shown in Figure 2-41.

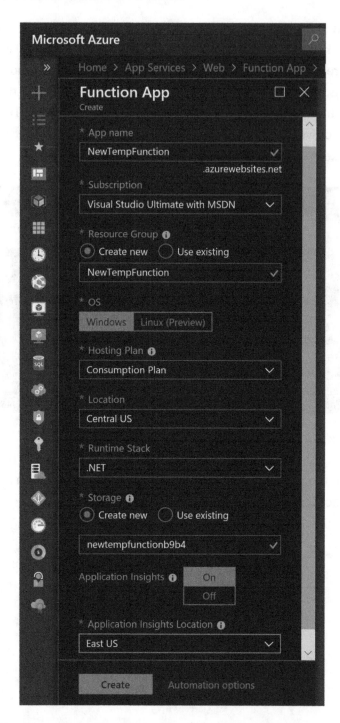

Figure 2-41. *NewTempFunction Azure Function App Service*

Click on the + button and a new HttpTrigger-based function called
HttpTriggerCSharp1, as shown in Figure 2-42.

Figure 2-42. *New HttpTrigger Azure function*

We can use the Integrate tab to configure new input/output bindings for the
HttpTriggerCSharp1 Azure function, which is created in the Azure portal, as shown in
Figure 2-43. Similarly, existing bindings will be displayed, as shown in Figure 2-44.

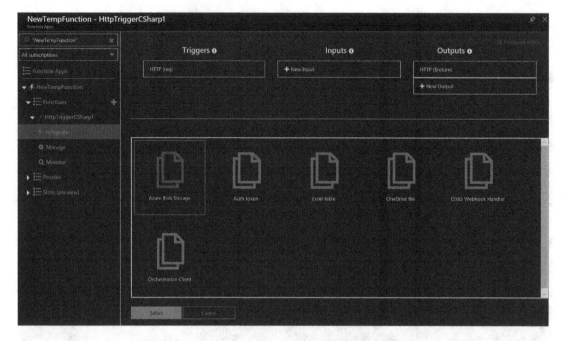

Figure 2-43. *New binding in the Integrate tab of the Azure Function*

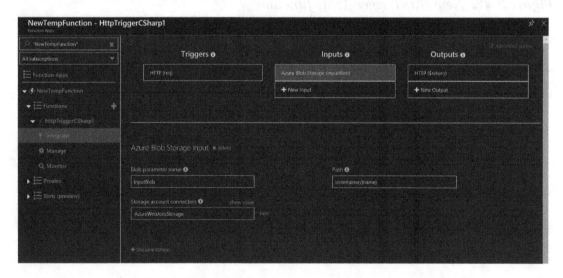

Figure 2-44. *Existing bindings in the Integrate tab of the Azure Function*

Note   We can create/modify the input/output bindings only for non-read-only functions. For the TweetBotFunction, we cannot use this tab because it is a read-only function with predefined bindings configured and published from Visual Studio.

We can directly create a function in the Azure portal. In that case, we can use the Integrate tab to configure bindings.

Azure Function's Proxies help forward the incoming request to a specific backend. We can create a proxy, as shown in Figure 2-45, where we specify the name of the proxy, route template to match the incoming request, allowed HTTP methods, and the backend URL to which the matched request should be forwarded. Proxy is a great feature that lets us break the large APIs into smaller, functional apps.

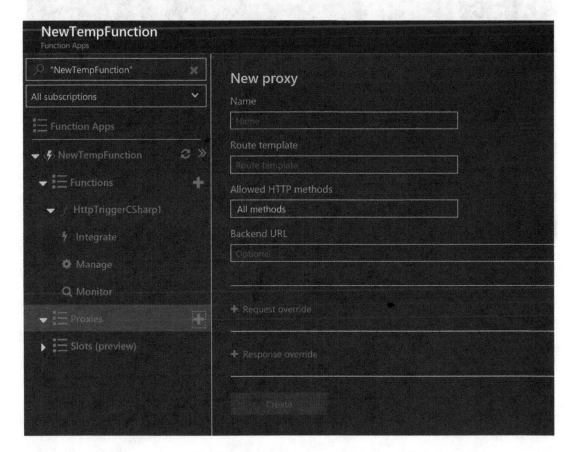

Figure 2-45. *Proxies in Azure Function*

Slots are another good feature in Azure Functions. We can configure different deployment slots that can have their own standalone deployments. This feature is very useful when we want to test our changes in the cloud before publishing the changes to the main environment. For example, we can test the changes in the staging environment before publishing them to the production environment. Slots are currently in the preview stage. To enable slots, we first need to turn on the Enable Deployment Slots (Preview) option from the Function App settings, as shown in Figure 2-46.

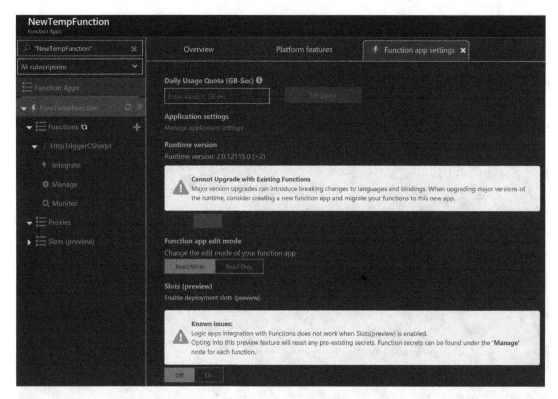

Figure 2-46. *Enable deployment slots in Azure Function*

We can create a slot, as shown in Figure 2-47. Give it a name and click on Create.

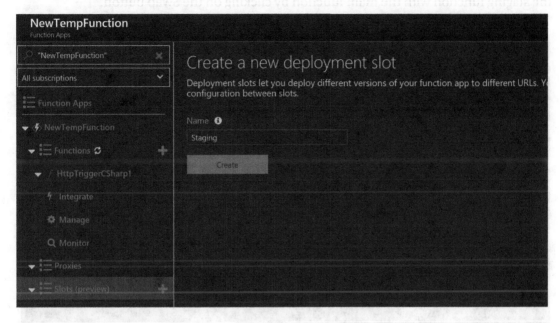

Figure 2-47. *Create a deployment slot in Azure Function*

The staging slot will have the Azure Function, as shown in Figure 2-48. We can swap the staging function with the main function by clicking on the Swap button.

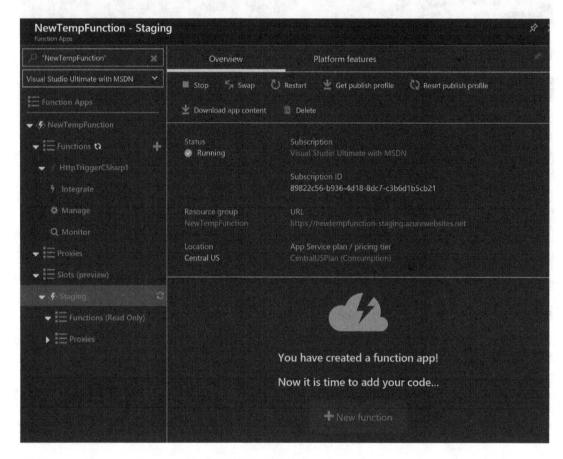

Figure 2-48. *Staging deployment slot in Azure Function*

Click on the Swap button to swap the Azure Function slot with another slot, as shown in Figure 2-49. Select the appropriate source and destination slots and click OK.

***Figure 2-49.** Swapping Azure Function slots*

The functions are swapped, as shown in Figure 2-50.

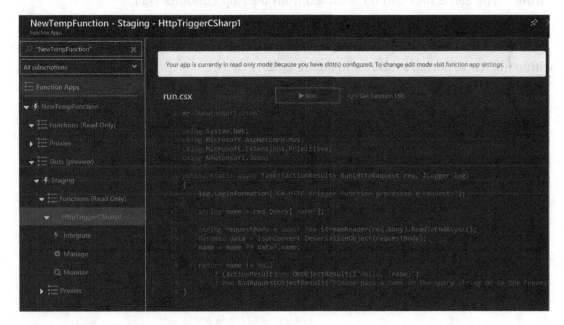

***Figure 2-50.** Swapped Azure Function slots*

Other important feature of the Azure Function app is the option to quickly glance the files related to Function in the View Files section, as shown in Figure 2-51.

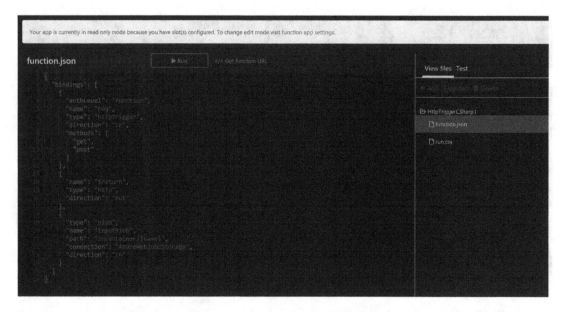

Figure 2-51. *View Files option of the Azure Function*

Note   The same files can be browsed from the App Editor as well.

The Azure Function app also comes with the default capability to run tests from within the Azure portal, as shown in Figure 2-52.

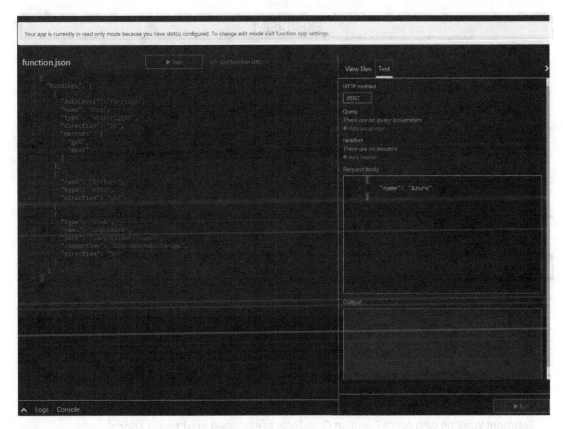

Figure 2-52. *Test an Azure function*

Note   We have explored most of the common Azure Function app features used in day-to-day operations. Some features, for example deployment slots, can be complex and extensive. They demand their own dedicated chapters for deep understanding.

In the context of this book, I explore all the necessary features and at the same time introduce all the relevant features at a high level. For more detailed information about these concepts or features, I recommend the Azure documentation at `https://docs.microsoft.com/en-us/azure/azure-functions/`.

EXERCISE 1

Create and run a simple Timer Trigger-based Azure Functions project using Azure Functions Core tools (CLI). So far in this chapter, we have used Visual Studio 2017 to develop and execute the Azure Functions project. Azure Functions development can also be achieved using the Azure Function Core Tools. The focus of this exercise is to familiarize you with core tools so you can learn how to use CLI to perform basic operations on the Azure Functions project.

Solution: Working with Azure Function Core Tools is explained in `https://docs.microsoft.com/en-us/azure/azure-functions/functions-run-local`.

EXERCISE 2

Publish a simple Timer Trigger-based Azure Functions project to an Azure Function app using Azure CLI and Azure Functions Core tools. In this chapter, we learned on how to deploy an Azure Functions project from Visual Studio. The intention of this exercise is to explore the Azure CLI and Azure Functions Core tools and automate the creation of an Azure Function app and then deploy the local project to Azure.

Solution: Working with Azure Function Core Tools is explained in `https://docs.microsoft.com/en-us/azure/azure-functions/functions-run-local`.

Create an Azure Function app using Azure CLI: `https://docs.microsoft.com/en-us/azure/azure-functions/functions-create-first-azure-function-azure-cli`.

Summary

In this chapter, you primarily focused on understanding the basics of Azure Functions. The brief details of Azure Functions—the core features, versions, and architecture—will help you identify the right business requirements that can be achieved by leveraging Azure Functions.

Later in the chapter, you signed up for a Twitter developer account and registered an application to access the Twitter Platform API. You created an API method in the `TwitterBot.Framework` project to retrieve the popular tweet based on a keyword with the help of `Tweetinvi`, an open source .NET C# library to access the Twitter REST API.

You created a Timer Trigger-based Azure Function in the `TwitterBot.`
`AzureFunctions` project and integrated it with `TwitterBot.Framework`. You learned
about different artifacts of an Azure Functions project. You created and configured a
custom Dependency Injection framework for Azure Functions.

You created the `TwitterAzureFunctions` Azure Function app and deployed the
`TwitterBot.AzureFunctions` project to it from Visual Studio. Finally, you explored
the different features of an Azure Function app, including logs and console windows,
platform features, the app editor, integrated tabs, and proxies and slots.

In the next chapter, you will learn the basics of the Azure Cosmos DB. You will
create a Tweet Notifier Azure Function by leveraging Azure Cosmos DB's change feed
mechanism.

References

1. https://azure.microsoft.com/en-us/blog/introducing-
   azure-functions/

2. https://azure.microsoft.com/en-in/blog/announcing-
   general-availability-of-azure-functions/

3. https://docs.microsoft.com/en-us/azure/azure-functions/
   functions-best-practices

4. https://docs.microsoft.com/en-us/azure/azure-functions/
   functions-versions

5. https://docs.microsoft.com/en-us/azure/azure-functions/
   durable-functions-overview

6. https://docs.microsoft.com/en-us/dotnet/standard/
   serverless-architecture/serverless-architecture

7. https://docs.microsoft.com/en-us/azure/azure-functions/
   functions-overview

8. https://docs.microsoft.com/en-us/azure/azure-functions/
   functions-host-json

9. https://docs.microsoft.com/en-us/azure/azure-functions/
   functions-run-local#local-settings-file

10. https://docs.microsoft.com/en-us/azure/azure-functions/
    functions-bindings-timer

11. https://docs.microsoft.com/en-us/azure/azure-functions/
    functions-triggers-bindings

12. https://blog.wille-zone.de/post/azure-functions-proper-
    dependency-injection/

13. https://github.com/Azure/azure-webjobs-sdk/issues/1865

CHAPTER 3

Exploring Azure Cosmos DB and Its Change Feed Mechanism

Twenty-first century software innovations and digital transformations not only changed traditional ways of operating businesses but also created new opportunities in different industries. As organizations started to adapt to different automation methodologies, the software industry began to experience unprecedented data growth. The cloud infrastructure, along with business intelligence tools, helped businesses securely store large volumes of data and process this data at high speeds with greater accuracy.

Platforms like Azure Storage, Azure HDInsight, and Amazon S3, along with different strategies that support these data models, like NoSQL, Big Data, Blob, and Graph, have not only made the data acquisition, ingestion, and transformation processes very simple and intuitive but have also helped developers create more innovative solutions. Gone are the days where software professionals had to deal with gigabytes of information; the current software applications demand a need to support and withstand terabytes to petabytes of information. The reliability of data storage and the flexibility in data modeling play a pivotal role in achieving great performance and high precision in mission-critical decision-making processes. A robust data storage must have the following features:

- Scalability, durability, low latency, and always on

- Global distribution, high availability, and disaster recovery

- Support for different data formats

- Good security and built-in performance

- Cost-optimized and good support for Big Data solutions

99

© Rami Vemula 2019
R. Vemula, *Integrating Serverless Architecture*, https://doi.org/10.1007/978-1-4842-4489-0_3

Azure Cosmos DB is Microsoft's globally distributed, multi-model database. It comes with all the default features of high throughput, elastically scaling, automatic indexing, and partitions. The Twitter Bot application uses Azure Cosmos DB's DocumentDB and its SQL API to perform data operations.

In this chapter, we:

- Explore the fundamentals of Azure Cosmos DB.

- Create a C# repository pattern implementation for Cosmos DB using SQL API.

- Understand the change feed mechanism of Cosmos DB.

- Design a data model for the Twitter Bot application.

- Integrate `TweetBotFunction` (developed in previous chapter) with Cosmos DB.

- Develop a Cosmos DB Trigger-based Azure Function that will get notifications from Cosmos DB.

Introduction to Azure Cosmos DB

Azure Cosmos DB is Microsoft's Azure Database Service. It's distributed globally and supports multiple data models, such as document, graph, key value, and column store. Cosmos DB is primarily built on top of Azure DocumentDB and it launched in May 2017.

Cosmos DB is a schema-free database; in other words, it's a typical NoSQL database. It supports different types of schema-free variants:

- **Documents:** Stores JSON documents.

- **Graph:** Stores data in graphs with vertices and edges.

- **Key Value:** Stores data in key and value pairs, for Azure table storage.

- **Column Store:** Stores the data using columns instead of rows.

Note   If relational data is a requirement, you should use the Azure SQL database, which is based on SQL Server.

Cosmos DB currently supports the following APIs to perform data operations. Figure 3-1 depicts the different data models and APIs of Cosmos DB.

- **SQL API:** Interacts with a document database for JSON data.

- **MongoDB API:** Existing MongoDB applications can leverage this API to interact with Cosmos DB.

- **Table API:** Supports Azure table storage operations.

- **Gremlin API:** Used to interact with graph data.

- **Cassandra API:** Existing Apache Cassandra applications (for example, apps dependent on column stores) can use this API to work with Cosmos DB.

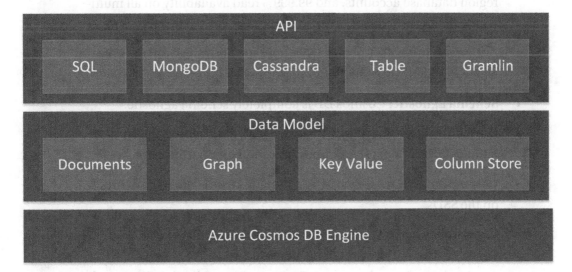

Figure 3-1. *Azure Cosmos data models and APIs*

Note   Each Cosmos DB API supports different programming models, such as .NET, Java, Node.js, Python, etc.

101

The main features of Cosmos DB are described here:

- **Turnkey global distribution:** Cosmos DB can be distributed across multiple regions. We can define read, write, and read/write regions, and Azure takes care of saving and retrieving data to closest region without any code or config changes.

- **Support for multiple data models and APIs:** Cosmos DB supports different data models, like document, graph, key value, and column store, which can be accessed through different APIs provided by different language SDKs, including SQL, MongoDB, Table, Gremlin, and Cassandra.

- **Always on:** Cosmos DB offers 99.99% availability SLA for all single-region database accounts, and 99.999% read availability on all multi-region database accounts.

- **Automatic indexes:** Cosmos DB automatically indexes all the data, which implicitly provides better performance queries.

- **Schema agnostic:** Cosmos DB is completely schema agnostic.

- **Horizontal storage scaling:** Cosmos DB dynamically scales to handle different data sizes through its container partitions.

- **Cost optimized:** We only pay for throughput and data (GBs) stored on the SSDs.

- **Consistency level:** Cosmos DB offers different levels of data read-write consistency levels—strong, bounded-staleness, session, consistent prefix, and eventual. Each consistency level differs based on how data is read during concurrent writes.

- **Automatic failovers:** Cosmos DB supports automatic failovers with the help of preferred locations configuration. If all the read regions have an outage, all the calls are redirected to a write region. If the write region has an outage, then another alternative region will be promoted as the write region.

- **Automatic backup and restore:** Cosmos DB automatically takes backups at regular intervals. In case of accidental DB deletion or data corruption, Azure support can restore backups for business continuity.

- **Low latency:** Cosmos DB guarantees low latency at the 99th percentile for various database operations. This is achieved because of global distribution of Cosmos DBs, where reads/writes are always performed in the region local to the client.

- **Security:** Cosmos DB provides encryption of data. This includes support for firewalls and IP access control, fine-grained access control using master keys and resource tokens, and Azure Key Vault support to store keys.

- **Time to live support:** Cosmos DB provides the ability to have documents automatically purged from the database after a period.

- **Support for change feed:** Automated notifications support on insert and update operations.

- **Multi-master (under preview):** Cosmos DB supports writing data to one region and it will propagate changes to other regions asynchronously with an uncompromised latency of less than 10ms.

Azure Cosmos DB is rapidly innovating, and Microsoft is planning to add new extensions in the SDK along with new platform features. Enhancements like support for paging, partial updates on documents, and support for group by, like, distinct clauses are planned in the near future. We can also expect support for more data models and different connectors to other Azure services. The long journey of Azure Cosmos DB has just started. Stay tuned.

Azure Cosmos DB Emulator

Azure Cosmos DB provides an emulator to support local development and testing. The emulator supports creating and querying JSON documents, provisioning and scaling collections, and executing stored procedures and triggers.

Note   The Azure Cosmos DB Emulator can be downloaded from `https://docs.microsoft.com/en-us/azure/cosmos-db/local-emulator`. Even though the emulator provides a similar Cosmos DB simulation, there can be differences with real Azure Cosmos DB. The emulator currently doesn't support the Table, Graph, and Cassandra APIs. Be cautious while developing applications using the emulator.

Once installed, the Cosmos DB Emulator can be started from the Windows Start menu, as shown in Figure 3-2.

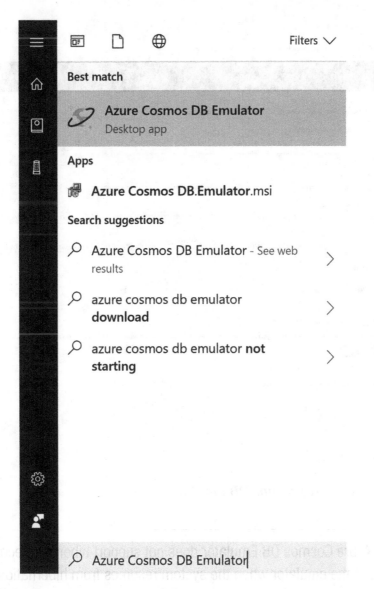

Figure 3-2. *Start the Azure Cosmos DB Emulator*

To check the emulator, we can navigate to `https://localhost:8081/_explorer/` `index.html` in any browser, as shown in Figure 3-3. We will use the `URI` and `Primary Key` settings to connect to the Cosmos DB Emulator from any application.

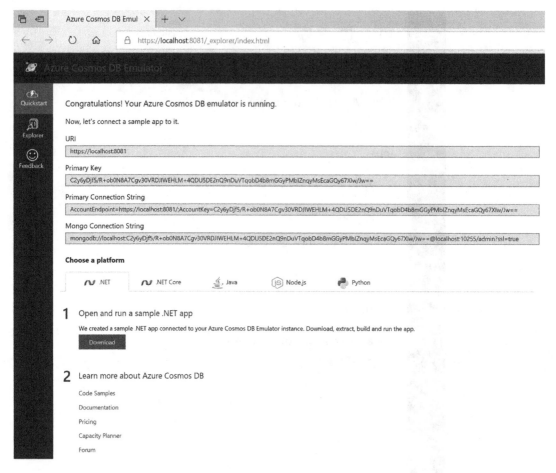

Figure 3-3. *The Azure Cosmos DB Emulator*

Note   The Azure Cosmos DB Emulator does not support hibernate recovery. You'll need to restart the emulator when the system resumes from hibernation. One other important thing to remember is to enable local firewall settings to allow TCP traffic for the emulator-related processes.

Azure Cosmos DB Repository Pattern

In this section, we are going to use Azure Cosmos DB with the SQL API (Documents) to build a robust data persistence store for the Twitter Bot application.

Note   The reason to use Azure Cosmos DB as the backend for the Twitter Bot application is its change feed mechanism. Azure Functions have built-in support to handle Cosmos DB Trigger events, which are based on change feed.

In this section, we create a generic C# repository pattern for Azure Cosmos DB. This repository pattern will let us work with any type of document (hashtags, tweets, etc.) in a generic way without duplicating the C# code.

We need to install the `Microsoft.Azure.DocumentDB.Core` nuget on the `TwitterBot.Framework` project, as shown in Figure 3-4.

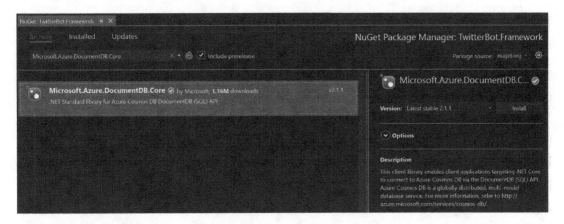

Figure 3-4. *Install the Microsoft.Azure.DocumentDB.Core nuget on the TwitterBot.Framework project*

In Chapter 2's section entitled "Creating Tweet Operations Framework Using the Tweetinvi Library," we created the `BaseType` class in the `Types` folder of the `TwitterBot.Framework` project. Update the `BaseType class` with the `JsonProperty` attribute for Id, as shown in Listing 3-1. `BaseType` is going to serve as the base model for all the Twitter Bot application models; it will hold all the common properties.

Listing 3-1. Updated BaseType Class

```csharp
using Newtonsoft.Json;
using System;
namespace TwitterBot.Framework.Types
{
    public class BaseType
    {
        [JsonProperty(PropertyName = "id")]
        public string Id { get; set; }
        public DateTime CreatedOn { get; set; }
        public string CreatedBy { get; set; }
        public DateTime ModifiedOn { get; set; }
        public string ModifiedBy { get; set; }
        public bool IsDeleted { get; set; }
    }
}
```

We created some sample models in Chapter 2 to demonstrate Azure Functions. The sample models do not hold all the required properties. The Twitter Bot application models will be designed in later sections of this chapter.

Create a folder called Data in the Contracts folder of the TwitterBot.Framework project. Create the IDocumentDbEntity interface in the Data folder, as shown in Listing 3-2. This interface will define the metadata of each entity collection that we are going to persist in Cosmos DB.

Note   Each document must have a partition key and a row key to uniquely identify it. Partition keys act as logical partitions for data and help Azure Cosmos DB distribute data across multiple physical partitions. We have already defined RowKey (id) in BaseType, which will be inherited by all entities.

For collections greater than 10GB, a partition key is required for better optimization. We are not going to use a partition key in any of the entities in the Twitter Bot application.

Listing 3-2. IDocumentDbEntity Interface

```
using System;
namespace TwitterBot.Framework.Contracts.Data
{
    public interface IDocumentDbEntity
    {
        Type EntityType { get; set; }
        string Name { get; set; }
    }
}
```

Create a new folder called `CosmosDB` in the `TwitterBot.Framework` project. This folder will hold the Cosmos DB related implementations of the contracts. Create the `DocumentDbEntity` class in the `CosmosDB` folder by inheriting from the `IDocumentDbEntity` interface, as shown in Listing 3-3.

Listing 3-3. DocumentDbEntity Class

```
using System;
using TwitterBot.Framework.Contracts.Data;
namespace TwitterBot.Framework.CosmosDB
{
    public class DocumentDbEntity : IDocumentDbEntity
    {
        public Type EntityType { get; set; }
        public string Name { get; set; }
    }
}
```

Creating a Document DB Context

In this section, we will create the IDocumentDbContext interface in the Data folder, as shown in Listing 3-4. IDocumentDbContext will hold all the information required to connect and operate against Cosmos DB. It will have the following properties:

- DatabaseId, EndpointUri, and AuthKey, which are required to connect to a Cosmos DB.

- IDocumentClient of the Microsoft.Azure.DocumentDb.Core nuget, which will help us interact with Cosmos DB by providing methods like CreateDatabaseAsync, CreateDocumentCollectionAsync, UpsertDocumentAsync, CreateDocumentQuery, etc.

- The EntityCollection list, which will hold all the entities of the Twitter Bot application.

- The CreateDatabaseAndCollectionsAsync method, which will ensure that the Twitter Bot application database and all its collections are created in the Cosmos DB.

Listing 3-4. IDocumentDbContext Interface

```
using Microsoft.Azure.Documents;
using System.Collections.Generic;
using System.Threading.Tasks;
namespace TwitterBot.Framework.Contracts.Data
{
    public interface IDocumentDbContext
    {
        string DatabaseId { get; set; }
        string EndpointUri { get; set; }
        string AuthKey { get; set; }
        IDocumentClient DocumentClient { get; }
        ICollection<IDocumentDbEntity> EntityCollection { get; }
        Task CreateDatabaseAndCollectionsAsync();
    }
}
```

Now we will create `DocumentDbContext` in the `CosmosDB` folder, as shown in
Listing 3-5. `DocumentDbContext` will implement `IDocumentDbContext`.

- The `DocumentClient` property will be populated from the
  `GetDocumentClient` private method. This method creates a new
  instance of `DocumentClient` with a new `ConnectionPolicy`. We
  need to pass an `Endpoint` and `Authentication` key to construct
  an `DocumentClient` instance. `ConnectionPolicy` is used to set the
  following important properties:

  - `ConnectionMode`: Defines how to connect to the Azure Cosmos
    DB Service—Direct or Gateway. Gateway (HTTPS) best suits
    applications running under corporate networks and where
    sockets are limited, for example Azure Functions. Direct mode is
    used to interact with Cosmos DB in TCP and HTTPS protocols.
    We will use Gateway mode, as we will be running the application
    through Azure Functions.

  - `ConnectionProtocol`: We will use HTTPS. Another available
    option is TCP.

  - `MaxConnectionLimit`: The default connection limit is 50. We
    can increase it (to 100), which will help us make multiple
    simultaneous connections.

  - `RetryOptions`: This option sets the retry options for request
    throttling. `MaxRetryAttemptsOnThrottledRequests` is used to
    define the number of times a retry should be performed before an
    exception is thrown. The `MaxRetryWaitTimeInSeconds` property
    allows the application to set a maximum wait time for all retry
    attempts.

  - `EnableEndpointDiscovery`: Based on this property,
    DocumentDB SDK will discover the current write and read
    regions to ensure requests are sent to the correct region based on
    the regions specified in the `PreferredLocations` property.

  - `EnableReadRequestsFallback`: This property is used to configure
    whether to allow reads to go to multiple regions configured on an
    account of the Azure Cosmos DB service.

- PreferredLocations: When EnableEndpointDiscovery is true
  and the value of this property is non-empty, the SDK uses the
  locations in this collection in the order they are specified to
  perform data operations. Otherwise, if the value of this property
  is not specified, the SDK uses the write region as the preferred
  location for all operations.

- Other properties: RequestTimeout can be used to specify the
  timeout value when connecting to the Azure Cosmos DB.
  MediaReadMode/MediaRequestTimeout can be specified when
  reading media content.

- EntityCollection will be populated from the GetDocumentEntities
  method. In GetDocumentEntities, we will create the list of all entities
  that will be stored in Cosmos DB. For each entity, we specify the type
  and collection name. Every time we add a new entity, we should
  update this list. We configured the Tweet class with TweetCollection.

- The CreateDatabaseAndCollectionsAsync method internally
  invokes the CreateDatabaseAsync and CreateCollectionAsync
  private methods. CreateDatabaseAsync is used to create the
  database using the CreateDatabaseIfNotExistsAsync method
  of DocumentClient. One collection per entity is created by using
  the CreateDocumentCollectionIfNotExistsAsync method of the
  DocumentClient instance.

Note We can use the RequestOptions class to configure the requests
issued against the Azure Cosmos DB Service. Similarly, we can use the
FeedOptions class to configure feeds from the Azure Cosmos DB Service.
The complete documentation can be found at https://docs.microsoft.
com/en-us/dotnet/api/microsoft.azure.documents.client.
requestoptions?view=azure-dotnet and https://docs.microsoft.
com/en-us/dotnet/api/microsoft.azure.documents.client.
feedoptions?view=azure-dotnet.

Listing 3-5. DocumentDbContext Class

```
using Microsoft.Azure.Documents;
using Microsoft.Azure.Documents.Client;
using System;
using System.Collections.Generic;
using System.Threading.Tasks;
using TwitterBot.Framework.Contracts.Data;
using TwitterBot.Framework.Types;

namespace TwitterBot.Framework.CosmosDB
{
    public class DocumentDbContext : IDocumentDbContext
    {
        private IDocumentClient _documentClient;
        private IList<IDocumentDbEntity> _documentDbEntities;

        public string EndpointUri { get; set; }
        public string AuthKey { get; set; }
        public string DatabaseId { get; set; }

        public IDocumentClient DocumentClient
        {
            get
            {
                if (_documentClient == null)
                {
                    _documentClient = GetDocumentClient();
                }
                return _documentClient;
            }
        }

        public ICollection<IDocumentDbEntity> EntityCollection
        {
            get
            {
                if (_documentDbEntities == null)
```

```
        {
            _documentDbEntities = GetDocumentEntities();
        }
        return _documentDbEntities;
    }
}

public async Task CreateDatabaseAndCollectionsAsync()
{
    await CreateDatabaseAsync(DatabaseId);
    foreach (var entity in EntityCollection)
    {
        await CreateCollectionAsync(DatabaseId, entity.Name);
    }
}

private IDocumentClient GetDocumentClient()
{
    var connectionPolicy = new ConnectionPolicy
    {
        ConnectionMode = ConnectionMode.Gateway,
        ConnectionProtocol = Protocol.Https,
        MaxConnectionLimit = 1000,
        RetryOptions = new RetryOptions {
        MaxRetryAttemptsOnThrottledRequests = 3,
        MaxRetryWaitTimeInSeconds = 30 },
        EnableEndpointDiscovery = true,
        EnableReadRequestsFallback = true
    };
    connectionPolicy.PreferredLocations.Add(LocationNames.SouthIndia);

    var client = new DocumentClient(new Uri(EndpointUri), AuthKey,
    connectionPolicy);
    return client;
}
```

```csharp
private List<IDocumentDbEntity> GetDocumentEntities()
{
    var entityCollection = new List<IDocumentDbEntity>()
    {
        new DocumentDbEntity { EntityType = typeof(Tweet), Name =
        "TweetCollection" }
    };
    return entityCollection;
}

private async Task<Database> CreateDatabaseAsync(string databaseId)
{
    var response = await DocumentClient.CreateDatabaseIfNotExistsAs
    ync(new Database { Id = databaseId });
    return response.Resource;
}

private async Task<DocumentCollection> CreateCollectionAsync(string
databaseId, string collectionName)
{
    var response = await DocumentClient.
    CreateDocumentCollectionIfNotExistsAsync(
        UriFactory.CreateDatabaseUri(databaseId),
        new DocumentCollection
        {
            Id = collectionName
        },
        new RequestOptions());

    return response.Resource;
}
}
}
```

Designing and Implementing a Document DB Repository

As we have a context class ready, we will define the IDocumentDbRepository contract of the repository pattern in the Data folder, as shown in Listing 3-6. IDocumentDbRepository uses C# generics to achieve code reusability. It contains the AddOrUpdateAsync, GetByIdAsync, RemoveAsync, WhereAsync, and TopAsync methods.

Listing 3-6. IDocumentDbRepository Class

```
using System;
using System.Linq;
using System.Linq.Expressions;
using System.Threading.Tasks;
using TwitterBot.Framework.Types;
namespace TwitterBot.Framework.Contracts.Data
{
    public interface IDocumentDbRepository<T> where T : BaseType
    {
        Task<T> AddOrUpdateAsync(T entity);
        Task<T> GetByIdAsync(string id);
        Task<bool> RemoveAsync(string id);
        Task<IQueryable<T>> WhereAsync(Expression<Func<T, bool>> predicate);
        Task<IQueryable<T>> TopAsync(Expression<Func<T, bool>> predicate,
        int n);
    }
}
```

Create the DocumentDbRepository class by implementing the IDocumentDbRepository interface in the CosmosDB folder, as shown in Listing 3-7. The DocumentDbRepository implementation consists of the following methods:

- The constructor takes an IDocumentDbContext instance as a parameter and holds it in a private variable. The DocumentCollection private variable is populated based on the type in context of DocumentDbRepository. These variables are required to perform data operations in other methods.

- `AddOrUpdateAsync` adds or updates the input entity by using the `IDocumentDbContext.DocumentClient`'s `UpsertDocumentAsync` method and returns the created resource. `UpsertDocumentAsync` takes a `DocumentCollection` link and entity as parameters.

- The `GetByIdAsync` method takes an `id` string as a parameter and fetches the entity by using the `CreateDocumentQuery` method of the `IDocumentDbContext.DocumentClient`, with a where predicate on an `Id` property. `CreateDocumentQuery` takes Collection URI as a parameter, which is constructed using the `UriFactory.CreateDocumentCollectionUri` method.

- The `RemoveAsync` method removes the entity by invoking the `RemoveDocumentAsync` method of `IDocumentDbContext.DocumentClient` and returns the success flag.

- The `WhereAsync` method takes an expression as an input parameter and returns all the entities matching the expression. This method uses the `CreateDocumentQuery` method of `IDocumentDbContext.DocumentClient` to fetch the results. `CreateDocumentQuery` takes the URI of the collection as input.

- The `TopAsync` method takes the expression and the total number of records to be returned as input parameters and returns the top results.

Listing 3-7. DocumentDbRepository Class

```
using Microsoft.Azure.Documents;
using Microsoft.Azure.Documents.Client;
using Newtonsoft.Json;
using System;
using System.Linq;
using System.Linq.Expressions;
using System.Net;
using System.Threading.Tasks;
using TwitterBot.Framework.Contracts.Data;
using TwitterBot.Framework.Types;
namespace TwitterBot.Framework.CosmosDB
```

```
{
    public class DocumentDbRepository<T> : IDocumentDbRepository<T> where T
    : BaseType
    {
        private IDocumentDbContext _context;
        private DocumentCollection _documentCollection;
        public DocumentDbRepository(IDocumentDbContext context)
        {
            _context = context;
            var entityMetadata = _context.EntityCollection.FirstOrDefault(p
            => p.EntityType == typeof(T));
            Task.Run(async () => _documentCollection = await _
            context.DocumentClient.ReadDocumentCollectionAsync(UriF
            actory.CreateDocumentCollectionUri(_context.DatabaseId,
            entityMetadata.Name))).Wait();
        }

        public async Task<T> AddOrUpdateAsync(T entity)
        {
            var upsertedDoc = await _context.DocumentClient.
            UpsertDocumentAsync(_documentCollection.SelfLink, entity);
            return JsonConvert.DeserializeObject<T>(upsertedDoc.Resource.
            ToString());
        }

        public async Task<T> GetByIdAsync(string id)
        {
            var result = await Task.Run(() => _context.DocumentClient.Cre
            ateDocumentQuery<T>(UriFactory.CreateDocumentCollectionUri(_
            context.DatabaseId, _documentCollection.Id))
                    .Where(p => p.Id == id).ToList());

            return result != null && result.Any() ? result.FirstOrDefault()
            : null;
        }
```

```csharp
public async Task<bool> RemoveAsync(string id)
{
    var result = await _context.DocumentClient.
    DeleteDocumentAsync(UriFactory.CreateDocumentUri(_context.
    DatabaseId, _documentCollection.Id, id));
    return result.StatusCode == HttpStatusCode.NoContent;
}

public async Task<IQueryable<T>> WhereAsync(Expression<Func<T,
bool>> predicate)
{
    return await Task.Run(() => _context.DocumentClient.CreateDocu
    mentQuery<T>(UriFactory.CreateDocumentCollectionUri(_context.
    DatabaseId, _documentCollection.Id))
            .Where(predicate));
}

public async Task<IQueryable<T>> TopAsync(Expression<Func<T, bool>>
predicate, int n)
{
    return await Task.Run(() => _context.DocumentClient.CreateDocu
    mentQuery<T>(UriFactory.CreateDocumentCollectionUri(_context.
    DatabaseId, _documentCollection.Id))
            .Where(predicate)
            .Take(n));
}
    }
}
```

The TwitterBot.Framework project structure is shown in Figure 3-5.

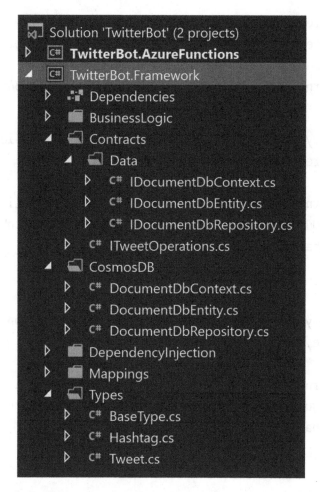

Figure 3-5. *The TwitterBot.Framework project*

Testing the Document DB Repository with a Console Application

In this section, we test the repository pattern implementation with a console application. Create a console application (.NET Core) under the TwitterBot solution. We need to add a TwitterBot.Framework project reference and install the Microsoft.Azure. DocumentDB.Core nuget package on the console application. Listing 3-8 shows the code to test the IDocumentDbRepository methods in a console app.

In the console app, the `Internalhandler` method tests the `IDocumentDbRepository` code. We create an instance of `DocumentDbContext` and assign the `AuthKey`, `DatabaseId`, and `EndpointUri` properties pointing to the Cosmos DB Emulator (`AuthKey` and `EndpointUri` can be found in Figure 3-3). We invoke the `CreateDatabaseAndCollectionsAsync` method to create the `TestDB` database along with `TweetCollection`. Then we create the `DocumentDbRepository` instance and invoke the `AddOrUpdateAsync`, `GetByIdAsync`, `RemoveAsync`, `WhereAsync`, and `TopAsync` methods with sample tweets, as shown in Listing 3-8.

Note   The console application is used merely to test the code. It has no relevance in the Twitter Bot application's business requirements.

Listing 3-8.   Console Application Code

```
using System;
using System.Threading.Tasks;
using TwitterBot.Framework.CosmosDB;
using TwitterBot.Framework.Types;

namespace ConsoleApp1
{
    class Program
    {
        static void Main(string[] args)
        {
            Task t = InternalHandler();
            t.Wait();
            Console.ReadLine();
        }

        private static async Task InternalHandler()
        {
            var context = new DocumentDbContext()
            {
                AuthKey = "C2y6yDjf5/R+ob0N8A7Cgv30VRDJIWEHLM+4QDU5DE2nQ9nD
                uVTqobD4b8mGGyPMbIZnqyMsEcaGQy67XIw/Jw==",
```

```
        DatabaseId = "TestDB",
        EndpointUri = "https://localhost:8081"
    };
    await context.CreateDatabaseAndCollectionsAsync();
    var documentRepo = new DocumentDbRepository<Tweet>(context);

    var id1 = Guid.NewGuid().ToString();
    var id2 = Guid.NewGuid().ToString();
    // Create Tweets
    var Tweet1 = await documentRepo.AddOrUpdateAsync(new Tweet { Id
    = id1, FullText = "This is Test!!!" });
    Console.WriteLine("===== Create =====");
    Console.WriteLine(Tweet1.FullText);
    Console.WriteLine("==================");
    var Tweet2 = await documentRepo.AddOrUpdateAsync(new Tweet { Id
    = id2, FullText = "This is second test!!!" });
    Console.WriteLine("===== Create =====");
    Console.WriteLine(Tweet2.FullText);
    Console.WriteLine("==================");

    // Update Tweet
    Tweet2 = await documentRepo.AddOrUpdateAsync(new Tweet { Id =
    id2, FullText = "This is 2nd test!!!" });
    Console.WriteLine("===== Update =====");
    Console.WriteLine(Tweet2.FullText);
    Console.WriteLine("==================");

    // Get By Id Tweet
    Tweet2 = await documentRepo.GetByIdAsync(id2);
    Console.WriteLine("===== GetByIdAsync =====");
    Console.WriteLine(Tweet2.FullText);
    Console.WriteLine("==================");

    // Where
    var tweets = await documentRepo.WhereAsync(p => p.FullText.
    Contains("e"));
    Console.WriteLine("===== Where =====");
```

```
foreach (var Tweet in Tweets)
{
    Console.WriteLine(Tweet.FullText);
}
Console.WriteLine("===================");

// Top
var topTweets = await documentRepo.TopAsync(p => p.FullText.
Contains("e"), 1);
Console.WriteLine("===== Top =====");
foreach (var Tweet in topTweets)
{
    Console.WriteLine(Tweet.FullText);
}
Console.WriteLine("===================");
    }
  }
}
```

If you run the console app, you'll see the output shown in Figure 3-6.

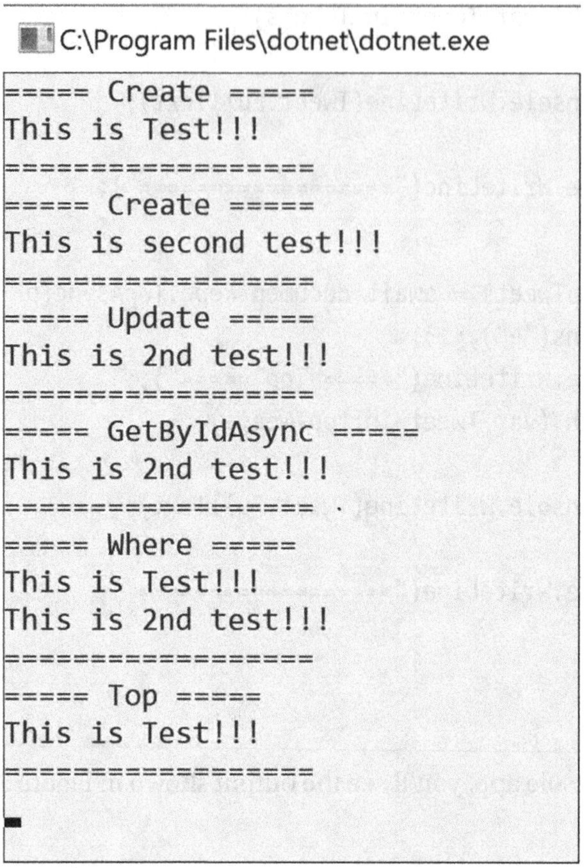

Figure 3-6. *Console app output*

We can check the data in the Data Explorer of the Cosmos DB Emulator, as shown in Figure 3-7. Navigate to the Explorer tab in the Cosmos DB Emulator. You'll see the TestDB database and the TweetCollection document collection. We can see that two tweets are listed in the Documents section.

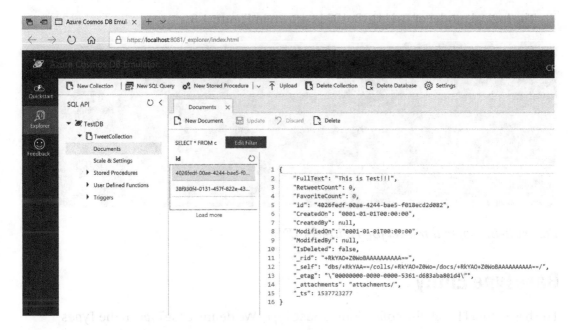

Figure 3-7. *Data Explorer of the Cosmos DB Emulator*

In later sections of this chapter, we will create an Azure Cosmos DB Service and integrate the IDocumentDbRepository with TweetBotFunction. Going forward, we will enhance IDocumentDbRepository and IDocumentDbContext with more methods and properties, which are required to support the Twitter Bot application's functionality.

Creating the Twitter Bot Application DB Model

In this section, we define the data model for the Twitter Bot application. The data model will be transformed into the Azure Cosmos DB collections and are used by different Azure Functions to save and retrieve information from the Cosmos DB. The Twitter Bot application primarily consists of the following models:

- Hashtags collection
- Tweets collection
- Users collection

The logical model of TwitterBotDB is shown in Figure 3-8.

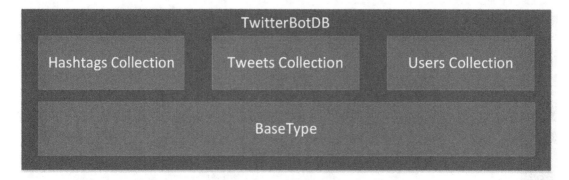

Figure 3-8. *Logical model for TwitterBotDB*

BaseType Entity

The base model for all the collections is BaseType. We define BaseType in the Types folder of the TwitterBot.Framework project. Update all the properties of BaseType to have a JsonProperty attribute, as shown in Listing 3-9. Having a JsonProperty attribute is useful in serializing the type into a minified version, thereby reducing the overall size of the document in Cosmos DB.

Listing 3-9. BaseType Class

```
using Newtonsoft.Json;
using System;
namespace TwitterBot.Framework.Types
{
    public class BaseType
    {
        [JsonProperty(PropertyName = "id")]
        public string Id { get; set; }

        [JsonProperty(PropertyName = "con")]
        public DateTime CreatedOn { get; set; }

        [JsonProperty(PropertyName = "cby")]
        public string CreatedBy { get; set; }
```

```
    [JsonProperty(PropertyName = "mon")]
    public DateTime ModifiedOn { get; set; }

    [JsonProperty(PropertyName = "mby")]
    public string ModifiedBy { get; set; }

    [JsonProperty(PropertyName = "isd")]
    public bool IsDeleted { get; set; }
    }
}
```

Hashtag Entity

The Hashtag entity (in the Types folder of the TwitterBot.Framework project) is going
to have Text, LastSyncedDateTime, and IsCurrentlyInQueue properties, as shown in
Listing 3-10. LastSyncedDatetime is useful in determining the sync priority of a hashtag.
IsCurrentlyInQueue will be used to determine whether a given hashtag is already
present in the queue for synchronization.

Listing 3-10. HashTag Class

```
using Newtonsoft.Json;
using System;
namespace TwitterBot.Framework.Types
{
    public class Hashtag : BaseType
    {
        [JsonProperty(PropertyName = "txt")]
        public string Text { get; set; }

        [JsonProperty(PropertyName = "lsdt")]
        public DateTime LastSyncedDateTime { get; set; }

        [JsonProperty(PropertyName = "iciq")]
        public bool IsCurrentlyInQueue { get; set; }

    }
}
```

Tweet Entity

The Tweet entity in the Types folder of the TwitterBot.Framework project will resemble a real-world tweet from Twitter. The Tweet entity will have the common attributes of a tweet, such as Text, Full Text, Tweet URL, Retweet Count, Favorite Count, Tweet Destroyed Flag, Tweet Created By, Tweet Created By URL, Tweet Created On, and a list of hashtags that are part of the tweet. The Tweet class is shown in Listing 3-11.

Listing 3-11. Tweet Class

```
using Newtonsoft.Json;
using System;
using System.Collections.Generic;
namespace TwitterBot.Framework.Types
{
    public class Tweet : BaseType
    {
        [JsonProperty(PropertyName = "txt")]
        public string Text { get; set; }

        [JsonProperty(PropertyName = "ftxt")]
        public string FullText { get; set; }

        [JsonProperty(PropertyName = "turl")]
        public string TweetUrl { get; set; }

        [JsonProperty(PropertyName = "rcnt")]
        public int RetweetCount { get; set; }

        [JsonProperty(PropertyName = "fcnt")]
        public int FavoriteCount { get; set; }

        [JsonProperty(PropertyName = "itd")]
        public bool IsTweetDestroyed { get; set; }

        [JsonProperty(PropertyName = "tcb")]
        public string TweetCreatedBy { get; set; }

        [JsonProperty(PropertyName = "tcbu")]
        public string TweetCreatedByUrl { get; set; }
```

```
    [JsonProperty(PropertyName = "tco")]
    public DateTime TweetCreatedOn { get; set; }

    [JsonProperty(PropertyName = "hts")]
    public ICollection<Hashtag> Hashtags { get; set; }

    }
}
```

User Entity

The User entity holds the attributes of the end user along with the preferences. Create the User class in the Types folder of the TwitterBot.Framework project, as shown in Listing 3-12. The User class will have a UserId property, which will be related to the user's identity. This class also holds a list of hashtags that the user subscribes to for notifications.

Listing 3-12. User Class

```
using Newtonsoft.Json;
using System;
using System.Collections.Generic;

namespace TwitterBot.Framework.Types
{
    public class User : BaseType
    {
        [JsonProperty(PropertyName = "uid")]
        public string UserId { get; set; }

        [JsonProperty(PropertyName = "hts")]
        public List<Hashtag> Hashtags { get; set; }
    }
}
```

Note   As the book progresses, based on the requirements, we will add new properties to the models and refresh the CosmosDB instance.

Integrating the Tweet Bot Function with the Cosmos DB

In this section, we integrate the TweetBotFunction that we developed in Chapter 2 with the Cosmos DB repository.

Let's get started by updating the AutoMapper mapping between the ITweet and Tweet types in the MappingProfile class with new properties, as shown in Listing 3-13. We are going to ignore the Hashtags property from the mapping process because we are going to use custom logic to map the hashtags list.

Note   AutoMapper automatically maps the properties between the source and destination if they have the same names. I am ignoring them in Listing 3-13.

Listing 3-13. Updated MappingProfile Class

```
using AutoMapper;
namespace TwitterBot.Framework.Mappings
{
    public class MappingProfile : Profile
    {
        public static void Activate()
        {
            Mapper.Initialize(cfg =>
            {
                cfg.CreateMap<Tweetinvi.Models.ITweet, Types.Tweet>()
                .ForMember(dest => dest.TweetUrl, opts => opts.MapFrom(src
                => src.Url))
                .ForMember(dest => dest.TweetCreatedBy, opts => opts.
                MapFrom(src => src.CreatedBy.Name))
                .ForMember(dest => dest.TweetCreatedByUrl, opts => opts.
                MapFrom(src => src.CreatedBy.Url))
                .ForMember(dest => dest.TweetCreatedOn, opts => opts.
                MapFrom(src => src.CreatedAt))
                .ForMember(dest => dest.Id, opts => opts.MapFrom(src =>
                src.IdStr))
```

```
        .ForMember(dest => dest.Hashtags, opts => opts.Ignore());
    });
  }
 }
}
```

Now we will update the `WebJobsExtensionStartup` class with the Cosmos DB repository configuration, as shown in Listing 3-14. We create a new instance of `DocumentDbContext` by passing the authentication key, endpoint URI, and database ID. Then we create the Cosmos DB instance and `TweetCollection` by invoking the `CreateDatabaseAndCollectionsAsync` method of `DocumentDbContext`. We proceed to register a singleton instance of `IDocumentDbContext` with the `DocumentDbContext` instance. Finally, we register a singleton instance of `IDocumentDbRepository<>` with `DocumentDbRepository<>`.

Note   Listing 3-14 has two different ways to register instances, one for `IDocumentDbContext` and another for `IDocumentDbRepository<>`. We use strong types with `typeof` resolution while registering generic interfaces with a generic implementation.

Listing 3-14. Updated WebJobsExtensionStartupclass

```
using Microsoft.Azure.WebJobs;
/* Code removed for brevity */
[assembly: WebJobsStartup(typeof(WebJobsExtensionStartup), "TwitterBot
Extensions Startup")]
namespace TwitterBot.AzureFunctions
{
    public class WebJobsExtensionStartup : IWebJobsStartup
    {
        public void Configure(IWebJobsBuilder builder)
        {
            MappingProfile.Activate();

            // CosmosDB Configuration
            var documentDbContext = new DocumentDbContext
```

```
    {
        AuthKey = "Twitter Bot Auth Key",
        DatabaseId = "TwitterBotDB",
        EndpointUri = "https://localhost:8081"
    };
    Task.Run(async () => await documentDbContext.
    CreateDatabaseAndCollectionsAsync()).Wait();
    builder.Services.AddSingleton<IDocumentDbContext>(documentDbCo
    ntext);
    builder.Services.AddSingleton(typeof(IDocumentDbRepository<>),
    typeof(DocumentDbRepository<>));

    builder.Services.AddSingleton<ITweetOperations>(
    new TweetOperations("umUgpc6eOVhGY5hROqN8HKxa9",
    "95eDHKsKcOxKvWbHqOdAso6GstdRzNq6AiWyRVR7qSayixQqWQ"));
    builder.Services.AddSingleton<InjectBindingProvider>();
    builder.AddExtension<InjectConfiguration>();
    }
  }
}
```

We will upgrade the TweetBotFunction, as shown in Listing 3-15. We make the Run method compatible for async method calls by using async with return type Task. Then we inject the IDocumentDbRepository<Tweet> instance into the Run method. The Run method of TweetBotFunction performs the following actions:

1. The Azure Function will retrieve the latest tweet from Twitter using the GetPopularTweetByHashtag method of ITweetOperations.

2. The retrieved tweet will be checked for its existence in TweetCollection of TwitterBotDB by using the GetByIdAsync method of IDocumentDbRepository<Tweet>.

3. If the tweet doesn't exist in the collection:

   • Add the current hashtag to the tweet's Hashtag collection.

   • Add the tweet to the TweetCollection by using the AddOrUpdateAsync method of IDocumentDbRepository<Tweet>.

4. If the tweet exists in the collection and the current hashtag isn't
    present in the tweet:

    •   Map the existing hashtags to the tweet and add the current
        hashtag to the tweet.

    •   Update the tweet to the collection by using the AddOrUpdateAsync
        method of IDocumentDbRepository<Tweet>.

Listing 3-15. Updated TweetBotFunction Class

```
using Microsoft.Azure.WebJobs;
using Microsoft.Extensions.Logging;
using System.Collections.Generic;
using System.Linq;
using System.Threading.Tasks;
using TwitterBot.Framework.Contracts;
using TwitterBot.Framework.Contracts.Data;
using TwitterBot.Framework.DependencyInjection;
using TwitterBot.Framework.Types;

namespace TwitterBot.AzureFunctions
{
    public static class TweetBotFunction
    {
        [FunctionName("TweetBotFunction")]
        public async static Task Run([TimerTrigger("0 */5 * * * *")]
        TimerInfo myTimer, ILogger log,
            [Inject]ITweetOperations tweetOperations, [Inject]
            IDocumentDbRepository<Tweet> tweetDbRepository)
        {
            var hashtag = new Hashtag { Text = "#justsaying" };
            // Retrieve the latest tweet.
            var tweet = tweetOperations.GetPopularTweetByHashtag(hashtag);
            if (tweet != null)
            {
                tweet.Hashtags = new List<Hashtag>();
                log.LogInformation($"Latest popular tweet for #justsaying :
                { tweet.FullText }");
```

```
            // Check if DB already has the tweet.
            var existingTweet = await tweetDbRepository.
            GetByIdAsync(tweet.Id);

            // If tweet is not present in DB, then add to DB.
            if (existingTweet == null)
            {
                tweet.Hashtags.Add(hashtag);
                // Add the tweet to DB.
                await tweetDbRepository.AddOrUpdateAsync(tweet);

                log.LogInformation($"Added Tweet in TweetCollection
                with Id : { tweet.Id }");
            }

            // Map DB Hashtags with latest Tweet.
            if (existingTweet != null && !existingTweet.Hashtags.Any(p
            => p.Text == hashtag.Text))
            {
                // Map the existing hashtags to tweet.
                tweet.Hashtags = existingTweet.Hashtags;
                // Add the current hashtag to tweet.
                tweet.Hashtags.Add(hashtag);
                // Update the tweet to DB.
                await tweetDbRepository.AddOrUpdateAsync(tweet);

                log.LogInformation($"Updated Tweet in TweetCollection
                with Id : { tweet.Id }");
            }
        }
    }
}
}
```

If you run the TweetBotFunction from Visual Studio, you should see the output in the Azure Functions CLI, as shown in Figure 3-9.

```
[9/28/2018 2:47:51 PM] Initializing Host.
[9/28/2018 2:47:51 PM] Host initialization: ConsecutiveErrors=0, StartupCount=1
[9/28/2018 2:47:51 PM] Starting JobHost
[9/28/2018 2:47:51 PM] Starting Host (HostId=ramivm-1710302376, InstanceId=b36da2cc-d481-4211-8905-f3c01d26bfd1, Version
=2.0.12115.0, ProcessId=7964, AppDomainId=1, Debug=False, FunctionsExtensionVersion=)
[9/28/2018 2:47:51 PM] Generating 1 job function(s)
[9/28/2018 2:47:51 PM] Found the following functions:
[9/28/2018 2:47:51 PM] TwitterBot.AzureFunctions.TweetBotFunction.Run
[9/28/2018 2:47:51 PM]
[9/28/2018 2:47:51 PM] Host initialized (374ms)
[9/28/2018 2:47:51 PM] The next 5 occurrences of the 'TwitterBot.AzureFunctions.TweetBotFunction.Run' schedule will be:
[9/28/2018 2:47:51 PM] 9/28/2018 2:50:00 PM
[9/28/2018 2:47:51 PM] 9/28/2018 2:55:00 PM
[9/28/2018 2:47:51 PM] 9/28/2018 3:00:00 PM
[9/28/2018 2:47:52 PM] 9/28/2018 3:05:00 PM
[9/28/2018 2:47:52 PM] 9/28/2018 3:10:00 PM
[9/28/2018 2:47:52 PM]
[9/28/2018 2:47:52 PM] Host started (721ms)
[9/28/2018 2:47:52 PM] Job host started
Hosting environment: Production
Content root path: C:\Users\ramiadmin\OneDrive\TwitterBot\TwitterBot.AzureFunctions\bin\Debug\netstandard2.0
Now listening on: http://0.0.0.0:7071
Application started. Press Ctrl+C to shut down.
Listening on http://0.0.0.0:7071/
Hit CTRL-C to exit...
[9/28/2018 2:47:57 PM] Host lock lease acquired by instance ID '00000000000000000000000014B8D3A4'.
[9/28/2018 2:50:01 PM] Executing 'TweetBotFunction' (Reason='Timer fired at 2018-09-28T14:50:00.0273309+00:00', Id=2ecdd
82f-bc44-41e3-b1df-8feda14dde4a)
[9/28/2018 2:50:03 PM] Latest popular tweet for #justsaying : Have not met/spoken with a single armed forces officer (se
rving or retired)  yet who thinks the 'surgical strikes festival' is a good idea. #JustSaying
Latest popular tweet for #justsaying : Have not met/spoken with a single armed forces officer (serving or retired)  yet
who thinks the 'surgical strikes festival' is a good idea. #JustSaying
[9/28/2018 2:50:03 PM] Added Tweet in TweetCollection with Id : 1045368116409237504
Added Tweet in TweetCollection with Id : 1045368116409237504
[9/28/2018 2:50:04 PM] Executed 'TweetBotFunction' (Succeeded, Id=2ecdd82f-bc44-41e3-b1df-8feda14dde4a)
```

Figure 3-9. *Output of TweetBotFunction*

The tweet will be saved to the `TweetCollection` of `TwitterBotDB` in the Cosmos DB Emulator, as shown in Figure 3-10.

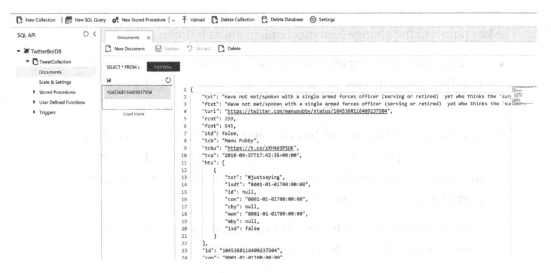

Figure 3-10. *TwitterBotDB in the Azure Cosmos DB Emulator Data Explorer*

> **Note**   In this section, we tested the integration of the `TweetBotFunction`
> with the Cosmos DB Emulator. Later in the chapter, we will execute the
> `TweetBotFunction` in integration with the Azure Cosmos DB Service.

Understanding Change Feed Support in Cosmos DB

One of the most important features of the Azure Cosmos DB service is the change feed
mechanism. It notifies different consumers about data updates. In the traditional SQL
world, we can compare the change feed with triggers that are fired on different data and
schema operations. By leveraging these notifications, we can build strong foundations for
real-time streaming and event-based computing applications, as shown in Figure 3-11.

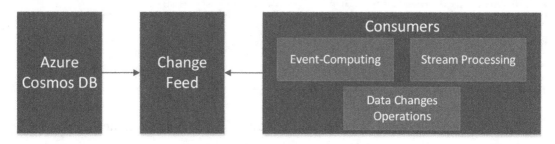

Figure 3-11.   *Change feed in Azure Cosmos DB*

The key points of the change feed mechanism are as follows:

- Change feed works for inserts and updates. Delete operations can be
  handled by soft deletes; otherwise, we should set the TTL expiry for
  the document and process it before the document expires.

- The most recent change of the document will be available in change
  feed and it appears only once for consumer processing. The changes
  are sorted by the modification time within a partition; sorting across
  partitions are not guaranteed.

- Change feed is enabled by default to all accounts and collections.
  There is no fixed period for change retention.

- Multiple consumers can process changes in parallel and in chunks. One collection can have multiple change feeds.

- Change feed works seamlessly in the case of failovers.

An application can connect to the Azure Cosmos DB change feed by using the following options:

- **Azure Functions:** A Cosmos DB Trigger Azure Function can process change feed messages for a specific collection. By default, Azure Functions poll the change feed every five seconds. That time interval can be changed by setting the feedPollTime parameter. We can scale Azure Functions to handle the change feed load; the only prerequisite to scale is to have every Azure Function instance have a different lease prefix.

- **.NET SDK for SQL API:** For more granular control on the change feed, we can use the SQL API SDK. We can use CreateDocumentChangeFeedQuery and iterate the change feed results.

- **Change Feed Processor Library:** This library simplifies the process of reading changes across partitions and multiple threads working in parallel. Using this library, there is no hassle of managing the partition keys, continuation tokens, and no need to poll collections manually, like in the SQL API SDK.

Change feed can also be accessed through Node.js SDK, the Java library, and Apache Spark.

Note   The SQL API SDK and Change Feed Processor Library implementations are out of scope of this book.

Azure Cosmos DB SDK's are continuously evolving with new features. At present, there is no support for features like exception handling and reprocessing of failed document notifications. In case of exceptions during processing, an application should have the logic to hold the erroneous document in a different persistent medium and process it separately.

We are going to use a Cosmos DB Trigger-based Azure Function in the Twitter Bot application to listen to the TweetCollection change feed.

Implementing a Cosmos DB Trigger-Based Tweet Notifier Function

So far in this chapter, we have integrated TweetBotFunction with the Azure Cosmos DB, so that whenever a new tweet is fetched from Twitter, TweetBotFunction will insert it into TweetCollection. As an extension to the Twitter Bot application architecture, we will create an Azure Cosmos DB Trigger function that will get notifications from the TweetCollection change feed on new data inserts and updates.

Note   In later chapters, the Cosmos DB Trigger Azure Function will issue SignalR notifications to connected users. The detailed architecture can be found in Chapter 1, in the "Physical Architecture of the Twitter Bot Application" section.

Let's get started by creating a new Cosmos DB database in Azure, as described in this step-by-step process:

1.   Click on the Create a Resource option. The Cosmos DB will be listed under the Databases tab, as shown in Figure 3-12.

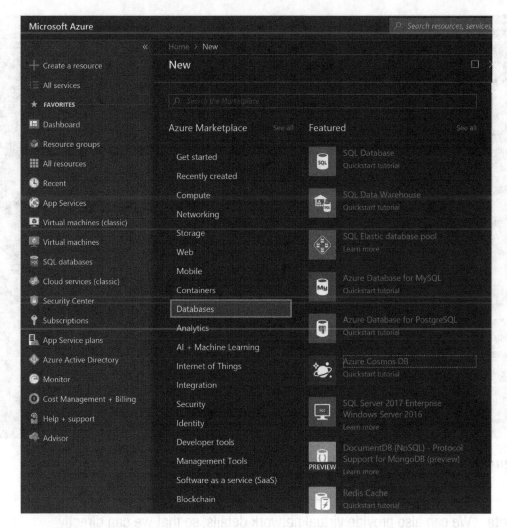

Figure 3-12.   *Create a new Azure Cosmos DB*

2. Select the subscription and the `TwitterBotApplication` resource
    group. Provide the instance name as `twitterbotdb` and location
    as Central US. Select SQL (or Core SQL) as the API and click on
    Review + Create, as shown in Figure 3-13.

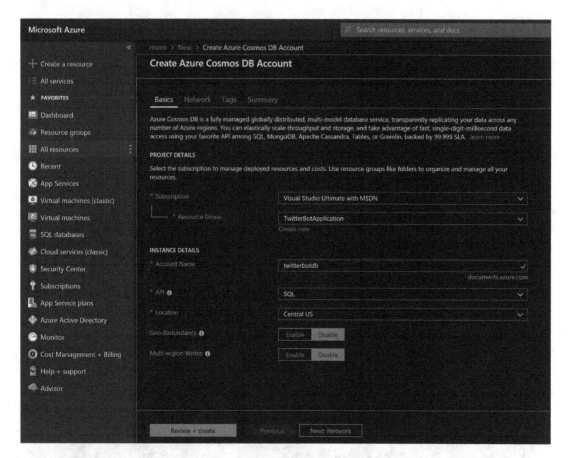

***Figure 3-13.** Provide Azure Cosmos DB details*

Note   We can also provide virtual network details, so that we can directly communicate to the Azure Cosmos DB from a virtual network. The Azure Cosmos DB instance can be tagged, which is helpful in categorizing the resources at the Azure portal.

Ignore these two sections and create the Cosmos DB instance.

---

3. Azure will validate all the inputs, as shown in Figure 3-14. Click the Create button.

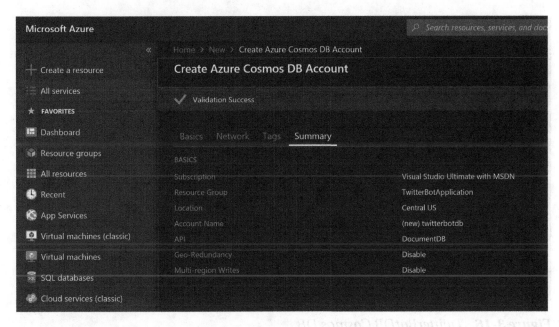

Figure 3-14.   *Create the Azure Cosmos DB*

4. The progress of Cosmos DB deployment will be displayed in the Azure portal, as shown in Figure 3-15.

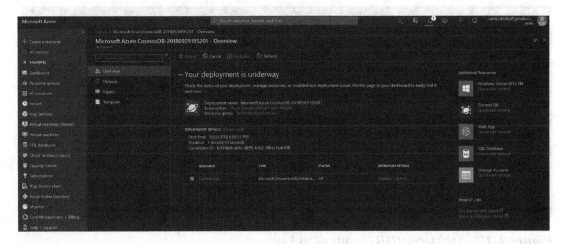

Figure 3-15.   *Azure Cosmos DB deployment progress*

5.   We can navigate to the new Cosmos DB from the Resource Group, as shown in Figure 3-16.

Figure 3-16.   *TwitterBotDB Cosmos DB*

6.   Keys that are required to connect to a Cosmos DB instance can be found in the Keys section, as shown in Figure 3-17.

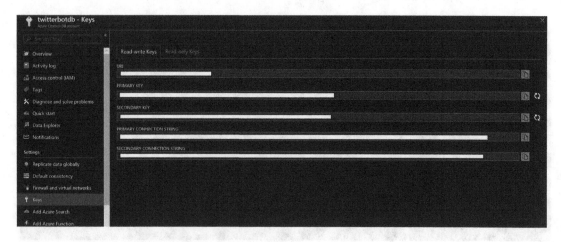

Figure 3-17.   *TwitterBotDB Cosmos DB keys*

Note   Make sure to protect the keys from unauthorized use. I have masked the keys in Figure 3-17 for security purposes.

Now that we have created `TwitterBotDB`, we can use its keys in `WebJobsExtensionStartup` of the `TweetBotFunction`, as shown in Listing 3-16.

Listing 3-16.   Updated WebJobsExtensionStartup Class

```
// CosmosDB Configuration
var documentDbContext = new DocumentDbContext
{
    AuthKey = "TwitterBotDB Primary Key",
    DatabaseId = "TwitterBotDB",
    EndpointUri = "TwitterBotDB URI"
};
```

At this point, we can run `TweetBotFunction` on the local machine. If we do so, we see the new `TweetCollection` in the Data Explorer tab of the Azure `TwitterBotDB`, as shown in Figure 3-18.

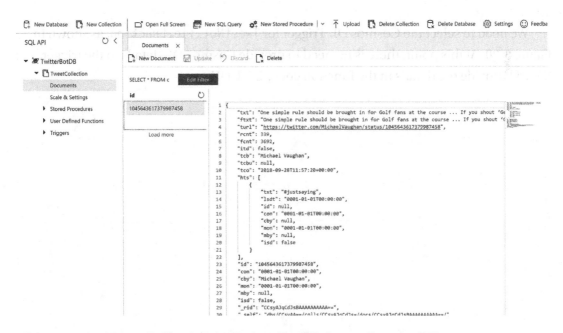

Figure 3-18.   *TweetCollection in TwitterBotDB Azure Cosmos DB*

Now we will create an Azure Cosmos DB Trigger Function in the `TwitterBot.`
`AzureFunctions` project, as shown in Figure 3-19. Right-click the `TwitterBot.`
`AzureFunctions` project. Then choose Add ➤ New Azure Function. Call it
`TweetNotifierFunction` and then click Add.

Figure 3-19. *Create TweetNotifierFunction*

We need to select the Cosmos DB Trigger for `TweetNotifierFunction`, as shown in
Figure 3-20. At this point, there is no need to provide Cosmos DB details to the trigger.
We will provide the details in the function code. Click OK.

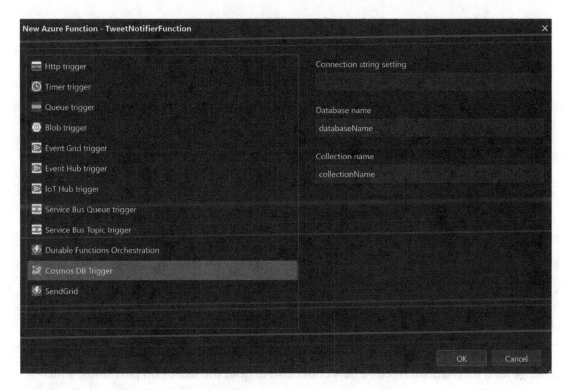

Figure 3-20. *Cosmos DB trigger for TweetNotifierFunction*

The default code of TweetNotifierFunction is shown in Listing 3-17. We need to pass the database name, collection name, and ConnectionString parameters. We will add ConnectionString in the app settings and use the name of the setting as an input to this parameter. The inserted or updated documents at Cosmos DB that triggered TweetNotifierFunction are available in the IReadOnlyList<Document> collection.

Listing 3-17. TweetNotifierFunction Class

```
using System.Collections.Generic;
using Microsoft.Azure.Documents;
using Microsoft.Azure.WebJobs;
using Microsoft.Extensions.Logging;
namespace TwitterBot.AzureFunctions
{
    public static class TweetNotifierFunction
    {
        [FunctionName("TweetNotifierFunction")]
```

```
    public static void Run([CosmosDBTrigger(
        databaseName: "databaseName",
        collectionName: "collectionName",
        ConnectionStringSetting = "",
        LeaseCollectionName = "leases")]IReadOnlyList<Document> input,
        ILogger log)
    {

        if (input != null && input.Count > 0)
        {
            log.LogInformation("Documents modified " + input.Count);
            log.LogInformation("First document Id " + input[0].Id);
        }
    }
}
}
```

The change feed mechanism is the base for Cosmos DB Trigger Azure function. The change feed mechanism needs a new collection to hold the leases on partitions, which are required to manage read operations between multiple workers. The lease collection is also used to hold the last checkpoints on different partitions. We will specify leases as LeaseCollectionName and set CreateLeaseCollectionIfNotExists to true.

Add the ConnectionString application setting in the local.settings.json file, as shown in Listing 3-18. The primary ConnectionString can be found in Figure 3-17.

Listing 3-18. Updated local.settings.json File

```
{
  "IsEncrypted": false,
  "Values": {
    "AzureWebJobsStorage": "UseDevelopmentStorage=true",
    "FUNCTIONS_WORKER_RUNTIME": "dotnet",
    "TwitterBotDB_ConnectionString": "TwitterBotDB Primary
    ConnectionString"
  }
}
```

Update the TweetNotifierFunction with the correct configuration, as shown in Listing 3-19.

Listing 3-19. Updated TweetNotifierFunction Class

```
using System.Collections.Generic;
using Microsoft.Azure.Documents;
using Microsoft.Azure.WebJobs;
using Microsoft.Extensions.Logging;
namespace TwitterBot.AzureFunctions
{
    public static class TweetNotifierFunction
    {
        [FunctionName("TweetNotifierFunction")]
        public static void Run([CosmosDBTrigger(
            databaseName: "TwitterBotDB",
            collectionName: "TweetCollection",
            ConnectionStringSetting = "TwitterBotDB_ConnectionString",
            LeaseCollectionName = "leases",
            CreateLeaseCollectionIfNotExists = true)]
            IReadOnlyList<Document> input, ILogger log)
        {
            if (input != null && input.Count > 0)
            {
                log.LogInformation("Documents modified " + input.Count);
                log.LogInformation("First document Id " + input[0].Id);
            }
        }
    }
}
```

Run the TwitterBot.AzureFunctions project. To test the TweetNotifierFunction, create a document manually in TweetCollection by using the New Document option in the Data Explorer tab of TwitterBotDB, as shown in Figure 3-21.

Figure 3-21. *Create a new document in TweetCollection*

The newly inserted document with an ID of Test123 will trigger the TweetNotifierFunction and the output will be displayed in Azure CLI, as shown in Figure 3-22.

```
Listening on http://0.0.0.0:7071/
Hit CTRL-C to exit...
Hosting environment: Production
Content root path: C:\Users\ramiadmin\OneDrive\TwitterBot\TwitterBot.AzureFunctions\bin\Debug\netstandard2.0
Now listening on: http://0.0.0.0:7071
Application started. Press Ctrl+C to shut down.
[9/29/2018 6:38:14 PM] Host lock lease acquired by instance ID '0000000000000000000000066B1D2B3'.
[9/29/2018 6:39:29 PM] Executing 'TweetNotifierFunction' (Reason='New changes on collection TweetCollection at 2018-09-2
9T18:39:29.6959349Z', Id=fb9608f1-b758-481d-bac4-e09008705389)
[9/29/2018 6:39:29 PM] Documents modified 1
Documents modified 1
[9/29/2018 6:39:29 PM] First document Id Test123
First document Id Test123
```

Figure 3-22. *TweetNotifierFunction output*

Note   After completion of this test, delete the test document from TweetCollection.

Now we will test both functions—TweetBotFunction and TweetNotifierFunction—by publishing them to Azure the TwitterAzureFunctions app. Right-click the TwitterBot.AzureFunctions project and click Publish. We can see the published functions, as shown in Figure 3-23.

Figure 3-23. *TweetBotFunction and TweetNotifierFunction in Azure TwitterAzureFunctions App Service*

Note   Publishing an Azure Function from Visual Studio is covered in Chapter 2's section entitled "Deploying the Function to an Azure Function App".

At this point, when we publish a functions project, we will have all the functions published to the same Azure Function app. In our case, TweetBotFunction and TweetNotifierFunction will both be published to the TwitterAzureFunctions app.

One way to mitigate this behavior is to create different projects for different Azure Functions.

We need to configure the TwitterBotDB_ConnectionString, which we previously configured in the local.settings.json file, in the TwitterAzureFunctions App Service, as shown in Figure 3-24. Navigate to the Application Settings option on the Platform

Features tab of the `TwitterAzureFunctions` App Service and add
`TwitterBotDB_ConnectionString` with the Cosmos DB Primary ConnectionString. Click
Save to save the settings.

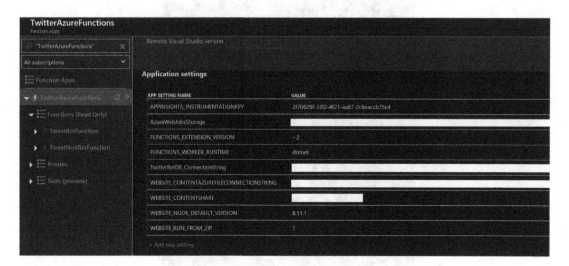

Figure 3-24. _Set the TwitterBotDB_ConnectionString in Application Settings of TwitterAzureFunctions App Service_

Now `TweetBotFunction` executes, as shown in Figure 3-25, and inserts data into the
`TweetCollection` of `TwitterBotDB`.

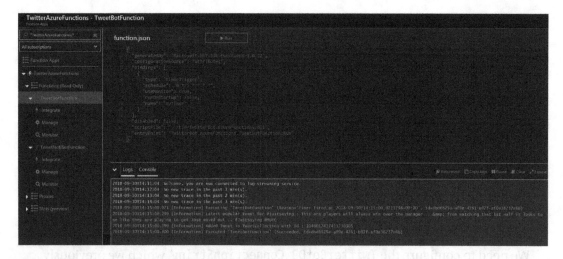

Figure 3-25. _Execution of TweetBotFunction_

Once data is inserted, `TweetNotifierFunction` gets notified, as shown in Figure 3-26.

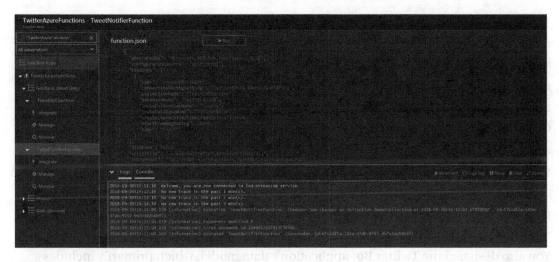

Figure 3-26. *Execution of TweetNotifierFunction*

Note   In this chapter, we have seen the entire workflow executed with a hardcoded hashtag, i.e., `#justsaying`. In the next chapter, we will make the workflow dynamic by fetching the hashtags from the Service Bus based on priority.

EXERCISE

In this chapter, we have seen how to consume `TweetCollection`'s change feed using an Azure Function. There are two other ways to read a collection's change feed—using SQL API SDK and using the change feed processor library. As part of this exercise, use either SQL API SDK or the change feed processor library to process change feeds of `TweetCollection`.

Solutions: Examples of the change feed processor library can be found at `https://github.com/Azure/azure-cosmosdb-dotnet/tree/master/samples/code-samples/ChangeFeedProcessorV2`.

A working example of SQL API SDK integration with change feed can be found at `https://github.com/Azure/azure-cosmosdb-dotnet/tree/master/samples/code-samples/ChangeFeed`.

Summary

You started off this chapter by learning about the important attributes of new generation data storage mechanisms and how Azure Cosmos DB is unique in achieving the requirements of different data applications. Cosmos DB is a globally distributed multi-model database that supports different data models, like documents, graph, key value, and column store. Cosmos DB provides different APIs—such as SQL, MongoDB, Table, Gremlin, and Cassandra—to perform data operations on different data models. You also learned the key features of Cosmos DB and installed the Cosmos DB Emulator to support local development and testing.

Later in the chapter, you implemented a generic implementation of a repository pattern to perform data operations on different collections in Cosmos DB. You tested the repository pattern with a console application by connecting to the Cosmos DB Emulator. You also designed the Twitter Bot application's data model, which primarily includes Tweet, Hashtag, and User collections.

You integrated `TweetBotFunction` (created in Chapter 2) with the `TwitterBotDB` Cosmos DB by injecting the repository instance of the `Tweet` type into `TweetBotFunction` through Dependency Injection. `TweetBotFunction's` code was upgraded to make sure duplicate tweets are not persisted and tweets are correctly associated with specific hashtags. You created a `TwitterBotDB` Cosmos DB instance in Azure and tested `TweetBotFunction` by integrating it with `TwitterBotDB`. You also published the latest `TweetBotFunction` to the `TwitterAzureFunctions` App Service.

You learned about the Cosmos DB change feed feature and created `TweetNotifierFunction` based on the Cosmos DB Trigger. You configured `TweetNotifierFunction` with the `TwitterBotDB` database and `TweetCollection` details. Finally, you published the `TweetNotifierFunction` to `TwitterAzureFunctions` and tested the entire workflow in coordination with `TweetBotFunction`.

In the next chapter, you will learn the basics of the Azure Service Bus. You will create a Tweet Scheduler Azure Function to prioritize hashtags in the Azure Service Bus.

References

1. https://docs.microsoft.com/en-us/azure/cosmos-db/
   introduction

2. https://docs.microsoft.com/en-us/azure/cosmos-db/
   performance-tips

3. https://docs.microsoft.com/en-us/azure/cosmos-db/
   partition-data

4. https://github.com/Crokus/cosmosdb-repo

5. https://docs.microsoft.com/en-us/azure/cosmos-db/
   change-feed

6. https://docs.microsoft.com/en-us/azure/azure-functions/
   functions-bindings-cosmosdb-v2

CHAPTER 4

Designing the Tweet Scheduler Function with Service Bus Integration

The fundamental design principles of a reliable and efficient software product are primarily based on factors like load and stress metrics, high availability and disaster recovery strategy, decoupled physical tiers, etc. The most frequently used technique in achieving a reliable product which can serve large loads is to scale the architecture, either by bringing in more servers (horizontal scaling) or by adding more CPU/RAM power to existing servers (vertical scaling). Horizontal scaling is considered the most effective technique compared to vertical scaling because it uses machine dynamics more efficiently.

Even though scaling solves most of the common reliability issues, at times this methodology falls short for applications that have tightly coupled layers and require every layer to scale independently. Scaling applications that employ non-centralized data, and state and cache management techniques can result in unexpected and inconsistent behaviors. Other factors that affect optimized scaling include synchronous communications between different systems, improper disaster management, and lack of segregation between different types of CPU/memory-intense workloads. The most common way to achieve optimized scaling is to decouple systems using service brokers through which independent systems can be scaled effectively.

155

In Chapters 2 and 3, we created the Twitter Bot application functions, which scan the Twitter platform for the latest popular tweets and capture their notifications through the Azure Cosmos DB. In this chapter, we enhance the Twitter Bot application design by decoupling hashtag prioritization with the tweet scanning logic. This is done by leveraging the Azure Service Bus.

Overall in this chapter, we:

- Learn about the basics of the Azure Service Bus and create a Hashtag Service Bus API.

- Design a TweetSchedulerFunction that will be responsible for prioritizing hashtags based on their last sync time.

- Upgrade the TweetBotFunction to look out for the prioritized hashtags in the Azure Service Bus Queue.

Note   As mentioned in Chapter 2's section entitled "Creating and Understanding the Basics of the Tweet Bot Azure Function," we will create an alternate implementation of the TweetBotFunction by leveraging the Service Bus trigger.

Creating and Configuring an Azure Service Bus Queue

Azure Service Bus is a message broker used for enterprise integration to decouple applications and services from each other. It provides reliable message queues and durable publish-subscribe messaging features. Azure Service bus primarily consists of namespaces that can be considered containers. Under each namespace are multiple queues and topics. Queues are used for point-to-point communications, whereas topics are useful in publish-subscribe scenarios. The following are some of the important features of Azure Service Bus:

- Guaranteed first in, first out (FIFO) using Sessions

- Auto-forwarding messages between queues or topics

- Dead-letter queue can contain unprocessed messages for inspection

- Set a schedule to deliver messages

- Support for deferred retrieval of messages

- Rules to define filters and actions

- Batching and transaction support for messages

- Message duplicate detection

- Disaster recovery

- Security with Shared Access Signatures (SAS), Role Based Access Control (RBAC), and Managed Service Identity

Let's get started by creating an instance of Azure Service Bus using this step-by-step process.

1. Click on the Create a Resource option. Service Bus will be listed under the Internet of Things tab, as shown in Figure 4-1.

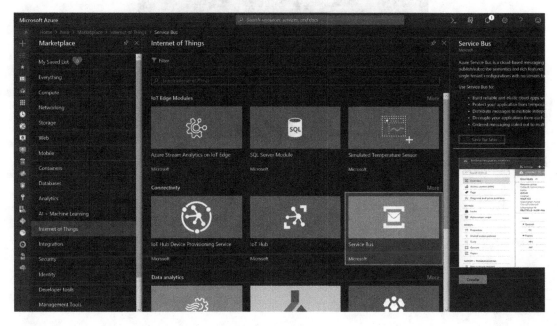

Figure 4-1. Create an Azure Service Bus instance

2. Create a Service Bus namespace under the
TwitterBotApplication resource group, as shown in Figure 4-2.
Enter the name twitterbotservicebus and select the standard
pricing tier. Select the Central US as the location. Click Create.

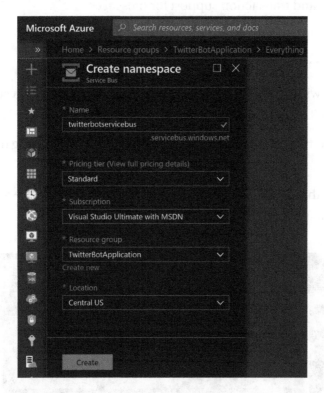

Figure 4-2. *Create the Azure Service Bus namespace*

3. The Service Bus is created, as shown in Figure 4-3.

Figure 4-3. *The TwitterBot Azure Service Bus*

To find the service bus connection string, which will be used to connect from any client, navigate to the Shared Access Policies tab, as shown in Figure 4-4.

Figure 4-4. *TwitterBot Service Bus Shared Access Policies tab*

Click on the RootManageSharedAccessKey policy. You can find the Primary Connection String in the right pane, as shown in Figure 4-5.

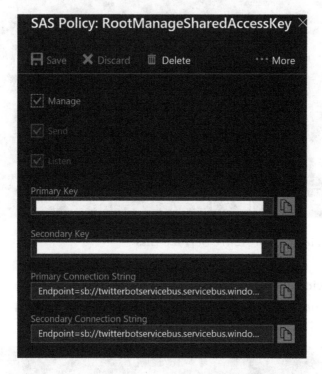

Figure 4-5. *TwitterBot Service Bus connection string details*

Note   Make sure to protect the connection strings from unauthorized use. I masked the keys in Figure 4-5 for security purposes.

To enjoy duplicate detection and the other features of the Service Bus Queue, we need to enable the standard messaging tier option for scaling, as shown in Figure 4-6.

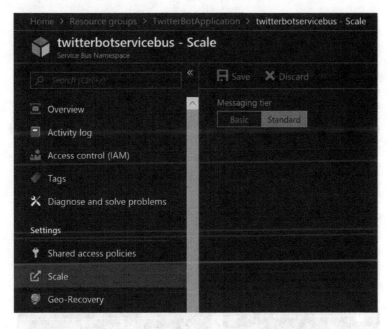

Figure 4-6. *Set the standard messaging tier option for scaling*

Now we create a Service Bus Queue by following this step-by-step process.

1. Navigate to the Queues tab, as shown in Figure 4-7.

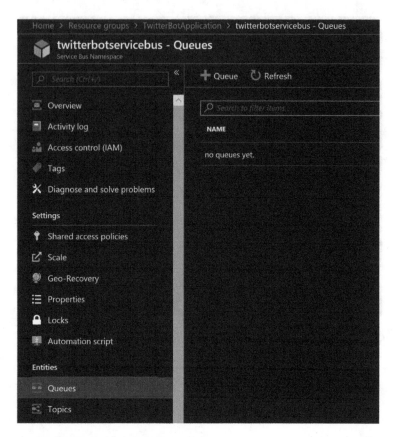

Figure 4-7. *Create a new Service Bus Queue*

2. Click on the + Queue option and enter details of the Hashtag Queue, as shown in Figure 4-8. Enter the name of the queue as HashTagQueue. Enable the Session and Duplicate Detection features. Select 1GB as the max queue size. Click on Create.

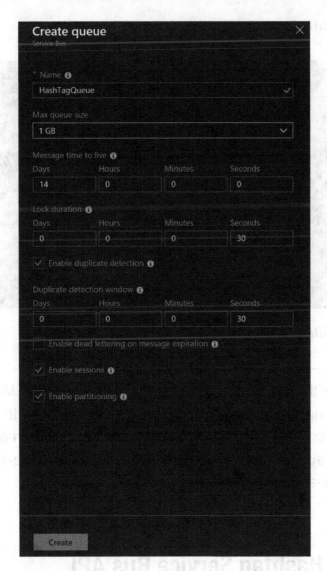

Figure 4-8. *Hashtag Queue*

3.   The HashTagQueue is created, as shown in Figure 4-9.

Figure 4-9.   *Hashtag Queue overview*

Note   Currently there is no local emulator for Azure Service Bus. Microsoft
recommends using an on-premise service bus as a substitute for the emulator. The
user voice is recorded at `https://feedback.azure.com/forums/216926-`
`service-bus/suggestions/2565564-provide-a-service-bus`
`-emulator-on-a-local-computer`.

Creating a Hashtag Service Bus API

In this section, we create a simple C# wrapper around Service Bus operations for
the Twitter Bot application. Install the `Microsoft.Azure.ServiceBus` Nuget on the
`TwitterBot.Framework` project, as shown in Figure 4-10.

Figure 4-10. *Install the Microsoft.Azure.ServiceBus nuget on the TwitterBot. Framework project*

Create a folder called `ServiceBus` under the `Contracts` folder of the `TwitterBot. Framework` project. Create an `IServiceBusContext` interface under the `ServiceBus` folder, as shown in Listing 4-1. `IServiceBusContext` holds the `ConnectionString` details of the Service Bus instance along with the `QueueName`. It also holds the `SessionId`, which indicates messages should be tagged to achieve first in, first out (FIFO) order. `OperationTimeout` is used to specify the timeout value for the retrieve operation and `MaxConcurrentMessagesToBeRetrieved` specifies the number of messages that can be retrieved from the Service Bus using a single session object.

Listing 4-1. ISeverviceBusContext Class

```
using System;
namespace TwitterBot.Framework.Contracts.ServiceBus
{
    public interface IServiceBusContext
    {
        string ConnectionString { get; set; }
        string QueueName { get; set; }
        string SessionId { get; set; }
        int MaxConcurrentMessagesToBeRetrieved { get; set; }
        TimeSpan OperationTimeout { get; set; }
    }
}
```

165

Create a folder called `ServiceBus` under the `TwitterBot.Framework` project. Create the `ServiceBusContext` class and implement the `IServiceBusContext` interface, as shown in Listing 4-2.

Listing 4-2. ServiceBusContext Class

```
using System;
using TwitterBot.Framework.Contracts.ServiceBus;
namespace TwitterBot.Framework.ServiceBus
{
    public class ServiceBusContext : IServiceBusContext
    {
        public string ConnectionString { get; set; }
        public string QueueName { get; set; }
        public string SessionId { get; set; }
        public int MaxConcurrentMessagesToBeRetrieved { get; set; }
        public TimeSpan OperationTimeout { get; set; }
    }
}
```

Create an `IServiceBusOperations` interface under the `ServiceBus` folder in the contracts of the `TwitterBot.Framework` project, as shown in Listing 4-3. `IServiceBusOperations` holds the methods to send and receive messages from the Azure Service Bus Queue.

Listing 4-3. IServiceBusOperations Class

```
using Microsoft.Azure.ServiceBus;
using System.Collections.Generic;
using System.Threading.Tasks;
namespace TwitterBot.Framework.Contracts.ServiceBus
{
    public interface IServiceBusOperations
    {
        Task SendMessageAsync(string id, string message);
        Task<List<Message>> ReceiveMessagesAsync();
    }
}
```

Create a ServiceBusOperations class under the ServiceBus folder of the TwitterBot.Framework project and implement IServiceBusOperations, as shown in Listing 4-4. The following are the key points of this implementation.

- ServiceBusOperation's constructor takes the IServiceBusContext instance through which IMessageSender and ISessionClient instances are created. IMessageSender is used to send messages to the Service Bus Queue. ISessionClient is used to receive messages from the Service Bus Queue.

- The SendMessageAsync method sends the message to the Service Bus Queue instance using IMessageSender. Id (mapped to MessageId) is used for duplicate detection of message. SessionId is used to tag messages for a particular session to achieve a guaranteed first in, first out order.

- ReceiveMessagesAsync fetches a session object by using ISessionClient, through which messages can be retrieved from the Service Bus Queue. Later this method loops through the MaxConcurrentMessagesToBeRetrieved value to limit the number of messages retrieved using a single session object. Inside the loop, the message is fetched using the ReceiveAsync method of the session object. If message is null, we break the loop indicating that there no new messages to be fetched from the Service Bus Queue. Otherwise, we hold the message in a list, mark the message for deletion on the queue using the CompleteAsync method, and proceed with the loop to fetch the next available message. Finally, the messages are returned to the calling method.

Listing 4-4. ServiceBusOperations Class

```
using Microsoft.Azure.ServiceBus;
using Microsoft.Azure.ServiceBus.Core;
using System;
using System.Collections.Generic;
using System.Text;
using System.Threading.Tasks;
```

```csharp
using TwitterBot.Framework.Contracts.ServiceBus;
namespace TwitterBot.Framework.ServiceBus
{
    public class ServiceBusOperations : IServiceBusOperations
    {
        private IServiceBusContext _serviceBusContext;
        private IMessageSender _messageSender;
        private ISessionClient _sessionClient;
        public ServiceBusOperations(IServiceBusContext serviceBusContext)
        {
            _serviceBusContext = serviceBusContext;
            _messageSender = new MessageSender(serviceBusContext.
            ConnectionString, serviceBusContext.QueueName);
            _sessionClient = new SessionClient(serviceBusContext.
            ConnectionString, serviceBusContext.QueueName);
        }

        public async Task<List<Message>> ReceiveMessagesAsync()
        {
            var messages = new List<Message>();
            IMessageSession session = await _sessionClient.
            AcceptMessageSessionAsync(_serviceBusContext.SessionId);

            if (session == null)
            {
                return messages;
            }
            for (int i = 0; i < _serviceBusContext.
            MaxConcurrentMessagesToBeRetrieved; i++)
            {
                Message message = await session.ReceiveAsync
                (_serviceBusContext.OperationTimeout);
```

```
        if (message == null)
        {
            break;
        }

        messages.Add(message);
        await session.CompleteAsync(message.SystemProperties.
        LockToken);
    }
    await session.CloseAsync();

    return messages;
}

public async Task SendMessageAsync(string id, string message)
{
    await _messageSender.SendAsync(new Message(Encoding.UTF8.
    GetBytes(message))
    {
        MessageId = id,
        SessionId = _serviceBusContext.SessionId
    });
    }
  }
}
```

The folder structure of the TwitterBot.Framework project is shown in Figure 4-11.

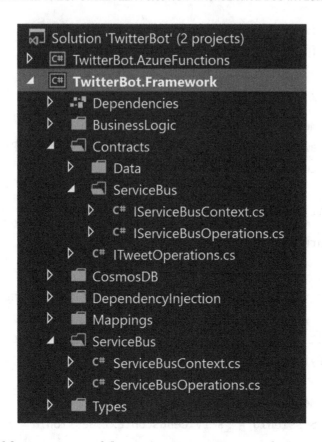

Figure 4-11. *Folder structure of the TwitterBot.Framework project*

Testing the Service Bus API with a Console Application

In this section, we test the Service Bus API with the Hashtag type by using a console application. First, create a Console Application (.NET Core) under the TwitterBot solution. We need to add a TwitterBot.Framework project reference to the console application. Install the Microsoft.Azure.ServiceBus Nuget package on the console application.

In the console app, the Internalhandler method tests the IServiceBusOperations code, as shown in Listing 4-5. We first create the instance of ServiceBusContext and set the required configuration. We configure it to retrieve two messages per batch and 500ms as the operation timeout value. We also provide a session and queue name. Then we create an instance of ServiceBusOperations by passing the ServiceBusContext instance. We create the list of sample hashtags and invoke the SendMessageAsync method of ServiceBusOperations with one hashtag at a time to send a message to the Service Bus Queue.

Once all the messages are created, we invoke the ReceiveMessagesAsync method of ServiceBusOperations to retrieve messages in batches and write the output to the console window.

Listing 4-5. Console Application Test

```
using Newtonsoft.Json;
using System;
using System.Collections.Generic;
using System.Linq;
using System.Text;
using System.Threading;
using System.Threading.Tasks;
using TwitterBot.Framework.ServiceBus;
using TwitterBot.Framework.Types;
namespace ConsoleApp1
{
    class Program
    {
        static void Main(string[] args)
        {
            Task t = InternalHandler();
            t.Wait();
            Console.ReadLine();
        }

        static async Task InternalHandler()
        {
            var serviceBusContext = new ServiceBusContext()
            {
                ConnectionString = "Service Bus Primary Connectionstring"
                QueueName = "HashTagQueue",
                MaxConcurrentMessagesToBeRetrieved = 2,
                SessionId = "TwitterBotApplication",
                OperationTimeout = TimeSpan.FromMilliseconds(500)
            };
```

```csharp
var serviceBusOperations = new ServiceBusOperations(serviceBusC
ontext);

// Create Hashtags
List<Hashtag> hashtags = new List<Hashtag>();
for (int i = 1; i <= 10; i++)
{
    hashtags.Add(new Hashtag { Id = $"{i}", Text =
    $"#justsaying{i}", IsCurrentlyInQueue = true });
}

// Send messages.
foreach (var hashtag in hashtags)
{
    await serviceBusOperations.SendMessageAsync(hashtag.Id,
    JsonConvert.SerializeObject(hashtag));
}
// Receive all Session based messages.
while (true)
{
    Thread.Sleep(TimeSpan.FromSeconds(3));
    var messages = await serviceBusOperations.
    ReceiveMessagesAsync();
    if (messages != null && messages.Any())
    {
        foreach (var message in messages)
        {
            var messageText = Encoding.UTF8.GetString(message.
            Body);
            var hashTag = JsonConvert.DeserializeObject<Hashtag>
            (messageText);
            Console.WriteLine(hashTag.Text);
        }
    }
```

```
        else
        {
            Console.WriteLine("No messages received!!!");
        }
      }
    }
  }
}
```

HashTagQueue reflects the new messages count, as shown in Figure 4-12.

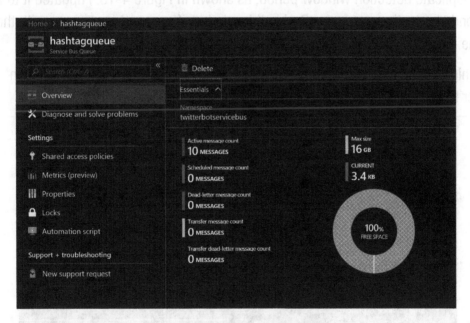

Figure 4-12. *Active messages count in HashTagQueue*

The output of the console application is shown in Listing 4-6.

Listing 4-6. Output of the Console Application

```
#justsaying1
#justsaying2
#justsaying3
#justsaying4
#justsaying5
#justsaying6
```

```
#justsaying7
#justsaying8
#justsaying9
#justsaying10
No messages received!!!
No messages received!!!
```

Note   If we run the console app again, we might not see the same output because of the duplicate detection support of Azure Service Bus. We can change the duplicate detection window period, as shown in Figure 4-13. I updated it to 20 seconds for testing purposes. During this window if we send a message with the same message ID, it will be considered a duplicate and will be discarded.

It is highly recommended to use a smaller duplicate detection window value in order to achieve higher throughput.

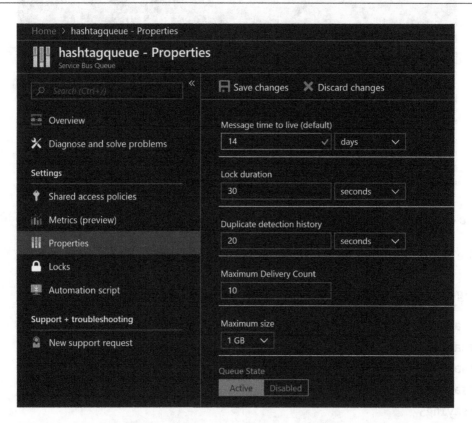

Figure 4-13. *Duplicate detection history setting for the Service Bus Queue*

Configuring the Service Bus API at the Azure Functions

In this section, we configure ISeviceBusContext and ISeviceBusOperations in the
TwitterBot.AzureFunctions project. Update the WebJobsExtensionStartup class, as
shown in Listing 4-7.

Listing 4-7. Configure IServiceBusContext and IServiceBusOperations in the
TwitterBot.AzureFunctions Project

```
using Microsoft.Azure.WebJobs;
using Microsoft.Azure.WebJobs.Hosting;
using Microsoft.Extensions.DependencyInjection;
using System;
using System.Threading.Tasks;
using TwitterBot.AzureFunctions;
using TwitterBot.Framework.BusinessLogic;
using TwitterBot.Framework.Contracts;
using TwitterBot.Framework.Contracts.Data;
using TwitterBot.Framework.Contracts.ServiceBus;
using TwitterBot.Framework.CosmosDB;
using TwitterBot.Framework.DependencyInjection;
using TwitterBot.Framework.Mappings;
using TwitterBot.Framework.ServiceBus;

[assembly: WebJobsStartup(typeof(WebJobsExtensionStartup), "TwitterBot
Extensions Startup")]
namespace TwitterBot.AzureFunctions
{
    public class WebJobsExtensionStartup : IWebJobsStartup
    {
        public void Configure(IWebJobsBuilder builder)
        {
            MappingProfile.Activate();
            // CosmosDB Configuration
```

```
var documentDbContext = new DocumentDbContext
{
    AuthKey = "TwitterBot Cosmos DB Authentication Key",
    DatabaseId = "TwitterBotDB",
    EndpointUri = "https://twitterbotdb.documents.azure.com:443/"
};
Task.Run(async () => await documentDbContext.
CreateDatabaseAndCollectionsAsync()).Wait();
builder.Services.AddSingleton<IDocumentDbContext>(documentDb
Context);
builder.Services.AddSingleton(typeof(IDocumentDbRepository<>),
typeof(DocumentDbRepository<>));

// Service Bus Configuration
var serviceBusContext = new ServiceBusContext()
{
    ConnectionString = "Primary Connectionstring of Service Bus",
    QueueName = "HashTagQueue",
    MaxConcurrentMessagesToBeRetrieved = 2,
    SessionId = "TwitterBotApplication",
    OperationTimeout = TimeSpan.FromMilliseconds(500)
};
builder.Services.AddSingleton<IServiceBusContext>(serviceBusCo
ntext);
builder.Services.AddSingleton<IServiceBusOperations>(new Servic
eBusOperations(serviceBusContext));

builder.Services.AddSingleton<ITweetOperations>
(new TweetOperations("umUgpc6eOVhGY5hROqN8HKxa9",
"95eDHKsKcOxKvWbHqOdAso6GstdRzNq6AiWyRVR7qSayixQqWQ"));
builder.Services.AddSingleton<InjectBindingProvider>();
builder.AddExtension<InjectConfiguration>();
    }
  }
}
```

In the next sections, we use the Service Bus API to interact with the Hashtag Queue and perform data operations on the Hashtags collection.

Creating a Tweet Scheduler Function Using the Hashtag Service Bus API

In this section, we create a Tweet Scheduler Azure Function that will prioritize the hashtags for TweetBotFunction. We use a Timer Trigger for the new TweetSchedulerFunction:

1. The TweetSchedulerFunction will first connect to the TwitterBotDB Cosmos DB.

2. It will query and fetch all the hashtags that have not been synced in the last 10 minutes, based on LastSyncedDateTime, and that are not currently in the queue, based on the IsCurrentlyInQueue value. The query will also include hashtags that have been in the Service Bus Queue for more than an hour.

3. TweetSchedulerFunction will save the hashtags to the TwitterBot Service Bus.

4. Finally, it will mark the hashtag's IsCurrentlyInQueue value to true and save it back to the Cosmos DB.

Let's get started by configuring the hashtag entity and its collection in the Cosmos BD entities, as shown in Listing 4-8. Update the GetDocumentEntities method of the DocumentDbContext class by including a DocumentDbEntity instance with the hashtag type set to EntityType and HashtagCollection set to Name.

Note   HashtagCollection will be created next time, when we restart the Function app.

Listing 4-8. Configure Hashtag Entity and Its Collection in DocumentDbContext

```
private List<IDocumentDbEntity> GetDocumentEntities()
{
    var entityCollection = new List<IDocumentDbEntity>()
    {
        new DocumentDbEntity { EntityType = typeof(Tweet), Name =
        "TweetCollection" },
        new DocumentDbEntity { EntityType = typeof(Hashtag), Name =
        "HashtagCollection" }
    };
    return entityCollection;
}
```

Create a new Timer Trigger Azure Function called TweetSchedulerFunction, as shown in Figure 4-14. Right-click the TwitterBot.AzureFunctions project and choose Add ➤ New Azure Function. Call this function TweetSchedulerFunction. Choose Add ➤ Select Timer Trigger type and update the schedule to run every minute. Then click OK.

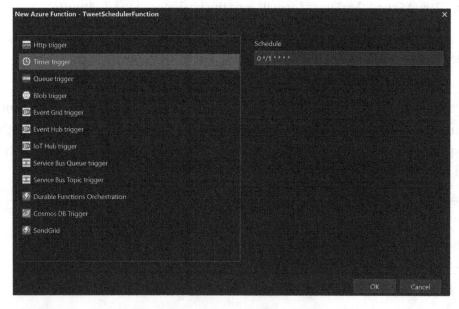

Figure 4-14. *Timer Trigger for TweetSchedulerFunction*

Update the TweetSchedulerFunction code, as shown in Listing 4-9. Inject
IServiceBusOperations and IDocumentDbRepository<Hashtag> instances into the
function through Dependency Injection. We will use WhereAsync of IDocumentDbReposit
ory<Hashtag> to fetch the hashtags that have not been synced in the last 10 minutes and
are currently not loaded at the Service Bus Queue along with hashtags that have been in
the queue for more than an hour.

We iterate each hashtag and send it to Service Bus by using the SendMessageAsync
method of the IServiceBusOperations. We then update the hashtag's
IsCurrentlyInQueue to true at the HashtagCollection of the TwitterBot Cosmos
DB. We also log the function start and end messages.

Listing 4-9. TweetSchedulerFunction Class

```
using System;
using System.Threading.Tasks;
using Microsoft.Azure.WebJobs;
using Microsoft.Extensions.Logging;
using Newtonsoft.Json;
using TwitterBot.Framework.Contracts.Data;
using TwitterBot.Framework.Contracts.ServiceBus;
using TwitterBot.Framework.DependencyInjection;
using TwitterBot.Framework.Types;

namespace TwitterBot.AzureFunctions
{
    public static class TweetSchedulerFunction
    {
        [FunctionName("TweetSchedulerFunction")]
        public async static Task Run([TimerTrigger("0 */1 * * * *")]
        TimerInfo myTimer, ILogger log,
            [Inject]IServiceBusOperations serviceBusOperations,
            [Inject]IDocumentDbRepository<Hashtag> hashTagRepository)
        {
            log.LogInformation($"TweetSchedulerFunction started execution
            at: {DateTime.Now}");
```

```csharp
            // Get Hashtags from TwitterBot Cosmos DB.
            var hashtags = await hashTagRepository.WhereAsync(p =>
            (!p.IsCurrentlyInQueue && p.LastSyncedDateTime < DateTime.
            UtcNow.AddMinutes(-10))
            || (p.IsCurrentlyInQueue && p.LastSyncedDateTime < DateTime.
            UtcNow.AddHours(-1)));
            foreach (var hashtag in hashtags)
            {
                // Queue the hashtags.
                await serviceBusOperations.SendMessageAsync(hashtag.Id,
                JsonConvert.SerializeObject(hashtag));

                // Mark the hashtags as currently in queue.
                hashtag.IsCurrentlyInQueue = true;
                await hashTagRepository.AddOrUpdateAsync(hashtag);
            }

            log.LogInformation($"TweetSchedulerFunction completed execution
            at: {DateTime.Now}");
        }
    }
}
```

To test the function, we need to set up test data at `HashtagCollection`. Add sample JSON documents, as shown in Listing 4-10, to `HashtagCollection` using the Data Explorer tab of TwitterBot Cosmos DB. Add multiple documents with the data, like #news, #world, etc. Make sure you have different ID values for each document.

Listing 4-10. Sample JSON Document

```json
{
 "txt": "#justsaying",
 "lsdt": "0001-01-01T00:00:00",
 "iciq": false,
 "id": "1046012417413730305",
 "con": "0001-01-01T00:00:00",
 "cby": "Rami",
 "mon": "0001-01-01T00:00:00",
```

```
"mby": null,
"isd": false,
"_rid": "CCsyAPouL+0BAAAAAAAAAA==",
"_self": "dbs/CCsyAA==/colls/CCsyAPouL+0=/docs/CCsyAPouL+0BAAAAAAAAAA==/",
"_etag": "\"0000457d-0000-0000-0000-5bbcf3b00000\"",
"_attachments": "attachments/",
"_ts": 1539109808
}
```

Note   In later chapters, we will populate the hashtags in `HashtagCollection` from a web application based on the user's subscription.

We will test `TweetSchedulerFunction` in the next section, where we integrate `TweetBotFunction` with a TwitterBot Azure Service Bus instance to fetch the queued hashtags and refresh them against Twitter.

Upgrading the Tweet Bot Function with Azure Service Bus Integration

In this section, we integrate `TweetBotFunction` with the TwitterBot Azure Service Bus by using an `IServiceBusOperations` implementation. The primary purpose of this integration is to enable `TweetBotFunction` to dynamically fetch the prioritized hashtags from the Service Bus and process them against Twitter.

Update `TweetBotFunction`, as shown in Listing 4-11. We inject `IServiceBusOperations` and `IDocumentDbRepository<Hashtag>` instances into the `TweetBotFunction` by leveraging Dependency Injection. Then the available messages at the Service Bus are retrieved using the `ReceiveMessagesAsync` method of `IServiceBusOperations`. The retrieved hashtag messages are deserialized and iterated in a loop to fetch the latest popular tweet from Twitter. At the end, each hashtag's `LastSyncedDateTime` is updated with `DateTime.UtcNow` and `IsCurrentlyInQueue` set to `false` (these properties should be updated so that `TweetSchedulerFunction` will again process the hashtag after a certain time interval).

Note   We can extend ITweetOperations to process multiple hashtags in parallel. For code simplicity, parallel processing is out of the scope of this book.

Listing 4-11. Updated TweetBotFunction Class

```
using Microsoft.Azure.WebJobs;
using Microsoft.Extensions.Logging;
using Newtonsoft.Json;
using System;
using System.Collections.Generic;
using System.Linq;
using System.Text;
using System.Threading.Tasks;
using TwitterBot.Framework.Contracts;
using TwitterBot.Framework.Contracts.Data;
using TwitterBot.Framework.Contracts.ServiceBus;
using TwitterBot.Framework.DependencyInjection;
using TwitterBot.Framework.Types;

namespace TwitterBot.AzureFunctions
{
    public static class TweetBotFunction
    {
        [FunctionName("TweetBotFunction")]
        public async static Task Run([TimerTrigger("0 */5 * * * *")]
        TimerInfo myTimer, ILogger log,
            [Inject]ITweetOperations tweetOperations,
            [Inject]IDocumentDbRepository<Tweet> tweetDbRepository,
            [Inject]IServiceBusOperations serviceBusOperations,
            [Inject]IDocumentDbRepository<Hashtag> hashTagRepository)
        {
            var hashtagMessagess = await serviceBusOperations.
            ReceiveMessagesAsync();
            var hashtags = hashtagMessagess.Select(p => JsonConvert.Deseria
            lizeObject<Hashtag>(Encoding.UTF8.GetString(p.Body)));
```

```csharp
foreach (var hashtag in hashtags)
{
    // Retrieve the latest tweet.
    var tweet = tweetOperations.GetPopularTweetByHashtag(hashtag);
    if (tweet != null)
    {
        tweet.Hashtags = new List<Hashtag>();
        log.LogInformation($"Latest popular tweet for {hashtag.
        Text} : { tweet.FullText }");

        // Check if DB already has the tweet.
        var existingTweet = await tweetDbRepository.
        GetByIdAsync(tweet.Id);

        // If tweet is not present in DB, then add to DB.
        if (existingTweet == null)
        {
            tweet.Hashtags.Add(hashtag);
            // Add the tweet to DB.
            await tweetDbRepository.AddOrUpdateAsync(tweet);
            log.LogInformation($"Added Tweet in TweetCollection
            with Id : { tweet.Id }");
        }

        // Map DB Hashtags with latest Tweet.
        if (existingTweet != null && !existingTweet.Hashtags.
        Any(p => p.Text == hashtag.Text))
        {
            // Map the existing hashtags to tweet.
            tweet.Hashtags = existingTweet.Hashtags;
            // Add the current hashtag to tweet.
            tweet.Hashtags.Add(hashtag);
            // Update the tweet to DB.
            await tweetDbRepository.AddOrUpdateAsync(tweet);

            log.LogInformation($"Updated Tweet in
            TweetCollection with Id : { tweet.Id }");
        }
    }
}
```

183

```
// Update the hashtag's Last sync Date time with current
time and currently in queue as false.
hashtag.IsCurrentlyInQueue = false;
hashtag.LastSyncedDateTime = DateTime.UtcNow;
await hashTagRepository.AddOrUpdateAsync(hashtag);
        }
    }
}
}
```

Let's test the complete flow by running the TweetBotFunction, TweetSchedulerFunction, and TweetNotifierFunction Azure Functions in a local development environment. Press F5 in Visual Studio to launch Azure Functions CLI. The functions will be started, as shown in Figure 4-15.

```
[10/11/2018 3:51:17 PM]  Initializing Host.
[10/11/2018 3:51:17 PM]  Host initialization: ConsecutiveErrors=0, StartupCount=1
[10/11/2018 3:51:17 PM]  Starting JobHost
[10/11/2018 3:51:17 PM]  Starting Host (HostId=ramivm-1710302376, InstanceId=98c25824-e122-431c-9770-da270500b0f2, Versio
n=2.0.12115.0, ProcessId=7656, AppDomainId=1, Debug=False, FunctionsExtensionVersion=)
[10/11/2018 3:51:17 PM]  Generating 3 job function(s)
[10/11/2018 3:51:20 PM]  Found the following functions:
[10/11/2018 3:51:20 PM]  TwitterBot.AzureFunctions.TweetBotFunction.Run
[10/11/2018 3:51:20 PM]  TwitterBot.AzureFunctions.TweetNotifierFunction.Run
[10/11/2018 3:51:20 PM]  TwitterBot.AzureFunctions.TweetSchedulerFunction.Run
[10/11/2018 3:51:20 PM]
[10/11/2018 3:51:20 PM]  Host initialized (2681ms)
[10/11/2018 3:51:21 PM]  The next 5 occurrences of the 'TwitterBot.AzureFunctions.TweetBotFunction.Run' schedule will be:
[10/11/2018 3:51:21 PM]
[10/11/2018 3:51:21 PM]  10/11/2018 3:55:00 PM
[10/11/2018 3:51:21 PM]  10/11/2018 4:00:00 PM
[10/11/2018 3:51:21 PM]  10/11/2018 4:05:00 PM
[10/11/2018 3:51:21 PM]  10/11/2018 4:10:00 PM
[10/11/2018 3:51:21 PM]  10/11/2018 4:15:00 PM
[10/11/2018 3:51:21 PM]
[10/11/2018 3:51:21 PM]  Executing 'TweetSchedulerFunction' (Reason='Timer fired at 2018-10-11T15:51:21.3711472+00:00', I
d=eb8d7d6d-44d3-48ea-a1da-447f414d48e1)
[10/11/2018 3:51:21 PM]  TweetSchedulerFunction started execution at: 10/11/2018 3:51:21 PM
TweetSchedulerFunction started execution at: 10/11/2018 3:51:21 PM
[10/11/2018 3:51:28 PM]  TweetSchedulerFunction completed execution at: 10/11/2018 3:51:28 PM
TweetSchedulerFunction completed execution at: 10/11/2018 3:51:28 PM
[10/11/2018 3:51:28 PM]  Executed 'TweetSchedulerFunction' (Succeeded, Id=eb8d7d6d-44d3-48ea-a1da-447f414d48e1)
[10/11/2018 3:51:28 PM]  The next 5 occurrences of the 'TwitterBot.AzureFunctions.TweetSchedulerFunction.Run' schedule wi
ll be:
[10/11/2018 3:51:28 PM]  10/11/2018 3:52:00 PM
[10/11/2018 3:51:28 PM]  10/11/2018 3:53:00 PM
[10/11/2018 3:51:28 PM]  10/11/2018 3:54:00 PM
[10/11/2018 3:51:28 PM]  10/11/2018 3:55:00 PM
[10/11/2018 3:51:28 PM]  10/11/2018 3:56:00 PM
[10/11/2018 3:51:28 PM]
[10/11/2018 3:51:28 PM]  Host started (11227ms)
[10/11/2018 3:51:28 PM]  Job host started
Hosting environment: Production
Content root path: C:\Users\ramiadmin\OneDrive\TwitterBot\TwitterBot.AzureFunctions\bin\Debug\netstandard2.0
Now listening on: http://0.0.0.0:7071
Application started. Press Ctrl+C to shut down.
```

Figure 4-15. *Execute all Tweet Bot Azure Functions*

TweetSchedulerFunction executes and we can see the hashtag messages being queued in the TwitterBot Service Bus HashTagQueue, as shown in Figure 4-16.

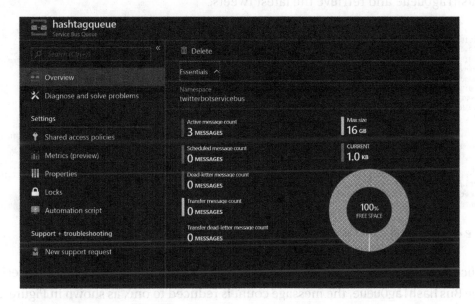

Figure 4-16. *Hashtag messages in the TwitterBot Service Bus HashTagQueue*

The status of hashtags in the TwitterBot Cosmos DB will be marked as "currently in queue" by setting IsCurrentlyInQueue (iciq) to true, as shown in Figure 4-17.

Figure 4-17. *IsCurrentlyInQueue set to true for a hashtag in the TwitterBot Cosmos DB*

After some time, `TweetBotFunction` will be executed, as shown in Figure 4-18. It will pull the first two prioritized hashtag messages from the TwitterBot Service Bus `HashTagQueue` and retrieve the latest tweets.

```
[10/11/2018 3:55:00 PM] Executing 'TweetBotFunction' (Reason='Timer fired at 2018-10-11T15:55:00.0129723+00:00', Id=9243
c4ad-3478-4117-8ae3-f177d4b4ce9e)
[10/11/2018 3:55:07 PM] Latest popular tweet for #justsaying : Looks like there is a plan underway to crash the markets
#justsaying
Latest popular tweet for #justsaying : Looks like there is a plan underway to crash the markets #justsaying
[10/11/2018 3:55:08 PM] Added Tweet in TweetCollection with Id : 1050188166081040384
Added Tweet in TweetCollection with Id : 1050188166081040384
[10/11/2018 3:55:10 PM] Latest popular tweet for #news : ?????AKB48?????????∞?NEWS?TWICE 9???????
https://t.co/xVDdb4909c

 #AKB48 #???46 #??46 #TWICE #NEWS #???? #nogizaka46 #????? #?? @nogizaka46 @keyakizaka46 @JYPETWICE_JAPAN @JYPETWICE
Latest popular tweet for #news : ?????AKB48?????????∞?NEWS?TWICE 9???????
https://t.co/xVDdb4909c

 #AKB48 #???46 #??46 #TWICE #NEWS #???? #nogizaka46 #????? #?? @nogizaka46 @keyakizaka46 @JYPETWICE_JAPAN @JYPETWICE
[10/11/2018 3:55:10 PM] Added Tweet in TweetCollection with Id : 1049875932318748672
Added Tweet in TweetCollection with Id : 1049875932318748672
[10/11/2018 3:55:11 PM] Executed 'TweetBotFunction' (Succeeded, Id=9243c4ad-3478-4117-8ae3-f177d4b4ce9e)
```

Figure 4-18. *TweetBotFunction execution*

Once `TweetBotFunction` fetches the first two hashtag messages from the TwitterBot Service Bus `HashTagQueue`, the message count is reduced to one, as shown in Figure 4-19.

Figure 4-19. *Pending messages in HashTagQueue*

The processed hashtags are updated with `IsCurrentlyInQueue` set to `false` and `LastSyncedDateTime` set to `DateTime.UtcNow`, as shown in Figure 4-20.

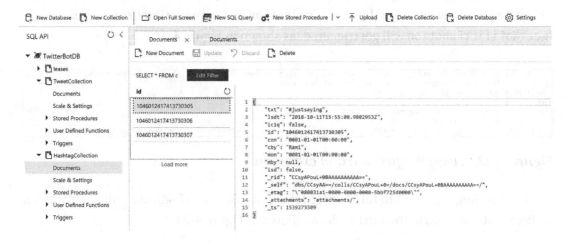

Figure 4-20. *Processed hashtags status in HashTagQueue*

TweetBotFunction will push the retrieved tweets to TweetCollection, as shown in Figure 4-21.

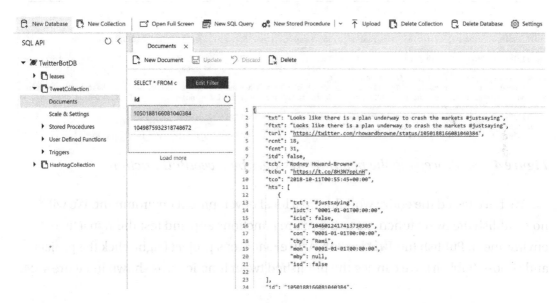

Figure 4-21. *Latest tweets in TwitterBot Cosmos DB TweetCollection*

As we have new tweets in the `TweetCollection` of the TwitterBot Cosmos DB, `TweetNotifierFunction` will get triggered, as shown in Figure 4-22.

```
[10/11/2018 3:55:11 PM] Executing 'TweetNotifierFunction' (Reason='New changes on collection TweetCollection at 2018-10-
11T15:55:11.4158023Z', Id=48296d0e-3402-48f1-9b68-e149e11c4585)
[10/11/2018 3:55:11 PM] Documents modified 2
Documents modified 2
[10/11/2018 3:55:11 PM] First document Id 1050188166081040384
First document Id 1050188166081040384
[10/11/2018 3:55:11 PM] Executed 'TweetNotifierFunction' (Succeeded, Id=48296d0e-3402-48f1-9b68-e149e11c4585)
```

Figure 4-22. *TweetNotifierFunction execution*

The pending messages in the TwitterBot Service Bus `HashTagQueue` will be processed by `TweetBotFunction` in the next cycle, as shown in Figure 4-23.

Note   In later chapters, we will integrate `TweetNotifierFunction` with the Azure SignalR Service. For now, it is a placeholder to get Cosmos DB Trigger notifications.

```
[10/11/2018 4:00:00 PM] Executing 'TweetBotFunction' (Reason='Timer fired at 2018-10-11T16:00:00.0250803+00:00', Id=ab54
b89b-457f-4c09-8af5-1e793292e530)
[10/11/2018 4:00:04 PM] Latest popular tweet for #world : To all our friends in #India and around the #World who celebra
te, best wishes on the occasion of the nine days of #Navratri2018 that started today and the actual beginning of the #Fe
stiveSeason #HappyNavratri https://t.co/AHlnuOBxeE
Latest popular tweet for #world : To all our friends in #India and around the #World who celebrate, best wishes on the o
ccasion of the nine days of #Navratri2018 that started today and the actual beginning of the #FestiveSeason #HappyNavrat
ri https://t.co/AHlnuOBxeE
[10/11/2018 4:00:04 PM] Added Tweet in TweetCollection with Id : 1050015639421808640
Added Tweet in TweetCollection with Id : 1050015639421808640
[10/11/2018 4:00:05 PM] Executed 'TweetBotFunction' (Succeeded, Id=ab54b89b-457f-4c09-8af5-1e793292e530)
```

Figure 4-23. *Processing the pending messages by TweetBotFunction*

We have tested the entire workflow in a local development environment. We will now publish the tweet functions to the Azure Functions app and test them in a live environment. Publish the `TwitterBot.AzureFunctions` project (right-click the project and choose Publish). We can see the published tweet functions, as shown in Figure 4-24.

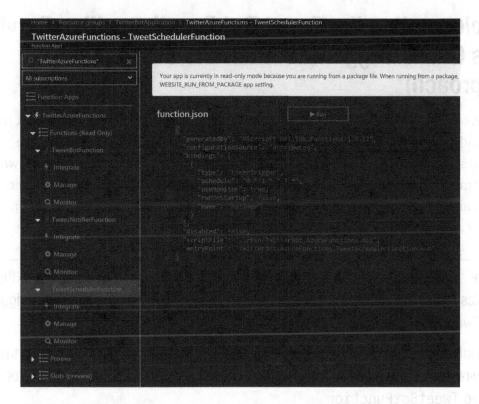

Figure 4-24. *Published Tweet functions at the Azure Functions app*

All the functions—TweetSchedulerFunction, TweetBotFunction, and
TweetNotifierFunction—will work seamlessly and the entire workflow will be executed
in one loop, just like what we experienced in the local environment.

Note   Executions of a specific function can be monitored from the logs tab of the
function in the Azure portal.

Implementing the Tweet Bot Function with a Service Bus Queue Trigger (an Alternate Sessionless Approach)

In this section, we discuss and implement an alternative design for TweetBotFunction. Currently, TweetBotFunction is a Timer Trigger function that's executed every five minutes. We will design a Service Bus Queue trigger function that will get notified when a new message is queued in the Azure Service Bus. In the Service Bus Queue trigger function, we perform the same operation of retrieving the latest popular tweet from Twitter and updating it in the TwitterBot Cosmos DB.

Note   Refer to the section in Chapter 2 entitled "Creating and Understanding the Basics of the Tweet Bot Azure Function," for detailed analysis on choosing a trigger for TweetBotFunction.

The intention of this section is to demonstrate an alternative way to approach the requirement. For the rest of the chapters, we will proceed with the Timer Trigger-based TweetBotFunction.

The Service Bus trigger-based Azure Function will not work with session-enabled Service Bus Queues (https://github.com/Azure/azure-functions-host/issues/563).

To test the Service Bus trigger-based TweetBotFunction, we will delete the existing session-based HashTagQueue and recreate it without session support, as shown in Figure 4-25.

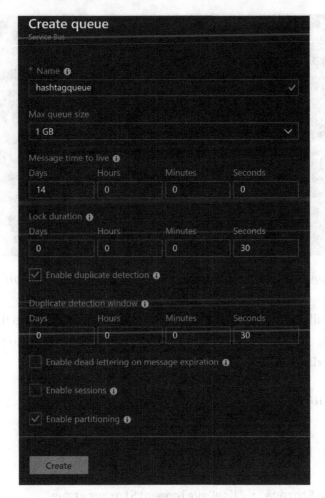

Figure 4-25. *Create a hashtag queue without enabling sessions*

Let's get started by creating a Service Bus Queue trigger function called TweetBotServiceBusTriggerFunction. Right-click the TwitterBot. AzureFunctions project and choose Add ➤ New Azure Function. Call it TweetBotServiceBusTriggerFunction. Then click OK. Select the Service Bus Queue trigger template, as shown in Figure 4-26. Click OK.

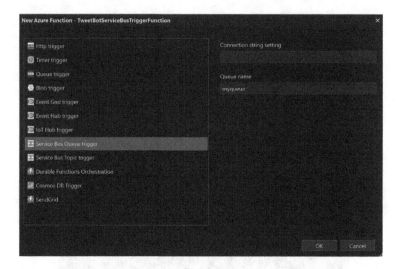

Figure 4-26. *TweetBotServiceBusTriggerFunction trigger selection*

Add a setting called `TwitterBotServiceBus_ConnectionString` to the `local.settings.json` file, as shown in Listing 4-12, with the value pointing to the connection string of the TwitterBot Azure Service Bus (found in Figure 4-5).

Listing 4-12. TwitterBot Service Bus ConnectionString Setting

```
{
  "IsEncrypted": false,
  "Values": {
    "AzureWebJobsStorage": "UseDevelopmentStorage=true",
    "FUNCTIONS_WORKER_RUNTIME": "dotnet",
    "TwitterBotDB_ConnectionString": "TwitterBot Cosmos DB ConnectionString",
    "TwitterBotServiceBus_ConnectionString": "TwitterBot Service Bus
    ConnectionString"
  }
}
```

Update the `TweetBotServiceBusTriggerFunction` class, as shown in Listing 4-13. The function has a Service Bus input binding that takes the queue name `HashTagQueue` and `ConnectionString` as inputs. The Azure Functions framework will automatically bind the queued message to the `myQueueItem` variable. We can deserialize `myQueueItem` into a hashtag object and proceed with the existing core logic of `TweetBotFunction`.

Listing 4-13. Updated TweetBotServiceBusTriggerFunction Class

```
using Microsoft.Azure.WebJobs;
using Microsoft.Extensions.Logging;
using Newtonsoft.Json;
using System;
using System.Collections.Generic;
using System.Linq;
using System.Threading.Tasks;
using TwitterBot.Framework.Contracts;
using TwitterBot.Framework.Contracts.Data;
using TwitterBot.Framework.DependencyInjection;
using TwitterBot.Framework.Types;

namespace TwitterBot.AzureFunctions
{
    public static class TweetBotServiceBusTriggerFunction
    {
        [FunctionName("TweetBotServiceBusTriggerFunction")]
        public async static Task Run([ServiceBusTrigger("hashtagqueue",
        Connection = "TwitterBotServiceBus_ConnectionString")]string
        myQueueItem,
            ILogger log,
            [Inject]ITweetOperations tweetOperations,
            [Inject]IDocumentDbRepository<Tweet> tweetDbRepository,
            [Inject]IDocumentDbRepository<Hashtag> hashTagRepository)
        {
            var hashtag = JsonConvert.DeserializeObject<Hashtag>(myQueueItem);
            // Retrieve the latest tweet.
            var tweet = tweetOperations.GetPopularTweetByHashtag(hashtag);
            if (tweet != null)
            {
                tweet.Hashtags = new List<Hashtag>();
                log.LogInformation($"Latest popular tweet for {hashtag.
                Text} : { tweet.FullText }");
```

```
// Check if DB already has the tweet.
var existingTweet = await tweetDbRepository.
GetByIdAsync(tweet.Id);

// If tweet is not present in DB, then add to DB.
if (existingTweet == null)
{
    tweet.Hashtags.Add(hashtag);
    // Add the tweet to DB.
    await tweetDbRepository.AddOrUpdateAsync(tweet);

    log.LogInformation($"Added Tweet in TweetCollection
    with Id : { tweet.Id }");
}

// Map DB Hashtags with latest Tweet.
if (existingTweet != null && !existingTweet.Hashtags.Any
(p => p.Text == hashtag.Text))
{
    // Map the existing hashtags to tweet.
    tweet.Hashtags = existingTweet.Hashtags;
    // Add the current hashtag to tweet.
    tweet.Hashtags.Add(hashtag);
    // Update the tweet to DB.
    await tweetDbRepository.AddOrUpdateAsync(tweet);
    log.LogInformation($"Updated Tweet in TweetCollection
    with Id : { tweet.Id }");
}
}

// Update the hashtag's Last sync Date time with current time
and currently in queue as false.
hashtag.IsCurrentlyInQueue = false;
hashtag.LastSyncedDateTime = DateTime.UtcNow;
await hashTagRepository.AddOrUpdateAsync(hashtag);
    }
  }
}
```

Run the `TwitterBot.AzureFunctions` project from Visual Studio. The tweet functions—`TweetBotServiceBusTriggerFunction`, `TweetSchedulerFunction`, and `TweetNotifierFunction`—will start, as shown in Figure 4-27.

Note   To exclude the original `TweetBotFunction` from execution, we can comment out the `FunctionName` attribute on the Run method.

```
[10/12/2018 2:29:56 PM] Initializing Host.
[10/12/2018 2:29:56 PM] Host initialization: ConsecutiveErrors=0, StartupCount=1
[10/12/2018 2:29:56 PM] Starting JobHost
[10/12/2018 2:29:56 PM] Starting Host (HostId=ramivm-1710302376, InstanceId=99b38c82-d706-44f6-9e42-8fa97d5a9c5c, Versio
n=2.0.12115.0, ProcessId=7748, AppDomainId=1, Debug=False, FunctionsExtensionVersion=)
[10/12/2018 2:29:56 PM] Generating 3 job function(s)
[10/12/2018 2:29:58 PM] Found the following functions:
[10/12/2018 2:29:58 PM] TwitterBot.AzureFunctions.TweetBotServiceBusTriggerFunction.Run
[10/12/2018 2:29:58 PM] TwitterBot.AzureFunctions.TweetNotifierFunction.Run
[10/12/2018 2:29:58 PM] TwitterBot.AzureFunctions.TweetSchedulerFunction.Run
[10/12/2018 2:29:59 PM]
[10/12/2018 2:29:59 PM] Host initialized (2690ms)
```

Figure 4-27. *Tweet functions execution from Visual Studio*

`TweetBotServiceBusTriggerFunction` will be executed, as shown in Figure 4-28.

```
[10/12/2018 2:30:07 PM] Executing 'TweetBotServiceBusTriggerFunction' (Reason='New ServiceBus message detected on 'hasht
agqueue'.', Id=905843eb-b390-46ee-a782-8256103139f3)
[10/12/2018 2:30:09 PM] Latest popular tweet for #justsaying : Hagia Sophia's famous minarets are 60m tall. #justsaying
https://t.co/NOml59ZrSh[10/12/2018 2:30:09 PM] Latest popular tweet for #world : The main reason that the majority of #e
mployees around the #world are unhappy with their #jobs, #managers, bossy #colleagues &amp; their
 #workenvironment is that they forget to ask the right questions &amp; evaluate their new employers before accepting the
 #job offer. ????

#workforce https://t.co/8mJ8MUeYsr[10/12/2018 2:30:09 PM] Latest popular tweet for #news : ?????·??????????????30?????????
??? #TBSNEWS #tbs #news #SNS #?? #???? #????  #2000? https://t.co/x5eXYBLtoN
Latest popular tweet for #news : ?????·??????????????30??????????? #TBSNEWS #tbs #news #SNS #?? #???? #????  #2000? https
://t.co/x5eXYBLtoN

Latest popular tweet for #world : The main reason that the majority of #employees around the #world are unhappy with the
ir #jobs, #managers, bossy #colleagues &amp; their
 #workenvironment is that they forget to ask the right questions &amp; evaluate their new employers before accepting the
 #job offer. ????

#workforce https://t.co/8mJ8MUeYsr

Latest popular tweet for #justsaying : Hagia Sophia's famous minarets are 60m tall. #justsaying https://t.co/NOml59ZrSh
[10/12/2018 2:30:10 PM] Added Tweet in TweetCollection with Id : 1050446131967221760
Added Tweet in TweetCollection with Id : 1050446131967221760
[10/12/2018 2:30:10 PM] Added Tweet in TweetCollection with Id : 1050231731591110657
Added Tweet in TweetCollection with Id : 1050231731591110657
[10/12/2018 2:30:10 PM] Executed 'TweetBotServiceBusTriggerFunction' (Succeeded, Id=905843eb-b390-46ee-a782-8256103139f3
)
[10/12/2018 2:30:10 PM] Executed 'TweetBotServiceBusTriggerFunction' (Succeeded, Id=cfe974a2-dd12-4da6-8176-56192c0d29cb
)
[10/12/2018 2:30:11 PM] Added Tweet in TweetCollection with Id : 1050407191616937985
Added Tweet in TweetCollection with Id : 1050407191616937985
[10/12/2018 2:30:11 PM] Executed 'TweetBotServiceBusTriggerFunction' (Succeeded, Id=914c4c11-41bb-4fdb-9ee2-024e9060935f
)
```

Figure 4-28. *Execution of TweetBotServiceBusTriggerFunction*

The entire flow of three Tweet Azure Functions —TweetBotServiceBusTriggerFunction, TweetSchedulerFunction, and TweetNotifierFunction—will continue to work as is.

Before we publish the TweetBotServiceBusTriggerFunction to the Azure Function app, we need to create the TwitterBotServiceBus_ConnectionString setting under the Application Settings tab of the TwitterAzureFunctions app, as shown in Figure 4-29.

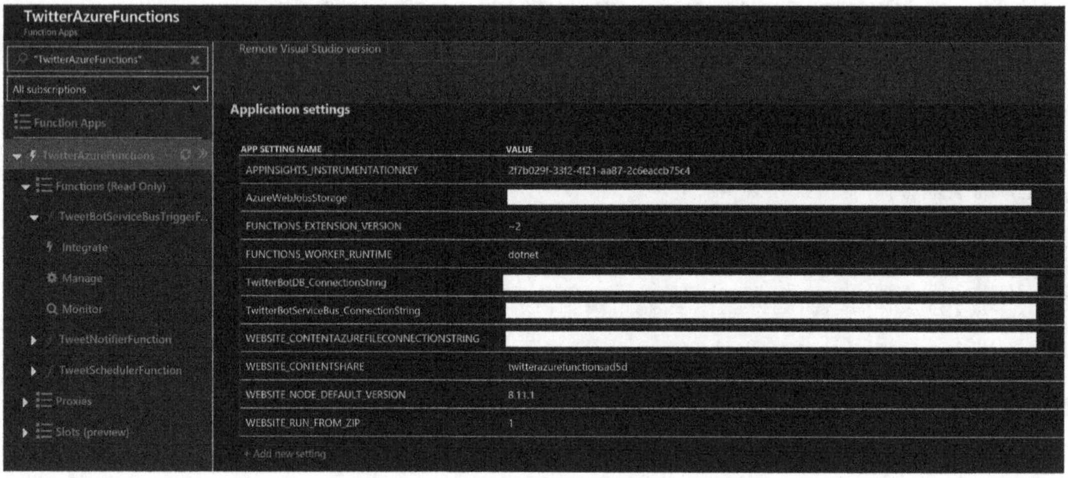

Figure 4-29. *Add the TwitterBotServiceBus_ConnectionString setting*

Now we can publish the TwitterBot.AzureFunctions project to the TwitterAzureFunctions Azure Function App, as shown in Figure 4-30. All the functions will work seamlessly in the Azure environment.

Figure 4-30   *TweetBotServiceBusTriggerFunction in the Azure Function app*

This way we can replace a Timer Trigger function with the Service Bus Queue trigger function in the Twitter Bot application.

Note   Going forward, we are going to use the Timer Trigger-based `TweetBotFunction`. Revert the following changes in the `TwitterBot.AzureFunctions` project.

1. Uncomment the `FunctionName` attribute on `TweetBotFunction`.

2. Comment the `FunctionName` attribute on the `TweetBotServiceBusTriggerFunction`.

3. Delete the `HashTagQueue` from the TwitterBot Azure Service Bus and recreate it by enabling the session.

Twitter Bot Application Architecture Checkpoint

At this junction of the book, we will take a pause in development to recap the Twitter Bot application architecture developed so far. We have completed the implementation of highlighted part of the architecture, as displayed in Figure 4-31.

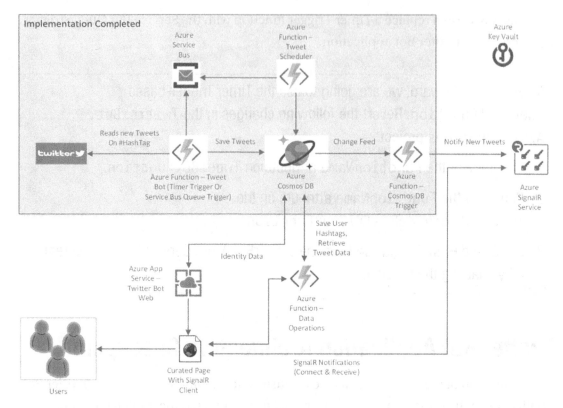

Figure 4-31. *Twitter Bot application architecture*

The following are the key points achieved so far during the journey in this book.

- Developed a custom framework to interact with the Tweetinvi library to retrieve the latest tweets from Twitter.

- Designed the Cosmos DB Twitter Bot application data model.

- Implemented a Cosmos DB Repository pattern.

- Designed a custom Dependency Injection module.

- Implemented a custom API to interact with Azure Service Bus.

- Created TweetSchedulerFunction, a Timer Trigger-based Azure Function to prioritize hashtags using the Service Bus Queue from Cosmos DB.

- Developed TweetBotFunction, an Azure Function based on Timer Trigger to interact with Twitter and retrieve the latest tweet information based on prioritized hashtags by leveraging the custom tweet framework. Created a Service Bus Queue trigger variant of the Azure Function to demonstrate an alternative approach.

- Developed TweetNotifierFunction, a Cosmos DB Trigger-based Azure Function, which will be notified about inserts and updates of tweet data at Cosmos DB.

- Deployed all functions to the Azure environment and tested the end-to-end workflow, as demonstrated in Figure 4-31.

In the next chapters, we will focus on developing the Twitter Bot web application and integrating the entire flow with the Azure SignalR Service.

EXERCISE 1

In this chapter, we created a C# API for session-based Azure Service Bus messages. Now develop a similar Service Bus C# API for sessionless messages.

Solution: Getting started with Azure Service Bus is explained in https://docs. microsoft.com/en-us/azure/service-bus-messaging/service-bus-dotnet-get-started-with-queues.

More C# Samples can be found at https://github.com/Azure/azure-service-bus/tree/master/samples.

EXERCISE 2

Azure Service Bus Queues are best suitable for applications with a single consumer of messages. In the case of multiple consumers looking for the same messages, Azure Service Bus Topics and Subscriptions are the right choice. Topics and Subscriptions support the publish/subscribe pattern.

As part of this exercise, develop a C# client by leveraging the Microsoft.Azure. ServiceBus nuget to send messages using TopicClient and receive messages using SubscriptionClient.

Note: Getting started with Azure Service Bus Topics is explained in https://docs. microsoft.com/en-us/azure/service-bus-messaging/service-bus-dotnet-how-to-use-topics-subscriptions.

Summary

You started off this chapter by learning about the strategies related to scaling software applications, such as horizontal and vertical scaling. You learned that optimized scaling can be achieved by decoupling multiple layers of the application into independent layers.

You learned the basics of the Azure Service Bus and its features. You created an instance of an Azure Service Bus for the Twitter Bot application with a queue that supports duplicate detection and sessions. You proceeded to create a C# API to send and receive messages to the Service Bus Queue and tested it with a console application. You configured hashtag collection at `DocumentDbContext` and the Service Bus API at the `WebJobsExtensionStartup` of the `TwitterBot.AzureFunctions` project.

You designed a `TweetSchedulerFunction`, a Timer Trigger-based Azure Function that prioritizes hashtags using the Azure Service Bus Queue from the TwitterBot Cosmos DB. You upgraded `TweetBotFunction` with the Service Bus API to fetch messages from the TwitterBot Service Bus in batches and use them to retrieve the latest popular tweets. You tested the entire flow in the Azure environment by running `TweetSchedulerFunction`, `TweetBotFunction`, and `TweetNotifierFunction` with sample hashtag data.

You created an alternate version of `TweetBotFunction` using a Service Bus Queue trigger. You also learned that Service Bus Queue triggers don't work for session based messages. For testing, you created a Service Bus Queue and disabled the session-based messaging feature. You published and tested the new variant of `TweetBotFunction` along with other functions in the Azure environment.

Finally, we concluded the chapter by recapping the Twitter Bot application architecture and reviewed all the components developed so far in this book. In the next chapter, you will integrate Azure Functions with the Azure Key Vault service to secure application secrets and explore the concepts of logging and exception handling in Azure Functions.

References

1. https://docs.microsoft.com/en-us/azure/service-bus-messaging/service-bus-messaging-overview.

2. https://github.com/Azure/azure-service-bus/tree/master/samples/DotNet/GettingStarted/Microsoft.Azure.ServiceBus/SessionSendReceiveUsingSessionClient.

3. https://docs.microsoft.com/en-us/azure/service-bus-messaging/duplicate-detection.

CHAPTER 5

Handling Secrets and Exceptions in Azure Functions

The robustness and reliability of a software application is heavily dependent on the security of the information provided to the customers and other stakeholders. Even though different access control strategies provide first-level defenses to user data at the application level, we should equally emphasize on securing all logical and infrastructure layers, especially persistence stores, from malicious attacks that can breach the sensitive data and infrastructure configuration. Securing application and infrastructure is achieved many ways, such as managing user identities through authentication and authorization protocols, enhancing server security through strong firewalls, securing configuration information at centralized vaults, etc.

In Chapter 4, we created a Tweet scheduler function that, along with the Tweet bot and Notifier Functions, constitutes the core business orchestration of the Twitter Bot application. In this chapter, we focus on securing the Azure Functions configuration. In the first part of this chapter, we:

- Secure the configuration information of the Twitter Bot application by leveraging the Azure Key Vault service.

- Upgrade the Twitter Bot Azure Functions to securely connect and access secrets from the Azure Key Vault.

Exception handling plays a key role in achieving greater operational control and easier maintenance of software. The goal of exception handling is to present the users with standard but meaningful error messages about system failures and unhandled exceptions. The exception handling module should ensure that system

203

© Rami Vemula 2019
R. Vemula, *Integrating Serverless Architecture*, https://doi.org/10.1007/978-1-4842-4489-0_5

sensitive information, such as details about the application code, persistent medium, and infrastructure, are never disclosed to end customers, as this information helps hackers breach the system. Generally, exception handling and logging frameworks go hand in hand, with the former handling exceptions and the later logging exception details to storage.

In the second part of this chapter, we:

- Explore the built-in logging capabilities of Azure Functions that leverage Azure Application Insights to log information.

- Develop an exception handling model for the Twitter Bot Azure Functions.

Getting Started with Azure Key Vault

Azure Key Vault is a Microsoft cloud service used to securely store and access sensitive application information, especially keys, passwords, certifications, etc. It is primarily used to decouple the application from the secrets and helps organizations prevent information theft. Prior to Key Vault, most software applications held sensitive configuration information within their own configuration files. The main problem with this approach is the lack of control over access to the configuration files. Anyone who has access to the configuration files via source control, infrastructure, etc., can easily acquire the secrets, which increases the chances of potential misuse.

Azure Key Vault primarily provides the following services:

- Securely stores and manages tokens, passwords, connection strings, etc.

- Creates and controls encryption keys.

- Provisions, manages, and deploys certificates.

- Supports Hardware Security Modules (HSM) for maximum data protection.

Secrets stored in Azure Key Vault can only be accessed by an application or user whose identity is verified through authentication and authorization. We can also monitor the access history of keys and secrets through Key Vault logging.

Register a Managed Service Identity for the Azure Function App

To retrieve secrets from Azure Key Vault, we need to register a Managed Secured Identity for the TwitterAzureFunctions Azure Function app with the Azure Active Directory. A managed identity from the Azure Active Directory allows the TwitterAzureFunctions app to easily access any Azure Active Directory protected resources, including Azure Key Vault. Navigate to the Platform Features tab of the TwitterAzureFunctions app and click on Managed Service Identity, as shown in Figure 5-1.

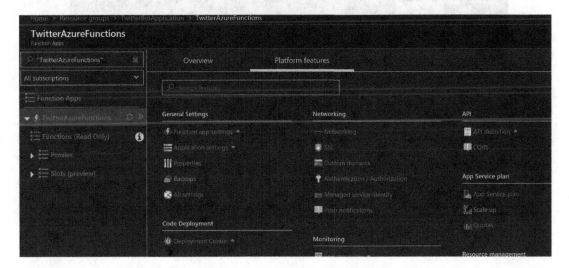

Figure 5-1. *Enable Managed Service Identity on the TwitterAzureFunctions app*

Turn on Managed Service Identity, as shown in Figure 5-2. Click Save.

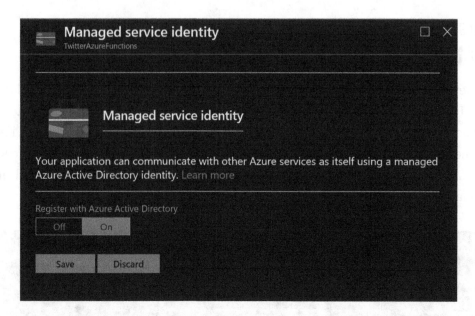

Figure 5-2. Turn on Managed Service Identity in the TwitterAzureFunctions app

---

Note   Enabling Managed Service Identity will create the MSI_ENDPOINT and
MSI_SECRET environment variables for TwitterAzureFunctions. These values
will be internally used by the Azure Key Vault nuget to get the authentication token
used to communicate with Key Vault.

Creating an Azure Key Vault and Configuring Its Access Policies

We will create an instance of Azure Key Vault and configure the access policies for the
TwitterAzureFunctions service principal at Key Vault, as described in the following
step-by-step process.

1. Click on the Create a Resource option. Key Vault will be listed
    under the Security tab, as shown in Figure 5-3.

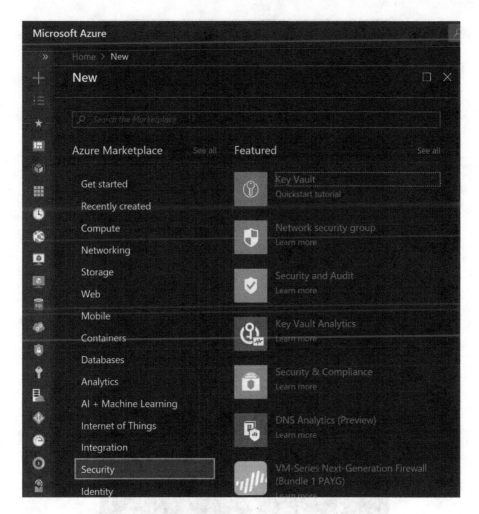

Figure 5-3. *Creating a new Azure Key Vault instance*

2. Enter the name TwitterBotKeyVault. Select
    TwitterBotApplication as a resource group and Central US as
    the location, as shown in Figure 5-4.

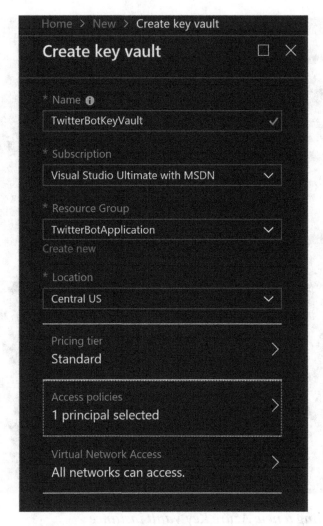

Figure 5-4. *Details of the Azure Key Vault instance*

3. We need to add the principal we created for the
    TwitterAzureFunctions Function app. Select the Access Policies
    tab, as shown in Figure 5-5.

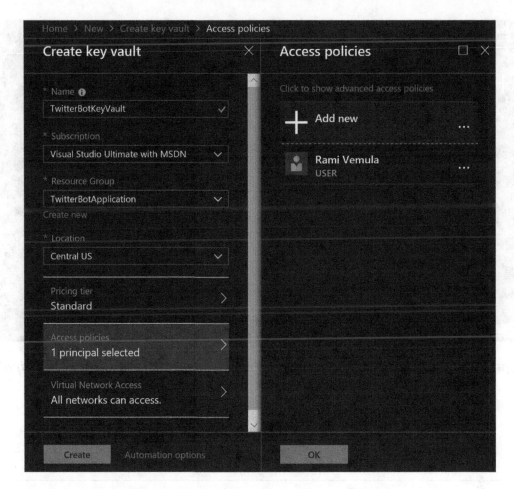

Figure 5-5. *Access Policies tab of the Azure Key Vault instance*

4. Click on Add New. Select the principal by searching for
   TwitterAzureFunctions, as shown in Figure 5-6. Click Select.

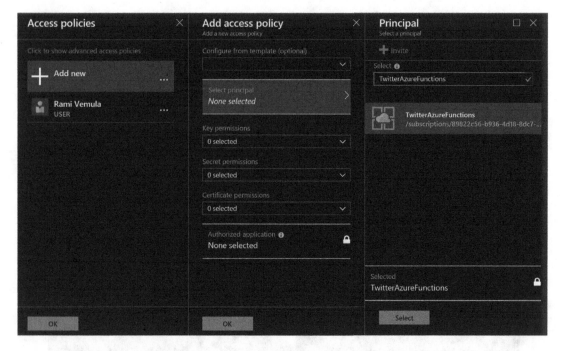

Figure 5-6. *Add an access policy by selecting the TwitterAzureFunctions principal*

5. Select the Get and List permissions for secrets, as shown in
    Figure 5-7, which are required to access one or more secrets from
    Key Vault.

Note   We are not going to use keys and certificates for the Twitter Bot application,
hence there is no need to grant permissions for their operations.

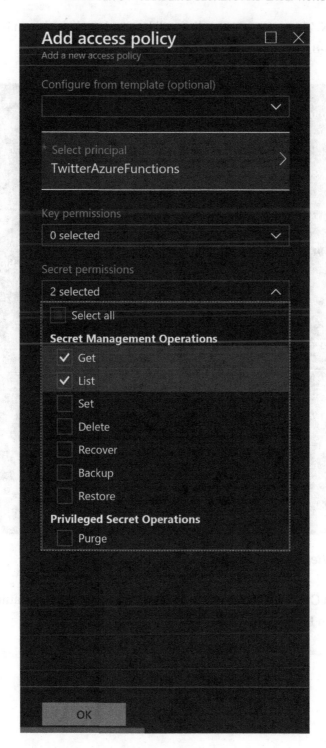

Figure 5-7. *Get and List permissions for secrets*

6. Click OK. The new access policy will be displayed, as shown in Figure 5-8.

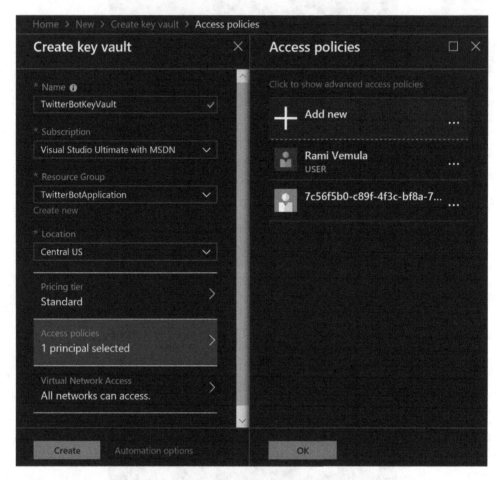

Figure 5-8. *TwitterAzureFunctions access policy*

7. Click on Create to create a new instance of the Azure Key Vault, as shown in Figure 5-9.

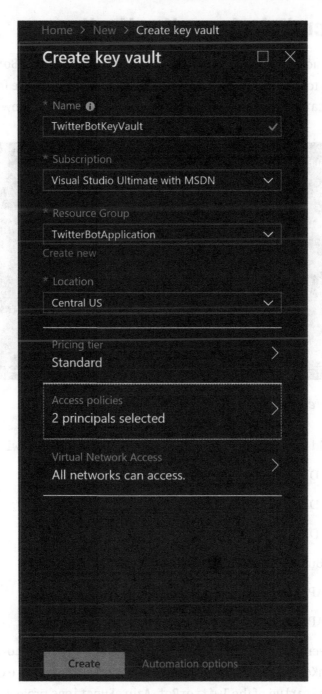

Figure 5-9.   *Create a TwitterBotKeyVault instance*

Storing Secrets in Azure Key Vault

In this section, we add Twitter Bot Application secrets to the `TwitterBotKeyVault` instance. Navigate to the newly created `TwitterBotKeyVault` instance from the `TwitterBotApplication` resource group. Select the Secrets tab, as shown in Figure 5-10.

Figure 5-10. *Secrets tab of TwitterBotKeyVault*

Now we will add the following Twitter Bot applications secrets to `TwitterBotKeyVault`:

- Cosmos DB Authentication Key

- Cosmos DB ConnectionString

- Cosmos DB URI

- Service Bus ConnectionString

- Twitter API Key

- Twitter API Secret

Add the first secret (`TwitterBotDbAuthKey`) to the Key Vault, as shown in Figure 5-11. `TwitterBotDbAuthKey` is `TwitterBotDB`'s authentication key, which we configured in `WebJobsExtensionStartup` of the `TwitterBot.AzureFunctions` project.

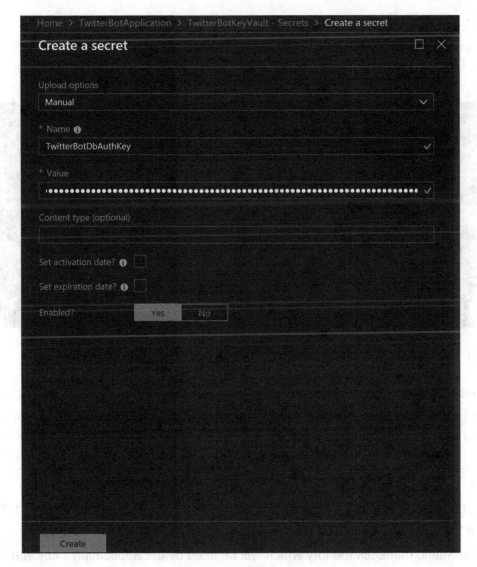

Figure 5-11. *Create a secret at TwitterBotKeyVault*

In the similar way, create the following secrets, as shown in Figure 5-12.

- `TwitterBotServiceBusConnectionString` (Service Bus ConnectionString)

- `TwitterBotDbConnectionString` (Cosmos DB ConnectionString)

- `TwitterAPIKey`

- `TwitterAPISecret`

- `TwitterBotDbUri` (Azure Cosmos DB URI, for example
  `https://localhost:8081`)

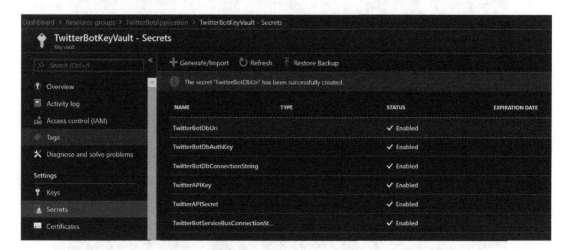

Figure 5-12.   *Secrets configured in TwitterBotKeyVault*

In the similar way, we can add more secrets, certificates, and keys to Key Vault.
We can easily manage the secrets in Key Vault because it provides fine grain control,
such as enabling/disabling the secrets, setting the activation, and setting expiry dates.

Note   Since we moved all the secrets to Azure Key Vault, we can remove the
settings from the `local.settings.json` file. If we are signed into Visual Studio
using the same Microsoft Azure Account, the application will work seamlessly
(Visual Studio manages identity which will be used by the application's key vault
configuration) in local debugging even without settings in the `local.settings.`
`json` file. Otherwise, we need to persist the settings in the `local.settings.`
`json` file.

From now on, let's assume that you are signed in to Visual Studio with the same
Azure Account. If you are not, do not forget to add the settings to the `local.`
`settings.json` file.

Getting Key Vault Secrets in Azure Functions

In this section, we upgrade the TwitterBot.AzureFunctions code to retrieve the secrets from TwitterBotKeyVault. Let's get started by installing the Microsoft.Extensions. Configuration.AzureKeyVault nuget package on the TwitterBot.AzureFunctions project, as shown in Figure 5-13.

Figure 5-13. *Install the Microsoft.Extensions.Configuration.AzureKeyVault nuget*

Update the WebJobsExtensionStartup class of the TwitterBot.AzureFunctions project, as shown in Listing 5-1. We will first read the default configuration through the IConfiguration instance using the IWebJobsBuilder's Services collection. We will create an instance of ConfigurationBuilder and add the default configuration to it using the AddConfiguration method.

Then we will add the Azure Key Vault configuration on top of the default configuration using the AddAzureKeyVault extension of ConfigurationBuilder. The final configuration is built using the Build method. Finally, the updated configuration instance is registered with IConfiguration using the AddSingleton extension of the IWebJobsBuilder.Services collection.

As shown in Listing 5-1, we need to update the Cosmos DB Auth Key, Cosmos DB URI, Service Bus ConnectionString, Twitter API Key, and Twitter API Secret with the values from the Configuration instance.

Listing 5-1. Updated WebJobsExtensionStartup Class

```
using Microsoft.Azure.WebJobs;
using Microsoft.Azure.WebJobs.Hosting;
using Microsoft.Extensions.Configuration;
using Microsoft.Extensions.DependencyInjection;
```

```csharp
using System;
/* Code removed for brevity. */

[assembly: WebJobsStartup(typeof(WebJobsExtensionStartup), "TwitterBot
Extensions Startup")]
namespace TwitterBot.AzureFunctions
{
    public class WebJobsExtensionStartup : IWebJobsStartup
    {
        public void Configure(IWebJobsBuilder builder)
        {
            MappingProfile.Activate();

            // Default configuration
            var serviceConfig = builder.Services.FirstOrDefault(s =>
            s.ServiceType.Equals(typeof(IConfiguration)));
            var defaultConfig = (IConfiguration)serviceConfig.
            ImplementationInstance;

            // Create a new config by merging default with Azure Key Vault
            configuration.
            string keyvaultName = "TwitterBotKeyVault";
            var config = new ConfigurationBuilder()
            .AddConfiguration(defaultConfig).AddAzureKeyVault($"https://
            {keyvaultName}.vault.azure.net/").Build();
            // Replace the existing config
            builder.Services.AddSingleton<IConfiguration>(config);

            // CosmosDB Configuration
            var documentDbContext = new DocumentDbContext
            {
                AuthKey = config["TwitterBotDbAuthKey"],
                DatabaseId = "TwitterBotDB",
                EndpointUri = config["TwitterBotDbUri"]
            };
```

```
Task.Run(async () => await documentDbContext.
CreateDatabaseAndCollectionsAsync()).Wait();
builder.Services.AddSingleton<IDocumentDbContext>(documentDbCo
ntext);
builder.Services.AddSingleton(typeof(IDocumentDbRepository<>),
typeof(DocumentDbRepository<>));

// Service Bus Configuration
var serviceBusContext = new ServiceBusContext()
{
    ConnectionString =
    config["TwitterBotServiceBusConnectionString"],
    QueueName = "HashTagQueue",
    MaxConcurrentMessagesToBeRetrieved = 2,
    SessionId = "TwitterBotApplication",
    OperationTimeout = TimeSpan.FromMilliseconds(500)
};
builder.Services.AddSingleton<IServiceBusContext>(serviceBusCo
ntext);
builder.Services.AddSingleton<IServiceBusOperations>(new Servic
eBusOperations(serviceBusContext));

builder.Services.AddSingleton<ITweetOperations>(new TweetOperat
ions(config["TwitterAPIKey"], config["TwitterAPISecret"]));
builder.Services.AddSingleton<InjectBindingProvider>();
builder.AddExtension<InjectConfiguration>();
        }
    }
}
```

TweetNotifierFunction should be updated with a ConnectionString setting, as shown in Listing 5-2.

Listing 5-2. Updated TweetNotifierFunction Class

```
/* Code Removed for brevity. */
[FunctionName("TweetNotifierFunction")]
public static void Run([CosmosDBTrigger(
    databaseName: "TwitterBotDB",
    collectionName: "TweetCollection",
    ConnectionStringSetting = "TwitterBotDbConnectionString",
    LeaseCollectionName = "leases",
    CreateLeaseCollectionIfNotExists = true)]IReadOnlyList<Document> input,
    ILogger log)
/* Code Removed for brevity. */
```

Likewise, `TweetBotServiceBusTriggerFunction` should be updated with the Service Bus `ConnectionString` setting, as shown in Listing 5-3.

Listing 5-3. Updated TweetBotServiceBusTriggerFunction Class

```
/* Code removed for brevity. */
[FunctionName("TweetBotServiceBusTriggerFunction")]
public async static Task Run([ServiceBusTrigger("hashtagqueue",
Connection = "TwitterBotServiceBusConnectionString")]string myQueueItem,
    ILogger log,
    [Inject]ITweetOperations tweetOperations,
    [Inject]IDocumentDbRepository<Tweet> tweetDbRepository,
    [Inject]IDocumentDbRepository<Hashtag> hashTagRepository)
/* Code removed for brevity. */
```

If you publish `TwitterBot.AzureFunctions` to the Azure environment, you'll see that all the functions will work just like before, but this time the configuration is coming from the Azure Key Vault.

Logging Support in Azure Functions

Application telemetry plays a crucial role in offering reliable maintenance and support services to end customers in production environments. Telemetry information is very useful in monitoring, troubleshooting, and analyzing system metrics and fault scenarios. Microsoft Azure offers the *Application Insights service,* which is used to capture mission-critical application metrics and analytics like request/response times, exceptions and errors, custom events, performance counters, host diagnostics, and more.

Note   Azure Application Insights is the Microsoft recommended way to capture, store, and persist application telemetry.

If Azure Functions are not configured with Application Insights, we can still enable logging using Azure Storage. To enable it, we need to set the AzureWebJobsDashboard application setting with a ConnectionString pointing to the Azure Storage. To disable it, we can simply delete the AzureWebJobsDashboard setting.

Azure Functions provides built-in integration with Azure Application Insights. We have integrated TwitterAzureFunctions with Application Insights at the time of creation, as shown in Figure 5-14. By default, Application Insights are turned on and the location is set to East US.

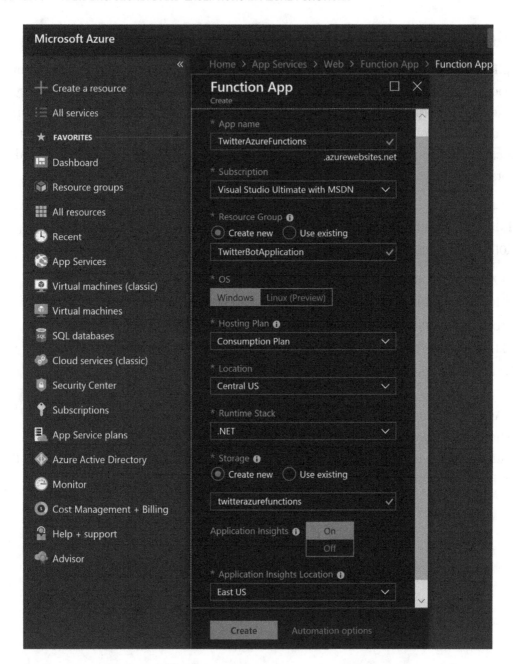

Figure 5-14. *Application Insights configuration at TwitterAzureFunctions creation*

If Application Insights are not configured at the time of creation of the Azure Function app, we can still configure it later. Consider the Application Insights instrumentation key, as shown in Figure 5-15.

Figure 5-15. *Application Insights instrumentation key*

We can configure the Application Insights instrumentation key at the Application Settings tab of `TwitterAzureFunctions`, as shown in Figure 5-16. We use the `APPINSIGHTS_INSTRUMENTATIONKEY` key with the Application Insights instrumentation key.

Figure 5-16. *Configure Application Insights Instrumentation key at TwitterAzureFunctions*

Now that we have Application Insights configured, we will see how to write logs from Azure Functions. `TweetBotFunction` already had the code to write logs, as shown in Listing 5-4. We inject the `ILogger` instance and use its `LogInformation` method to log the details.

Listing 5-4. TweetBotFunction Class

```
[FunctionName("TweetBotFunction")]
public async static Task Run([TimerTrigger("0 */5 * * * *")]TimerInfo
myTimer, ILogger log, /* Code Removed for brevity */)
{
    /* Code Removed for brevity */
    foreach (var hashtag in hashtags)
    {
        // Retrieve the latest tweet.
        var tweet = tweetOperations.GetPopularTweetByHashtag(hashtag);
        if (tweet != null)
        {
            tweet.Hashtags = new List<Hashtag>();
            log.LogInformation($"Latest popular tweet for {hashtag.Text}
            : { tweet.FullText }");
             /* Code Removed for brevity */
        }
    }
}
```

Note   Instead of ILogger, we can use a TraceWriter instance. TraceWriter doesn't support structured logging, which is very useful in parsing and querying logs compared to regular expression parsing of text logs.

To enable structure logging in TweetBotFunction, we can construct the log string as shown in Listing 5-5.

Listing 5-5. Structured Logging in the TweetBotFunction Class

```
log.LogInformation("Latest popular tweet for {hashtag} : {tweet}", hashtag.
Text, tweet.FullText);
```

Once we publish the TweetBotFunction, we can see the logs in Application Insights, as shown in Figure 5-17. We can filter the logs by category and time range.

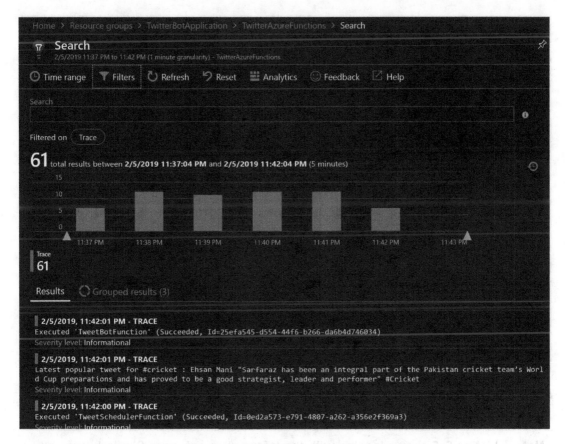

Figure 5-17. *Application Insight logs of TweetBotFunction*

By clicking on any trace instance, we can see the trace details, as shown in Figure 5-18. We can see the log message along with the original format. Custom data helps us achieve better querying and analytics capabilities.

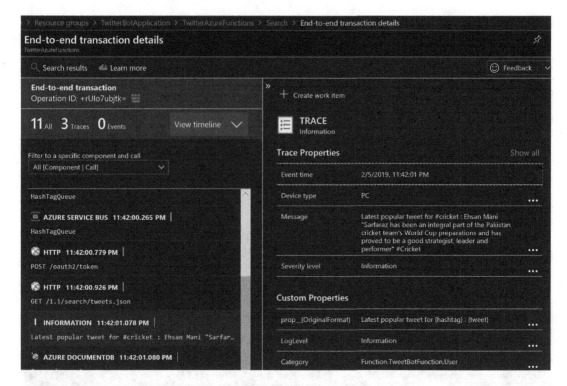

Figure 5-18. *Application Insight log details of TweetBotFunction*

Note   Listing 5-5 shows logging with the Information category. Similarly, we can log using other categories like Critical, Error, Warning, Debug, and Trace and using extension methods like `LogCritical`, `LogError`, etc. The None category can be used to suppress all logs for a category.

We can also track custom metrics using the `LogMetric` method.

We can explore other tabs of Application Insights to find information related to failures, performance, servers, etc., as shown in Figure 5-19.

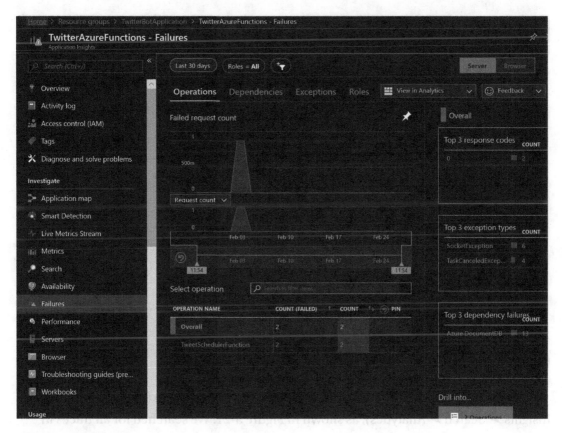

Figure 5-19. Application Insights tabs

Live Metrics streaming can be monitored, as shown in Figure 5-20.

Note   Application Insights can also be explored from Azure Function's Monitor tab.

Figure 5-20. *Application Insights Live Metrics streaming*

We can query Application Insights data using the Analytics tab (choose Application Insights ➤ Search ➤ Analytics), as shown in Figure 5-21. We searched for all traces in the last 24 hours that have a `customDimensions['prop__hashtag']` value of `'#world'`. `customDimensions` is the JSON data in which Application Insights holds our custom key value pairs from structured logging.

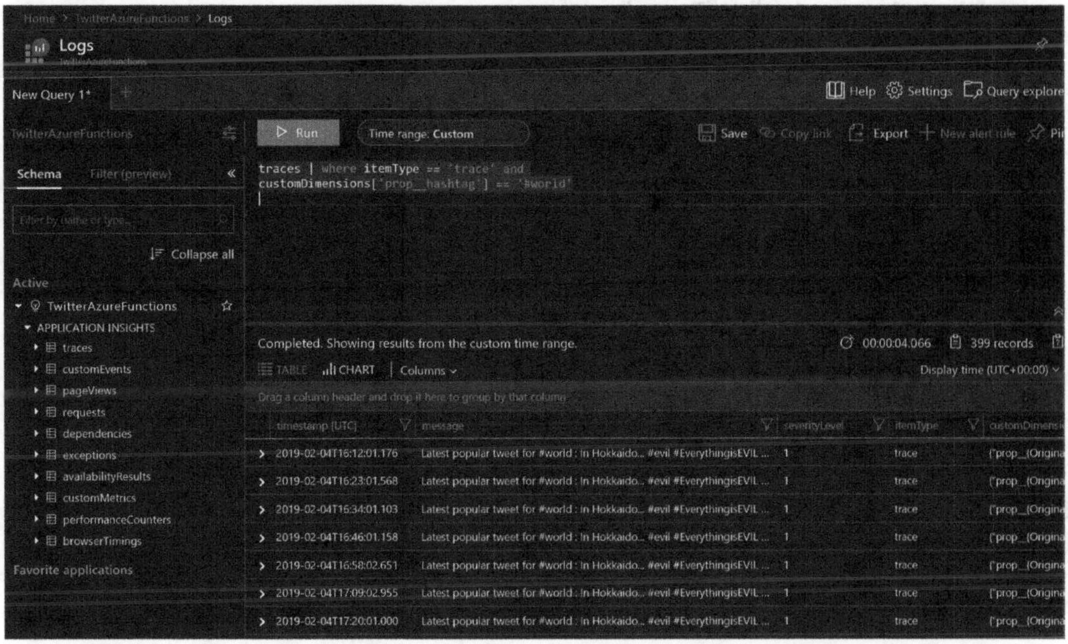

Figure 5-21. *Executing custom queries using Application Insights analytics*

We will configure Azure Function's `host.json` to set the logging levels for different categories, as shown in Listing 5-6. `fileLoggingMode` is used with the `always`, `never`, and `debugOnly` options to enable logging. `logLevel` suggests the different log levels used for different categories. In the example in Listing 5-6, we configured the Azure Function to log levels from Information and above, `Host.Results` logs levels of Warning and above.

Listing 5-6. Logging Configuration in the host.json File

```
{
  "version": "2.0",
  "logging": {
    "fileLoggingMode": "always",
    "logLevel": {
      "default": "Information",
      "Host": "Information",
      "Host.Results": "Warning",
      "Function": "Information",
```

```
      "Host.Aggregator": "Trace"
   }
  }
}
```

> **Note**   In Listing 5-6, we configured `Host` along with `Host.Results`, `Host.Aggregator`. Host configuration is applied for the overall host process. However, the configuration related to `Results` and `Aggregator` will take precedence over the overall `Host` configuration.

Having stated that Application Insights is the recommended approach for Azure Functions to log telemetry, we can also use third-party logging libraries like Log4Net, Serilog, etc. We can also build our own custom `ILogger` implementations, which are dependent on specific requirements.

Exception Handling in Azure Functions

In this section, we see how to handle exceptions in Azure Functions. There are multiple techniques to handle exceptions at a global level as well as at a function level. We will handle all exceptions using `IFunctionExceptionFilter`, which provides `FunctionExceptionContext` through which we can fetch the exception details and process them further.

> **Note**   By default, Azure Functions will log all exceptions to Application Insights. The main intention of this section is to demonstrate how to handle the exceptions through code.
>
> Function Filters are in preview. There can be potential breaking changes in future releases around the concepts narrated in this section. Please be cautious in applying them to real-world applications.

We are going to specifically handle exceptions from TweetBotFunction, where there is a potential chance of leaving hashtags in Server Bus Queue during exceptions. Assume we get an exception while processing a hashtag against Twitter (using TweetOperations). In such a case, the hashtag's IsCurrentlyInQueue will not be set to false at the Cosmos DB and the TweetSchedulerFunction will never pick up this hashtag for prioritization.

Let's get started by creating a new exception type. Create a folder called Exceptions in the TwitterBot.Framework project and create TwitterBotBusinessException, as shown in Listing 5-7. TwitterBotBusinessException has a Hashtags property which is used to hold the faulted hashtags that are not processed because of exceptions. The Message property is overridden to accommodate the concatenated string of the hashtag's text.

Listing 5-7. TwitterBotBusinessException Class

```
using System;
using System.Collections.Generic;
using TwitterBot.Framework.Types;
using System.Linq;

namespace TwitterBot.Framework.Exceptions
{
    public class TwitterBotBusinessException : Exception
    {
        public List<Hashtag> Hashtags { get; set; }
        public TwitterBotBusinessException(List<Hashtag> hashtags)
        {
            this.Hashtags = hashtags;
        }

        public override String Message
        {
            get
            {
                return String.Format("Exception Occurred while processing:
                {0}", String.Join(",", Hashtags.Select(p => p.Text)));
            }
        }
    }
}
```

Update the `TweetBotFunction` to throw `TwitterBotBusinessException`, as shown in Listing 5-8. We created a hashtag collection to hold the erroneous hashtags. This list will be populated within the `TRY...CATCH` block inside the `foreach` processing loop of hashtags. In the `catch` block, we log the exception and then add it to erroneous hashtag collection. Finally, if there are erroneous hashtags, we throw `TwitterBotBusinessException` with the erroneous hashtag collection.

Note   We will throw the `TwitterBotBusinessException` only after processing all the hashtags in the current context. We do not want to terminate the entire process because of an exception on a hashtag.

Listing 5-8. Update TweetBotFunction Class

```
using Microsoft.Azure.WebJobs;
/* Code Removed for brevity */
using TwitterBot.Framework.Exceptions;
using TwitterBot.Framework.Types;

namespace TwitterBot.AzureFunctions
{
    public static class TweetBotFunction
    {
        [FunctionName("TweetBotFunction")]
        public async static Task Run([TimerTrigger("0 */5 * * * *")]
        TimerInfo myTimer, ILogger log,
            [Inject]ITweetOperations tweetOperations,
            [Inject]IDocumentDbRepository<Tweet> tweetDbRepository,
            [Inject]IServiceBusOperations serviceBusOperations,
            [Inject]IDocumentDbRepository<Hashtag> hashTagRepository)
        {
            var erroredHashtags = new List<Hashtag>();
            /* Code Removed for brevity
            foreach (var hashtag in hashtags)
            {
```

```
try
{
    // Retrieve the latest tweet.
    var tweet = tweetOperations.GetPopularTweetByHashtag
    (hashtag);

    /* Code Removed for brevity */

    await hashTagRepository.AddOrUpdateAsync(hashtag);
}
catch(Exception ex)
{
    log.LogError(ex, ex.Message);
    erroredHashtags.Add(hashtag);
}
        }

        if (erroredHashtags.Any())
        {
            throw new TwitterBotBusinessException(erroredHashtags);
        }
    }
  }
}
```

Now we will create an exception filter attribute using IFunctionExceptionFilter to handle global unhandled exceptions. Create TwitterBotBusinessExceptionFilter in the Exceptions folder of the TwitterBot.Framework project, as shown in Listing 5-9.

TwitterBotBusinessExceptionFilter will implement IFunctionExceptionFilter, which primarily defines an exception filter. We inject an IDocumentDbRepository <Hashtag> instance into the filter, which is used to interact with the Cosmos DB hashtag collection. We implement the OnExceptionAsync method, which will check for exception of type TwitterBotBusinessException and invoke a private ProcessErroredHashtags method. ProcessErroredHashtags marks the hashtag at Cosmos DB as not currently in the queue by setting the IsCurrentlyInQueue to false using a IDocumentDbRepository <Hashtag> instance.

Listing 5-9. TwitterBotBusinessExceptionFilter Class

```
using Microsoft.Azure.WebJobs.Host;
using System.Collections.Generic;
using System.Linq;
using System.Threading;
using System.Threading.Tasks;
using TwitterBot.Framework.Contracts.Data;
using TwitterBot.Framework.Types;

namespace TwitterBot.Framework.Exceptions
{
    public class TwitterBotBusinessExceptionFilter : IFunctionExceptionFilter
    {
        private IDocumentDbRepository<Hashtag> _hashTagRepository;
        public TwitterBotBusinessExceptionFilter(IDocumentDbRepository<Hash
        tag> hashTagRepository)
        {
            _hashTagRepository = hashTagRepository;
        }

        public async Task OnExceptionAsync(FunctionExceptionContext
        exceptionContext, CancellationToken cancellationToken)
        {
            if (exceptionContext.Exception.InnerException is
            TwitterBotBusinessException)
            {
                var erroredHashtags = (exceptionContext.Exception.
                InnerException as TwitterBotBusinessException).Hashtags;
                await ProcessErroredHashtags(erroredHashtags);
            }
        }
        private async Task ProcessErroredHashtags(List<Hashtag> hashtags)
        {
```

```
        if (!hashtags.Any())
        {
            return;
        }

        foreach (var hashtag in hashtags)
        {
            hashtag.IsCurrentlyInQueue = false;
            await _hashTagRepository.AddOrUpdateAsync(hashtag);
        }
    }
  }
}
```

We register the `TwitterBotBusinessExceptionFilter` filter at the `WebJobsExtensionStartup` class of the `TwitterBot.AzureFunctions` project, as shown in Listing 5-10.

Listing 5-10. Register TwitterBotBusinessExceptionFilter at WebJobsExtensionStartup Class

```
// Exception Filter
  builder.Services.AddSingleton<IFunctionFilter,
TwitterBotBusinessExceptionFilter>();
```

Note   We can test the exception filter by simulating an exception scenario in `TweetBotFunction` and throwing any random exception from within the code.

Run all the functions in the local environment with an exception simulation. We can see `TwitterBotBusinessExceptionFilter` getting invoked as expected on exceptions. It resets the `IsCurrentlyInQueue` to `false` for all the hashtags that are in the context of exception filter.

Summary

You started off this chapter by learning about the importance of securing all logical and physical layers of the application from malicious threats and attacks. The main way to secure the application keys, secrets, and certificates is to store them in Key Vaults. Azure Key Vault is a cloud service provided by Microsoft that securely stores and accesses secret information like passwords, API keys, etc.

You created an Azure Key Vault instance and ported all the Twitter Bot application's secrets to it. You also enabled the Managed Service Identity for `TwitterAzureFunctions`, which is required for Azure Functions to communicate with Key Vault securely. You upgraded the `WebJobsExtensionStartup` class of `TwitterAzureFunctions` to utilize the configuration from Azure Key Vault.

You explored the concepts of Application Insights logging in Azure Functions. You learned about the importance of structured logging through built-in `ILogger` instances. You explored different sections of Application Insights and learned how to query the custom dimensions log information using the Analytics tab. You configured logging settings in the `host.json` file with specific log levels set to different categories.

You implemented exception handing in Azure Functions using the Function Filters (preview). You created a `TwitterBotBusinessException` exception type and updated `TweetBotFunction` to throw it along with faulted hashtags in case of exceptions. Finally, you designed `TwitterBotBusinessExceptionFilter` by implementing `IFunctionExceptionFilter`, which will reset the status of hashtags at the Azure Cosmos DB upon the event of a `TwitterBotBusinessException`.

In the next chapter, you will design and develop the Twitter Bot web application using ASP.NET Core.

References

1. https://docs.microsoft.com/en-us/azure/key-vault/key-vault-overview

2. https://integration.team/2017/09/25/retrieve-azure-key-vault-secrets-using-azure-functions-managed-service-identity/

3. https://github.com/Azure/azure-webjobs-sdk/issues/746

4. https://docs.microsoft.com/en-us/azure/azure-functions/
   functions-monitoring

5. https://github.com/Azure/azure-webjobs-sdk/wiki/
   Function-Filters

6. https://github.com/Azure/azure-webjobs-sdk/wiki/
   Function-Filters

7. https://github.com/Azure/azure-webjobs-sdk/issues/1865

CHAPTER 6

Designing and Developing the Twitter Bot Web Application

Ever since the Internet conquered the world with its digital revolution, the World Wide Web (WWW) became the Internet's primary face to present digital content to users in a readable format. Even with recent innovations around wearable technologies—for example, the Apple Watch, HoloLens, Google Glass etc.—the web is still considered a leader in data presentation because of its affordability, adaptability, and maintainability. Web applications have helped people around the globe overcome geographical barriers by sharing and reacting to critical information with a few clicks.

Over the last decade, web application development has gained significant momentum because of web technologies and the open source frameworks. Developers across the world are collaborating and developing next-generation software products by using open source platforms and tools. Microsoft started its open source journey by incorporating .NET Foundation, an independent organization to improve open source software development around the .NET ecosystem. Microsoft's .NET Core is an open source development platform that can be leveraged to deliver cross-platform solutions through web, cloud, and IoT applications and devices.

As part of .NET Core, Microsoft introduced the ASP.NET Core Framework, which is built from the ground up with a new modular design and support for cross-platform web application development. The ASP.NET Core development model has many new features and ground-breaking changes compared to the traditional ASP.NET MVC. ASP. NET Core web applications can run on all major operating systems, including Windows, MacOS, and Linux, with built-in support to execute on .NET Core and the .NET Framework.

© Rami Vemula 2019
R. Vemula, *Integrating Serverless Architecture*, https://doi.org/10.1007/978-1-4842-4489-0_6

In Chapter 5, we secured the Twitter Bot application's secrets by storing them in Azure Key Vault and implemented exception handing for the Twitter Azure Functions. In this chapter, we:

- Look at the core concepts of the ASP.NET Core Framework.

- Create the Twitter Bot web application and develop a theme by using Materialize CSS.

- Integrate the Twitter Identity Provider for authentication and persist the user information in Azure Cosmos DB.

- Develop a page to capture the user's hashtag preferences and display the latest popular tweets based on those preferences.

- Deploy the application to Azure App Service and test the entire flow.

Getting Started with ASP.NET Core

ASP.NET Core is a new, open source, cross-platform framework from Microsoft used to build modern web applications. It is designed from the ground up to create applications for web, cloud, mobile, and IoT services. As shown in Figure 6-1, ASP.NET Core is compatible with the .NET Framework and .NET Core and provides a unified approach to build web and web API solutions. The ASP.NET Core Framework provides an easy integration with the SignalR Framework, through which push notifications can be delivered to connected clients.

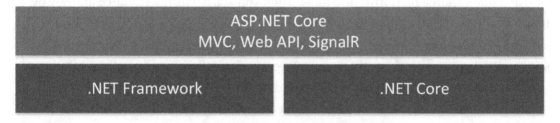

Figure 6-1. *Compatibility of ASP.NET Core with the .NET Framework and .NET Core*

The main features of the ASP.NET Core Framework are as follows:

- **Open source:** ASP.NET Core is open source under the Apache 2 license.

- **Cross-platform support:** ASP.NET Core applications can be developed and run on Windows, MacOS, and Linux operating systems.

- **Unified MVC and Web API approach:** In ASP.NET Core, MVC and Web APIs are both driven with a unified object model. A single namespace serves both the MVC and Web APIs, which removes any confusion from the older versions of ASP.NET.

- **Lightweight HTTP request pipeline:** Compared to previous versions of ASP.NET, most of the unwanted overheads are removed from ASP. NET Core, resulting in a lightweight HTTP pipeline. We can construct the HTTP pipeline by using the default framework middleware or through custom-developed middleware.

- **Modular design:** Starting with ASP.NET Core, there is no need to manage unwanted packages or references in the project (there is no System.Web.dll). We need to get only those nuget packages that we want for the application. In fact, ASP.NET Core itself is a nuget package.

- **Integration with client-side frameworks:** ASP.NET Core applications can easily integrate with client-side frameworks such as AngularJS, KnockoutJS, Gulp, Grunt, and Bower.

- **SignalR support:** ASP.NET Core has built-in compatibility with SignalR.

- **Improved performance:** ASP.NET Core's modular design and lightweight HTTP pipeline offer very good performance.

- **Dependency injection:** ASP.NET Core by default supports dependency injection.

- **Cloud-ready solutions:** ASP.NET Core solutions are optimized for cloud compatibility through an easy configuration system.

- **Containers support:** Applications developed using ASP.NET Core will have built-in support for containers like Docker, Kubernetes, etc.

- **Runs on the .NET Framework and .NET Core:** ASP.NET Core applications can run on the .NET Framework and on .NET Core runtimes. We have the flexibility of using traditional .NET Framework APIs that are not yet available in .NET Core.

- **Hosting:** ASP.NET Core supports IIS and self-hosting.

- **Tooling:** ASP.NET Core applications can be built using Visual Studio Code, Visual Studio IDE, or the .NET Core CLI. The new tooling enhances developer productivity in building, publishing, and creating Docker containers.

So far ASP.NET Core has been released in four major versions. The important updates of the releases are described here:

- **ASP.NET Core 1.0:**

  - Different project structure along with new project file format.

  - Default support for dependency injection.

  - Dynamic compilation using the Roslyn compiler.

  - `wwwroot` folder to hold static files.

  - Routes have new controller and action tokens.

  - Tag helpers and view components.

  - Configuration based on `Appsettings.json`.

  - `_ViewImports.cshtml` file to hold common namespaces across different views.

  - Bundling and minification is achieved through the `bundleconfig.json` file.

  - New filter types and much better control over filter execution.

  - New way to manage secure information on the development machine through user secrets.

  - Data access using Entity Framework Core.

- Configuring authentication and authorization is easy through ASP.NET Core Identity.

- New improvements to internationalization, logging, and exception handling features.

- **ASP.NET Core 1.1:**

  - Support for WebSockets.

  - New middleware for URL rewriting and caching.

  - View components as tag helpers.

  - Support for Azure Key Vault Configuration Provider and Azure App Service Logging Provider.

  - Middleware as MVC filters.

  - Cookie-based TempData provider.

  - WebListener server (an alternative for Kestral) for Windows with direct connection to the Internet.

- **ASP.NET Core 2.0:**

  - Razor pages and automatic pre-compilation.

  - ASP.NET Core metapackage.

  - Support for new Runtime store, which eliminates the packaging of references of metapackages.

  - Compatibility with .NET Standard 2.0.

  - New updates to Identity, Configuration, Logging, and Authentication configurations.

  - New SPA templates for Angular, Knockout, React, and Redux.

  - Kestral improvements.

  - Enhanced HTTP header support.

  - Host startup and Application Insights support.

- **ASP.NET Core 2.1:**

  - SignalR support.

  - Razor class libraries.

  - Improved HTTPS support.

  - Identity UI library and scaffolding helps in selectively adding the source code contained in the Identity Razor Class library.

  - GDPR (General Data Protection Regulation) support.

  - Support for integration tests.

  - WebSockets made transport channel for Kestral transport.

  - Updated SPA templates.

Note   ASP.NET Core is being actively developed in collaboration with the open source community. We can expect more features and enhancements in future releases. The latest information on ASP.NET Core can be found at `https://docs.microsoft.com/en-us/aspnet/core/`.

We are going to use the ASP.NET Core Razor Pages model for the Twitter Bot web application. Razor Pages is the recommended way to build UIs for web apps using ASP.NET Core. Razor Pages gives a flavor of old ASP.NET web pages by including model and controller code within the Razor Page itself. Razor Pages offers simple and fast development compared to MVC, where code resides along with the pages and provides a clear separation of concerns. Razor Pages can work along with ASP.NET Core MVC, which gives both options for the developers to develop smart web applications.

Note   To use Razor Pages, we need to install .NET Core 2.1 SDK or later. As described in the section entitled "Software Prerequisites" in Chapter 1, the book uses the .NET Core 2.1.401 SDK.

Creating and Understanding the Project Structure of an ASP.NET Core Web Application

In this section, we create an ASP.NET Core Web application project under the TwitterBot solution that serves as the Twitter Bot web application. We also consider the importance and relevance of different artifacts of an ASP.NET Core project.

Let's get started by creating a new ASP.NET Core web application project under the TwitterBot solution, as shown in Figure 6-2. Right-click the TwitterBot solution and choose Add ➤ New Project. Call it `TwitterBot.Web` and then click OK.

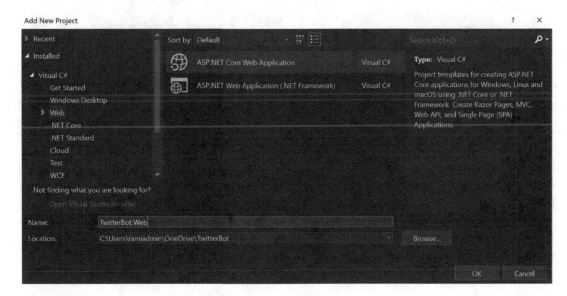

Figure 6-2.   *Create the TwitterBot.Web project*

Select .NET Core with ASP.NET Core 2.1 as the framework. Make sure the Web Application template is selected, as shown in Figure 6-3.

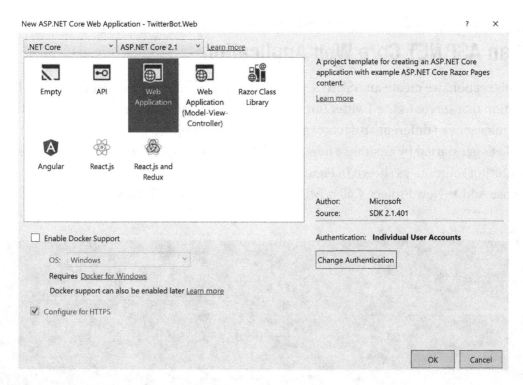

Figure 6-3. *Select the Web Application template for the TwitterBot.Web project*

To configure authentication, click on Change Authentication and select Individual User Accounts, as shown in Figure 6-4.

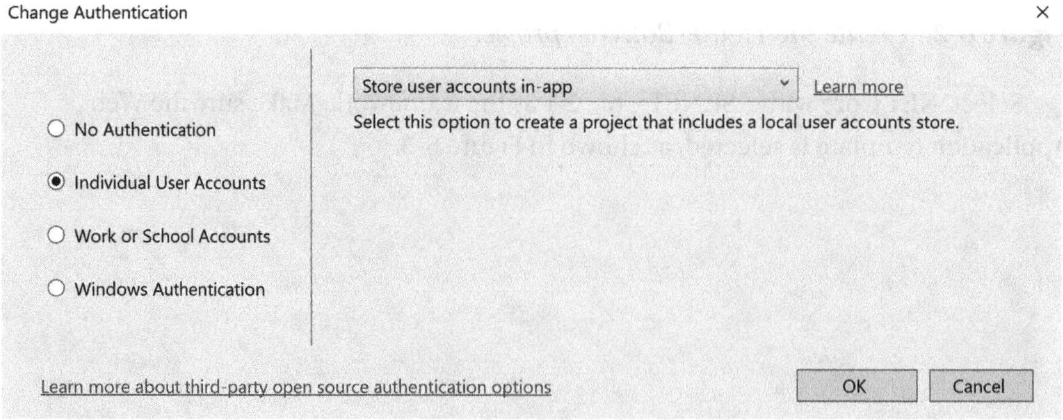

Figure 6-4. *Configure individual user accounts for the TwitterBot.Web project*

Click OK to create the project. Set TwitterBot.Web as the startup project in the solution and run it from Visual Studio. The home screen will be displayed, as shown in Figure 6-5.

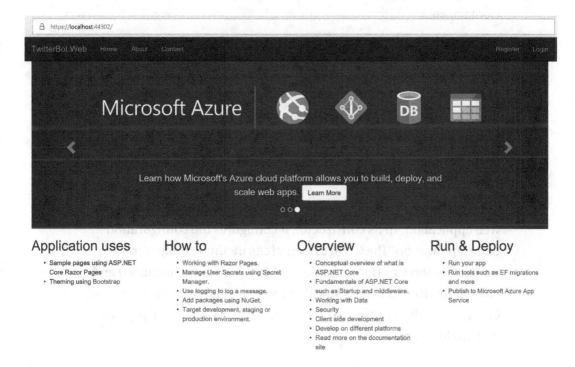

Figure 6-5. *Home screen of the TwitterBot.Web project*

The project structure in Visual Studio is shown in Figure 6-6.

- The wwwroot folder houses all the static files, including images, JavaScript files, stylesheets, etc.

- The Areas folder gives the logical separation of pages between modules.

- The `Data` folder holds the `DbContext` and `Initial` migrations for the ASP.NET Core Identity.

- The `Pages` folder holds all the different pages, such as Index, About, Contact, etc.

- The `appsettings.json` file holds the configuration of the application.

- The `Program` class is the starting point of an ASP.NET Core web application, which contains the `Main` entry point, making the ASP.NET Core Web application a true console application. The ASP.NET Core application requires a host to start the application and manage the application's lifetime. The `Program` class creates a new instance of `WebHostBuilder`, which is used to configure and launch the host.

- The `Startup` class configures the environment for the ASP.NET Core web application. In its constructor, it configures the configuration of the application. The `ConfigureServices` method configures framework services (for example, EF, MVC, and authentication) and custom services (business specific) using dependency injection. The `Configure` method is used to build the ASP.NET Core HTTP pipeline with middleware.

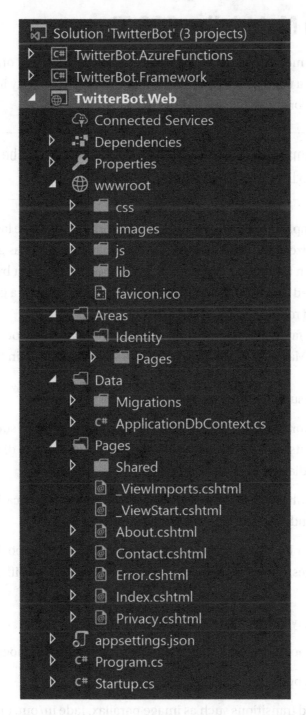

Figure 6-6. *Default project structure of the TwitterBot.Web project*

Designing a Materialize CSS Theme

Materialize CSS is a modern, responsive, frontend framework based on material design. It was developed by a team of students at Carnegie Mellon University in 2014. It is an open source framework available under the MIT License.

Note   More information about the Materialize CSS authors can be found at `http://materializecss.com/about.html`.

Just like Bootstrap, Materialize supports a 12-column responsive layout along with the offsets. Materialize comes with various navigation menus and has great compatibility for mobile navigation through its drag-out menu. It uses Roboto font by default, which can be easily changed to any other font family. Materialize provides a good set of helpers to format, align, and render text on various devices.

It also has, by default, responsive support for rendering media content such as images and videos. Materialize can be applied to a web application in two ways: via CSS/JS or SASS files.

Materialize CSS supports these additional features:

- Different form styles, buttons, and input controls. Built-in support for elements such as carousels, collapsible panels, feature discovery prompts, dialog boxes, tabs, and Scrollspy.

- Breadcrumbs to show the user's current site navigation location, and progress indicators to show the task status.

- Support for badges to show notifications, pushpins to fix positioning of messages, and cards to display different content from different objects.

- Different styles for collections and pagination.

- Great support for media content, and a wide range of iconography.

- Built-in support for modal popups.

- Effects and transitions such as image parallax, fade in/out, and waves.

Both Material Design and Materialize CSS were quickly adopted by the open source community. As a result, several free and paid themes have been developed by leveraging Materialize CSS. For the Twitter Bot web application, we are going to use one of the open source developed themes and tailor them to our needs.

We are going to use the Starter template, shown in Figure 6-7, as the base theme for the Twitter Bot web application. The Starter template, a free template offered by the Materialize CSS team, is the simplest template that we can start off with. We'll customize it based on the Twitter Bot web application's requirements.

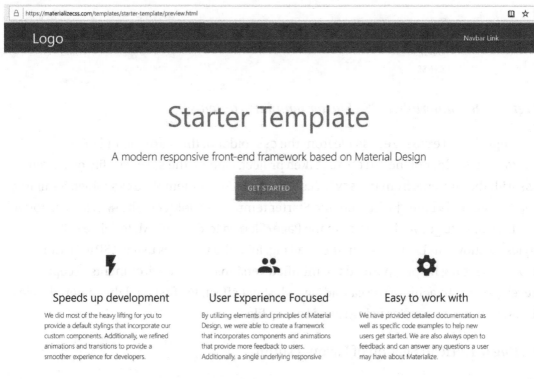

Figure 6-7. *The Starter template developed by the Materialize CSS team*

Note   The Starter template can be downloaded at `https://materializecss.com/getting-started.html`.

Creating a Layout Using the Materialize CSS Starter Template

In this section, we develop an ASP.NET Core layout by leveraging the Starter template from Materialize CSS. Let's get started by extracting the content of the Materialize CSS Starter template, as shown in Figure 6-8.

> This PC > Downloads > starter-template > starter-template

Name		File ownership	Date modified	Type
	css		11/24/2018 7:37 P...	File folder
	js		11/24/2018 7:37 P...	File folder
	index.html		11/24/2018 7:37 P...	HTML File
	LICENSE		11/24/2018 7:37 P...	File

Figure 6-8. *Materialize CSS Starter template contents*

Copy the `materialize.css` file from the `css` folder of the Starter template to the `wwwroot/css` folder of the `TwitterBot.Web` project. Update the `site.css` file of `wwwroot/css` with the contents from the `style.css` file of the Starter template `css` folder. Similarly, copy the `materialize.js` file from the Starter template `js` folder to the `wwwroot/js` folder.

Let's update `_Layout.cshtml` in the `Page/Shared` folder with Materialize CSS styles, as shown in Listing 6-1. In the `head` tag, load the CSS files using ASP.NET Core's `environment` tag helper. We load the minified versions for all environments except for development. To achieve the cascading stylesheet effect, we first load the material styles followed by custom styles using the `site.css` file.

Listing 6-1. Head Section of Layout.cshtml

```
<head>
    <meta charset="utf-8" />
    <meta http-equiv="Content-Type" content="text/html; charset=UTF-8" />
    <meta name="viewport" content="width=device-width, initial-scale=1,
    maximum-scale=1.0" />
    <title>Twitter Bot Application</title>

    <environment include="Development">
        <link rel="stylesheet" href="~/css/materialize.css" />
    </environment>
```

```
<environment exclude="Development">
    <link rel="stylesheet" href="~/css/materialize.min.css" />
</environment>
<link rel="stylesheet" href="~/css/site.css" />
<link href="https://fonts.googleapis.com/icon?family=Material+Icons"
rel="stylesheet">
</head>
```

We will have the header, main, and footer tags under the body tag, as shown in Listing 6-2. The header tag will hold the nav tag, which is used to display the brand logo and top navigation menu. The top navigation will also have a sidenav tag, which will be rendered on smaller devices.

The main tag will render the content page using the RenderBody helper. The footer tag will display the description of the Twitter Bot application and site links pointing to different social media accounts.

jQuery references are loaded after the footer tag using the environment tag helper. Custom jQuery code is loaded using the site.js file. The RenderSection helper is used to designate a place in layout to render content from the content pages.

Listing 6-2. Updated Layout.cshtml

```
<body>
    <header>
        <nav class="light-blue lighten-1" role="navigation">
            <div class="nav-wrapper container">
                <a id="logo-container" href="/" class="brand-logo">Twitter
                Bot</a>
                <ul class="right hide-on-med-and-down">
                    <li><a class="waves-effect waves-light btn modal-trigger
                    orange twitterLogin" href="#">Twitter Login</a></li>
                </ul>
                <ul id="nav-mobile" class="sidenav">
                    <li><a class="waves-effect waves-light btn modal-trigger
                    orange twitterLogin" href="#">Twitter Login</a></li>
                </ul>
                <a href="#" data-target="nav-mobile" class="sidenav-
                trigger"><i class="material-icons">menu</i></a>
```

```
            </div>
        </nav>
    </header>
    <main>
        @RenderBody()
    </main>
    <footer class="page-footer orange">
        <div class="container">
            <div class="row">
                <div class="col l6 s12">
                    <h5 class="white-text">About Us</h5>
                    <p class="grey-text text-lighten-4">
                        Twitter Bot Application let's you to fine tune the
                        information you are looking for at Twitter platform.
                        It provides a keyword subscription model, where
                        you specify your interests and we deliver you the
                        latest updates based on your subscriptions.
                    </p>
                </div>
                <div class="col l3 s12">
                    <h5 class="white-text">Settings</h5>
                    <ul>
                        <li><a class="white-text" href="#!">Sign Up</a></li>
                        <li><a class="white-text" href="#!">Sign In</a></li>
                        <li><a class="white-text" href="#!">Forgot
                        Password</a></li>
                    </ul>
                </div>
                <div class="col l3 s12">
                    <h5 class="white-text">Connect</h5>
                    <ul>
                        <li><a class="white-text" href="#!">Twitter</a></li>
                        <li><a class="white-text" href="#!">Facebook</a></li>
                        <li><a class="white-text" href="#!">LinkedIn</a></li>
                        <li><a class="white-text" href="#!">Blog</a></li>
```

```
            </ul>
          </div>
        </div>
      </div>
      <div class="footer-copyright">
        <div class="container">
          Powered by <a class="orange-text text-lighten-3"
          href="http://materializecss.com">Materialize</a>
        </div>
      </div>
    </footer>

    <!--  Scripts-->
    <environment exclude="Development">
      <script type="text/javascript" src="https://code.jquery.com/jquery-
      2.1.1.min.js"></script>
      <script src="~/js/materialize.min.js"></script>
    </environment>
    <environment include="Development">
      <script src="~/lib/jquery/dist/jquery.js"></script>
      <script src="~/js/materialize.js"></script>
    </environment>
    <script src="~/js/site.js"></script>

    @RenderSection("Scripts", required: false)
</body>
```

Now we implement the sticky footer, which always stays at the bottom of the page regardless of the content. Update site.css, as shown in Listing 6-3.

Listing 6-3. Sticky Footer Styles

```css
.icon-block {
    padding: 0 15px;
}

    .icon-block .material-icons {
        font-size: inherit;
    }
```

```
body {
    display: flex;
    min-height: 100vh;
    flex-direction: column;
}

main {
    flex: 1 0 auto;
}
```

Now we initiate the side navigation menu using the jQuery code in site.js, as shown in Listing 6-4.

Listing 6-4. Enable Side Navigation in site.js

```
(function ($) {
    $(function () {
        $('.sidenav').sidenav();
    });
})(jQuery);
```

Update the Index.cshtml file in the Pages folder, as shown in Listing 6-5. The first container displays the Twitter Bot application heading and an option to get started (which points to the same home page for now). The next container divides the page into three equal sections and displays the static informational text.

Listing 6-5. Updated Index.cshtml

```
@page
@model IndexModel
@{
    ViewData["Title"] = "Home page";
}

<div class="section no-pad-bot" id="index-banner">
    <div class="container">
        <br><br>
        <h1 class="header center orange-text">Twitter Bot Application</h1>
        <div class="row center">
```

```
        <h5 class="header col s12 light">An innovative social platform
        to find relevant information based on Keywords.</h5>
    </div>
    <div class="row center">
        <a href="/" id="download-button" class="btn-large waves-effect
        waves-light orange">Get Started</a>
    </div>
    <br><br>
  </div>
</div>

<div class="container">
  <div class="section">
      <!--   Icon Section    -->
      <div class="row">
          <div class="col s12 m4">
              <div class="icon-block">
                  <h2 class="center light-blue-text"><i class="material-
                  icons">flash_on</i></h2>
                  <h5 class="center">Curate your lists</h5>
                  <p class="light">
                      You can curate the information based on your
                      subscriptions to the keywords. You can add new
                      keywords based on your interests and remove
                      existing ones.
                      We always work on your latest interests.
                  </p>
              </div>
          </div>
          <div class="col s12 m4">
              <div class="icon-block">
                  <h2 class="center light-blue-text"><i class="material-
                  icons">group</i></h2>
                  <h5 class="center">Find latest Information</h5>
                  <p class="light">
```

```
                              Based on your subscriptions, we retrieve the latest
                              information from Twitter platform on a periodic
                              basis and display it to you.
                              If no information is available for a particular
                              keyword, we retry it on certain period of time.
                         </p>
                    </div>
               </div>
               <div class="col s12 m4">
                    <div class="icon-block">
                         <h2 class="center light-blue-text"><i class="material-
                         icons">settings</i></h2>
                         <h5 class="center">Auto Notifications</h5>
                         <p class="light">
                              We provide automatic notifications for the latest
                              content based on your subscriptions. In case you
                              miss the notification,
                              you can still browse the content because we save
                              the latest information in our database.
                         </p>
                    </div>
               </div>
          </div>
     </div>
     <br><br>
</div>
```

Run the TwitterBot.Web project. If you do so, the home page will be displayed, as shown in Figure 6-9.

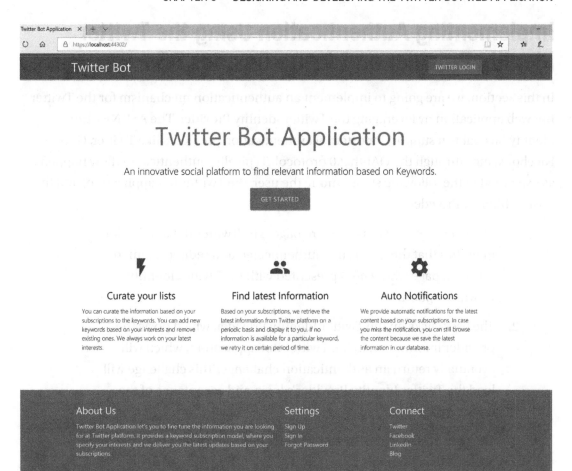

Figure 6-9.   *The Twitter Bot web application Home screen*

Note   We can similarly style other pages like About, Contact, etc. To focus on the pages relevant to the Twitter Bot application, I am skipping the styling of those pages for now.

Implementing Authentication Using the Twitter Identity Provider and Azure Cosmos DB

In this section, we are going to implement an authentication mechanism for the Twitter Bot web application by leveraging the Twitter Identity Provider. The ASP.NET Core identity has built-in support for external authentication providers like Twitter, Google, Facebook, etc., through the OAuth 2.0 protocol. Typically, authentication flow happens as explained in the following steps among the user, the Twitter Bot application, and the Twitter Identity Provider.

1. The user tries to access a secure page. The Twitter Bot application identifies that the user is not authenticated and redirects him to the login page where he is presented with the Twitter Identity Provider option.

2. The user clicks on the Twitter Identity Provider, which posts the provider information to the Twitter Bot application, which will eventually return an authentication challenge. This challenge will load the Twitter Identity Provider's login and acceptance of the consent page.

3. The user logs in to the Twitter Identity Provider challenge using his Twitter credentials.

4. The Twitter Identity Provider validates the credentials and redirects to the Twitter Bot application with a temporary access code.

5. The Twitter Bot application uses the code and retrieves the access token at the Twitter Identity Provider token endpoint.

6. Using the access token, any client can request the secured pages of the Twitter Bot application. ASP.NET Core also uses a default cookie-based authentication scheme in which an identity cookie is sent upon a successful authentication response to the user's browser. The browser will send this cookie to the Twitter Bot application on each subsequent request, through which the user will be allowed access.

Enable Sign-in Option on the Twitter Platform

As the first step in configuring authentication for the Twitter Bot web application, we need to enable the sign-in option for the `TwitterBotApplication` Twitter app. Edit the TwitterBotApplication Twitter app details and specify `https://localhost:44302/signin-twitter` (the URL of the Twitter Bot web application) as the callback URL, as shown in Figure 6-10. Click Save.

Note   The `TwitterBotApplication` is the Twitter app we created in Chapter 2. At the time of creation, we did not enable the signin option.

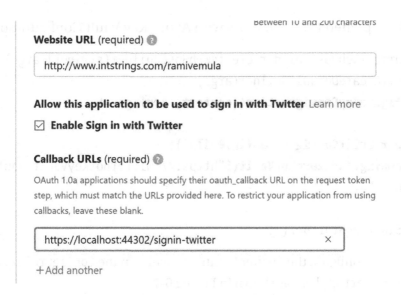

Figure 6-10.   *The Enable Signin option in the TwitterBotApplication Twitter app*

Configuring the Web App with the Twitter Authentication Settings from Azure Key Vault

In this section, we configure the Twitter Bot web application with the Twitter authentication service settings from Azure Key Vault. Install the `Microsoft.Extensions.Configuration.AzureKeyVault` nuget package in the `TwitterBot.Web` project, as shown in Figure 6-11.

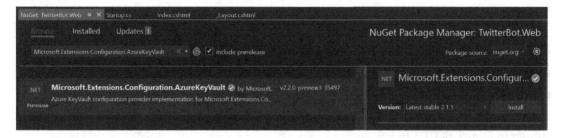

Figure 6-11. *Install the Microsoft.Extensions.Configuration.AzureKeyVault nuget on the TwitterBot.Web project*

Update the `CreateWebHostBuilder` method of the `Program` class, as shown in Listing 6-6.

Listing 6-6. Updated Program Class with Azure Key Vault Configuration

```
public static IWebHostBuilder CreateWebHostBuilder(string[] args) =>
    WebHost.CreateDefaultBuilder(args)
     .ConfigureAppConfiguration((context, config) =>
     {
         var builtConfig = config.Build();
         config.AddAzureKeyVault($"https://TwitterBotKeyVault.vault.azure.
         net/");
     })
     .UseStartup<Startup>();
```

Now we can configure the Twitter Identity Provider in the `ConfigureServices` method of the `Startup` class, as shown in Listing 6-7.

Note   Remove the existing code from the `ConfigureServices` method of the `Startup` class.

Listing 6-7. Updated ConfigureServices Method of the Startup Class

```
public void ConfigureServices(IServiceCollection services)
{
    services.AddAuthentication().AddTwitter(twitterOptions =>
    {
        twitterOptions.ConsumerKey = Configuration["TwitterAPIKey"];
        twitterOptions.ConsumerSecret = Configuration["TwitterAPISecret"];
    });

    services.AddMvc().SetCompatibilityVersion(CompatibilityVersion.
    Version_2_1);
}
```

Configuring ASP.NET Core Identity with Azure Cosmos DB

By default, ASP.NET Core Identity is configured to use a SQL database to store and retrieve the user's identity data. The Twitter Bot application does not use a SQL Server database; we need to configure TwitterBotDB Cosmos DB to act as the identity backend store. There is no direct API or nuget available from Microsoft (at this point in time) to configure a Cosmos DB as the identity backend store. We will use `CodeKoenig. AspNetCore.Identity.DocumentDb`, an open source nuget package, to configure TwitterBotDB as the identity backend.

Note CodeKoenig.AspNetCore.Identity.DocumentDb was developed by Bernhard Koenig. All credit goes to him for this implementation. You can find him at https://github.com/codekoenig.

Install the `CodeKoenig.AspNetCore.Identity.DocumentDb` nuget on the `TwitterBot.Web` project, as shown in Figure 6-12.

Figure 6-12. *Install the CodeKoenig.AspNetCore.Identity.DocumentDb nuget on the TwitterBot.Web project*

Before we configure the Cosmos DB Identity store, we need to create an ApplicationUser type. Create a folder called Identity in the TwitterBot.Web project and create the ApplicationUser class, as shown in Listing 6-8. The ApplicationUser type is used to create an instance for the logged-in user to hold his data, serialize it, and save it to Cosmos DB.

Listing 6-8. ApplicationUser Class

```
using AspNetCore.Identity.DocumentDb;
namespace TwitterBot.Web.Identity
{
  public class ApplicationUser : DocumentDbIdentityUser<DocumentDbIdentity
  Role>
  { }
}
```

Now we will configure the ASP.NET Core Identity with TwitterBotDB Cosmos DB instance, as shown in Listing 6-9. In the ConfigureServices method of the Startup class, we add a singleton instance of IDocumentClient with a new instance of DocumentClient, which takes the Cosmos DB URL, the authentication key, and the serialization settings. Create the private methods InitializeDatabaseAsync and InitializeCollectionAsync, which will take DocumentClient, DatabaseName, and CollectionName as input parameters and create the database and collection at Cosmos DB if they don't exist.

We add the ASP.NET Core Identity with ApplicationUser and DocumentDbIdentityRole types, followed by adding the document store using the AddDocumentDbStores extension method. We specify the database name and user store collection of the TwitterBotDB Cosmos DB. We also set the default login path to the home page.

Listing 6-9. Updated ConfigureServices Method of Startup Class

```
/* Code removed for brevity */
using Newtonsoft.Json;
using Microsoft.Azure.Documents;
using Microsoft.Azure.Documents.Client;
using AspNetCore.Identity.DocumentDb;
using TwitterBot.Web.Identity;
using System.Threading.Tasks;

namespace TwitterBot.Web
{
    public class Startup
    {
        /* Code removed for brevity */

        public void ConfigureServices(IServiceCollection services)
        {
            var databaseName = "TwitterBotDB";
            var identityCollectionName = "AptNetIdentity";
            var serializationSettings = new JsonSerializerSettings();

            var documentClient = new DocumentClient(
                new Uri(Configuration["TwitterBotDbUri"]),
                Configuration["TwitterBotDbAuthKey"],
                serializationSettings);

            services.AddSingleton<IDocumentClient>(documentClient);
            Task.Run(async () => await InitializeDatabaseAsync(document
            Client, databaseName)).Wait();
            Task.Run(async () => await InitializeCollectionAsync(document
            Client, databaseName, identityCollectionName)).Wait();

            services.AddIdentity<ApplicationUser, DocumentDbIdentityRole>()
                .AddDocumentDbStores(options =>
                {
                    options.UserStoreDocumentCollection =
                    identityCollectionName;
```

265

```
                options.Database = databaseName;
        });

    services.ConfigureApplicationCookie(options => options.LoginPath = "/");
        services.AddAuthentication().AddTwitter(twitterOptions =>
        {
            twitterOptions.ConsumerKey = Configuration["TwitterAPIKey"];
            twitterOptions.ConsumerSecret = Configuration["TwitterAPI
            Secret"];
        });

    /* Code removed for brevity */
    }

/* Code removed for brevity */

    private async Task InitializeDatabaseAsync(DocumentClient
    documentClient, string databaseName)
    {
        await documentClient.CreateDatabaseIfNotExistsAsync(new
        Database { Id = databaseName });
    }

private async Task InitializeCollectionAsync(DocumentClient documentClient,
string databaseName, string collectionName)
    {
        DocumentCollection collection = new DocumentCollection() { Id =
        collectionName };
        collection = await documentClient.CreateDocumentCollection
        IfNotExistsAsync(UriFactory.CreateDatabaseUri(databaseName),
        collection);
    }
    }
}
```

Note   As we are trying to store user information including claims in a collection at Azure Cosmos DB, we might get a `PlatformNotSupportedException`.

.NET Core throws a `PlatformNotSupportedException` when we try to serialize `ClaimsIdentity` using the `Newtonsoft.Json` package; see `https://github.com/JamesNK/Newtonsoft.Json/issues/1713`.

To mitigate this error, we will create a custom `JsonConverter`, which will serialize the claims.

Create the `JsonClaimConverter` class in the `Identity` folder of the `TwitterBot.Web` project, as shown in Listing 6-10. It will check for the type of `ClaimsPrincipal` object. If the type matches, it will serialize the dictionary containing the claims.

Listing 6-10. JsonClaimConverter Class

```
using Newtonsoft.Json;
using System;
using System.Collections.Generic;
using System.Security.Claims;

namespace TwitterBot.Web.Identity
{
    public class JsonClaimConverter : JsonConverter
    {
        public override bool CanConvert(Type objectType)
        {
            return (objectType == typeof(ClaimsPrincipal));
        }

        public override void WriteJson(JsonWriter writer, object value,
        JsonSerializer serializer)
        {
            var claimsDictionary = new Dictionary<string, string>();
            foreach(var claim in ((ClaimsIdentity)(value as
            ClaimsPrincipal).Identity).Claims)
```

```
        {
            claimsDictionary.Add(claim.Type, claim.Value);
        }

        new JsonSerializer().Serialize(writer, claimsDictionary);
    }
    public override object ReadJson(JsonReader reader, Type objectType,
    object existingValue, JsonSerializer serializer)
    {
        throw new NotImplementedException();
    }
    }
}
```

Add the newly created JsonClaimConverter to JsonSerializationSettings in the ConfigureServices method of the Startup class, as shown in Listing 6-11.

Listing 6-11. Configure JsonClaimConverter in the ConfigureServices Method of the Startup Class

```
var serializationSettings = new JsonSerializerSettings();
serializationSettings.Converters.Add(new JsonClaimConverter());

var documentClient = new DocumentClient(
    new Uri(Configuration["TwitterBotDbUri"]),
    Configuration["TwitterBotDbAuthKey"],
    serializationSettings);
```

Customizing ASP.NET Core's External Authentication Flow

So far in this chapter, we have completed most of the Twitter authentication setup for the Twitter Bot web application. Now we focus on customizing the entire authentication flow. Let's start by making the Twitter Login button trigger the authentication flow.

Note   We placed the Twitter Login button in the `Layout.cshtml` file in the previous section.

The Twitter Login button will post the Twitter provider to the `ExternalLogin` action of the `Account` controller. Place the `form` tag in `Layout.cshtml`, as shown in Listing 6-12. The `returnUrl` attribute points to `/tweet/index`, which we are going to create later in this chapter, and it is the secured page that's protected by the Twitter login. The `asp-page` attribute points to the `/Account/ExternalLogin` endpoint.

Listing 6-12. POST Identity Provider Option to ExternalLogin Endpoint

```
<!-- Login with Twitter -->
<form asp-area="Identity" asp-page="/Account/ExternalLogin" class="form-
horizontal loginForm" asp-route-returnUrl="/tweet/index" method="post">
    <input type="hidden" name="provider" value="Twitter" />
</form>
```

We handle the `Twitter Login` button click event in jQuery. Add the click event in `site.js`, as shown in Listing 6-13.

Listing 6-13. JQuery Click Event of Twitter Login Button

```
(function ($) {
    $(function () {
        $('.sidenav').sidenav();

        $('.twitterLogin').click(function () {
            $('.loginForm').submit();
        });
    });
})(jQuery);
```

Now we will handle the Logout option for the Twitter Bot application. Instead of placing the login/logout options in `Layout.cshtml`, we will construct the menu in `_LoginPartial.cshtml`. Update `_LoginPartial.cshtml` from the Page/Shared folder, as shown in Listing 6-14. We inject `SignInManager` into the view to check whether the user is currently signed in or not. `UserManager` is injected to retrieve the logged-in user's name. If the user is logged in, we will display the user's name and logout option. Otherwise, we will show the login option.

Note   We are using the same `_LoginPartial.cshtml` file to display normal and mobile compatible menu options. We can make this menu dynamic by using sections. Creating a configurable menu is out of the scope of this book.

Listing 6-14.   Updated _LoginPartial.cshtml

```
@using TwitterBot.Web.Identity
@inject SignInManager<ApplicationUser> SignInManager
@inject UserManager<ApplicationUser> UserManager

@if (SignInManager.IsSignedIn(User))
{
<form asp-area="Identity" asp-page="/Account/Logout" asp-route-returnUrl=
"@Url.Page("/Index", new { area = "" })" method="post" id="logoutForm"
class="navbar-right">
    <ul class="right hide-on-med-and-down">
        <li>
            <a href="#">Hello @UserManager.GetUserName(User)!</a>
        </li>
        <li>
            <button type="submit" class="waves-effect waves-light btn
            orange">Log out</button>
        </li>
    </ul>
    <ul id="nav-mobile" class="sidenav">
        <li>
            <a href="#">Hello @UserManager.GetUserName(User)!</a>
        </li>
```

```
    <li>
        <button type="submit" class="waves-effect waves-light btn
        orange">Log out</button>
    </li>
</ul>
<a href="#" data-target="nav-mobile" class="sidenav-trigger">
<i class="material-icons">menu</i></a>
</form>
}
else
{
    <ul class="right hide-on-med-and-down">
        <li><a class="waves-effect waves-light btn modal-trigger orange
        twitterLogin" href="#">Twitter Login</a></li>
    </ul>
    <ul id="nav-mobile" class="sidenav">
        <li><a class="waves-effect waves-light btn modal-trigger orange
        twitterLogin" href="#">Twitter Login</a></li>
    </ul>
    <a href="#" data-target="nav-mobile" class="sidenav-trigger"><i
    class="material-icons">menu</i></a>
}
```

Update the header tag of Layout.cshtml to load _LoginPartial.cshtml, as shown in Listing 6-15.

Listing 6-15. Updated Layout.cshtml

```
<header>
    <nav class="light-blue lighten-1" role="navigation">
        <div class="nav-wrapper container">
            <a id="logo-container" href="/" class="brand-logo">Twitter
            Bot</a>
```

```
            @await Html.PartialAsync("_LoginPartial")
        </div>
    </nav>
</header>
```

Note   By now you might have observed that there is no account controller and there are no other ASP.NET Core Identity artifacts like pages, classes, etc. in the `TwitterBot.Web` project.

ASP.NET Core 2.1 provides ASP.NET Core Identity as a Razor Class library. All the identity artifacts are coming from the Razor Class library and we can override them by selecting the scaffolding option. Using the scaffolder, we can selectively add the source code contained in the Identity Razor Class library (RCL).

Next in this chapter, we will override the default style of `ExternalLogin.cshtml` to reflect the material design.

Now we will scaffold `ExternalLogin.cshtml` and `Logout.cshtml`. The `ExternalLogin` class is used to capture the user's email ID and save it along with the identity information. Right-click the `TwitterBot.Web` project and then choose Add ➤ New Scaffolded Item, as shown in Figure 6-13.

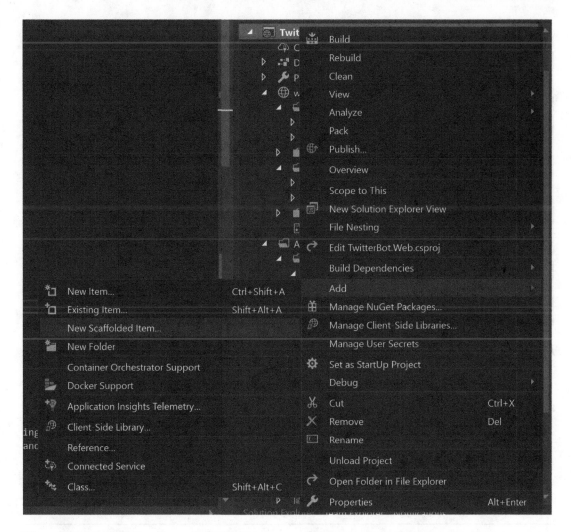

Figure 6-13. *Add a new scaffolded item to the TwitterBot.Web project*

Select Identity and click on Add, as shown in Figure 6-14.

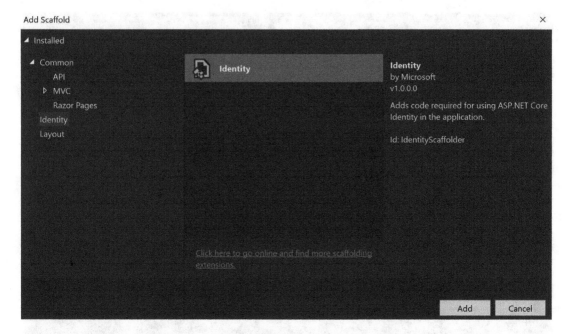

Figure 6-14. *Add the identity scaffolded item to the TwitterBot.Web project*

Select the Account/ExternalLogin and Account/Logout checkboxes and click Add, as shown in Figure 6-15.

Note   Although we are not using `ApplicationDbContext`, we need to select it as the Data Context class. Otherwise, the Add button will remain disabled. The user class option is available only upon new data context creation.

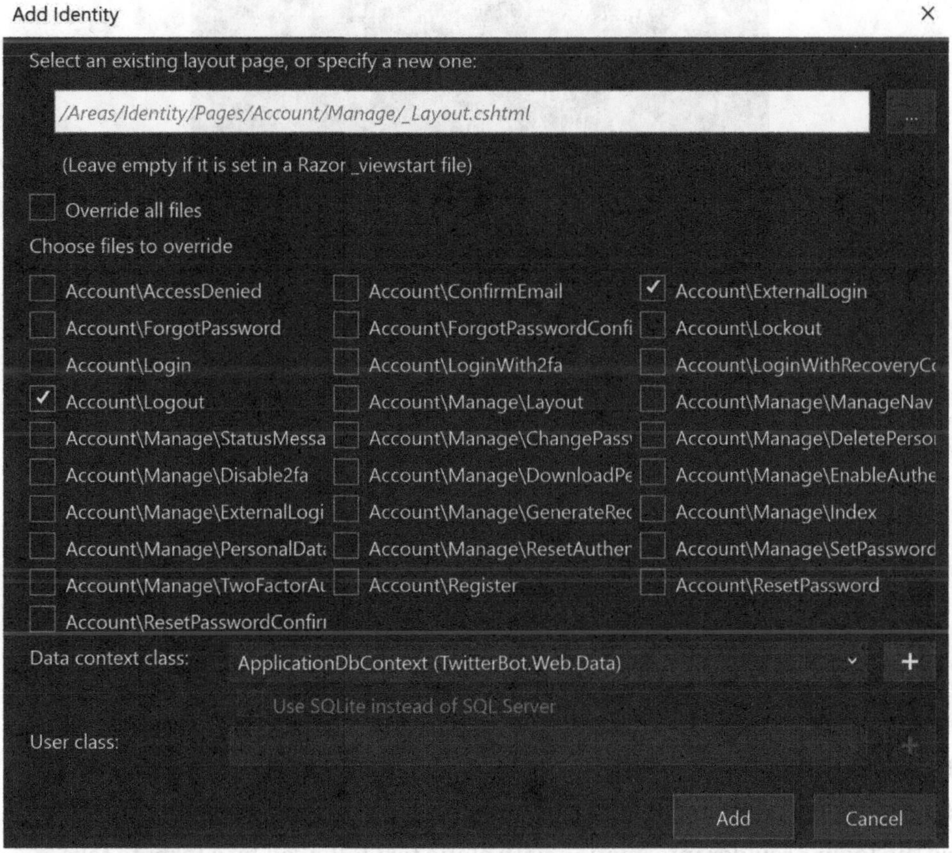

Figure 6-15. *Select ExternalLogin and Logout for scaffolding*

Both ExternalLogin.cshtml and Logout.cshtml are added to the Identity/Pages/
Account folder, as shown in Figure 6-16.

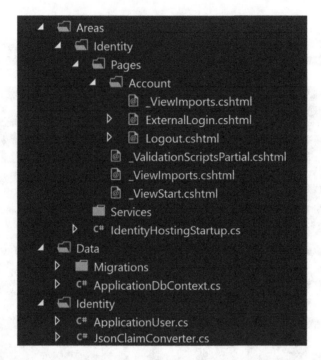

Figure 6-16. *The TwitterBot.Web Project structure*

Update `ExternalLogin.cshtml` with the Materialize CSS design, as shown in Listing 6-16. This page takes `ExternalLoginModel` as the input model. We display the login provider information with static text followed by a form to take email as input. A validation tag helper is used to display the validation message. `_ValidationScriptsPartial` is used to load the jQuery validation scripts.

Listing 6-16. Updated ExternalLogin.cshtml

```
@page
@model ExternalLoginModel
@{
    ViewData["Title"] = "Register";
}

<div class="row">
    <div class="col s3"></div>
    <div class="col s6">
        <div class="card blue-grey darken-1">
            <div class="card-content white-text">
```

```
            <span class="card-title">Email Registration</span>
            <p>
                You've successfully authenticated with <strong>@Model.
                LoginProvider</strong>.
                Please enter an email address for this site below and
                click the Register button to finish logging in.
            </p>
        </div>
        <div class="card-action white">
            <div class="row">
                <form asp-page-handler="Confirmation" asp-route-
                returnUrl="@Model.ReturnUrl" method="post">
                    <div class="input-field col s10">
                        <input placeholder="Enter Email" id="email"
                        type="text" name="Input.Email" class="validate">
                        <label for="email">Email</label>
                        <span asp-validation-for="Input.Email"
                        class="text-danger"></span>
                    </div>
                    <div class="input-field col s2">
                        <button type="submit" class="btn btn-
                        default">Register</button>
                    </div>
                </form>
            </div>
        </div>
    </div>

    <div class="col s3"></div>
</div>

@section Scripts {
    @await Html.PartialAsync("_ValidationScriptsPartial")
}
```

Now we need to update the ExternalLogin.cshtml.cs file by removing the IdentityUser references with the custom ApplicationUser type, as shown in Listing 6-17.

Listing 6-17. Updated ExternalLogin.cshtml.cs Class

```
/* Code removed for brevity */
using TwitterBot.Web.Identity;

namespace TwitterBot.Web.Areas.Identity.Pages.Account
{
    [AllowAnonymous]
    public class ExternalLoginModel : PageModel
    {
        private readonly SignInManager<ApplicationUser> _signInManager;
        private readonly UserManager<ApplicationUser> _userManager;
        private readonly ILogger<ExternalLoginModel> _logger;

        public ExternalLoginModel(
            SignInManager<ApplicationUser> signInManager,
            UserManager<ApplicationUser> userManager,
            ILogger<ExternalLoginModel> logger)
        {
            _signInManager = signInManager;
            _userManager = userManager;
            _logger = logger;
        }

/* Code removed for brevity */

        public async Task<IActionResult> OnPostConfirmationAsync(string
        returnUrl = null)
        {
            /* Code removed for brevity */

            if (ModelState.IsValid)
            {
                var user = new ApplicationUser { UserName = Input.Email,
                Email = Input.Email };
```

```
        /* Code removed for brevity */
    }

    LoginProvider = info.LoginProvider;
    ReturnUrl = returnUrl;
    return Page();
  }
 }
}
```

Note   In Listing 6-17, we changed `SignInManager` and `UserManager` from using `IdentityUser` to `ApplicationUser`. This manual change is required for now because we registered the ASP.NET Core Identity with `ApplicationUser`, which will eventually pass down to `SignInManager` and `UserManager` registrations.

You might wonder why `ApplicationUser` is not inherited from `IdentityUser`. It cannot be because it is already inherited from `DocumentDbIdentit yUser<DocumentDbIdentityRole>` and C# doesn't support multiple inheritance. Unfortunately, at this point in time, neither `IdentityUser` nor `DocumentDbIdentityUser` have interfaces through which we can inherit both.

We should do this manual change for all the Identity functionalities that we are planning to use with Cosmos DB as the backend. For the Twitter Bot application, we are only planning to use the external login and logout functionalities, so I limited the changes to that.

Similarly, we need to update `Logout.cshtml.cs` with the `SignInManager` instance, as shown in Listing 6-18.

Listing 6-18. Updated Logout.cshtml.cs Class

```
/* Code removed for brevity */
using TwitterBot.Web.Identity;

namespace TwitterBot.Web.Areas.Identity.Pages.Account
{
    [AllowAnonymous]
    public class LogoutModel : PageModel
    {
        private readonly SignInManager<ApplicationUser> _signInManager;
        private readonly ILogger<LogoutModel> _logger;

        public LogoutModel(SignInManager<ApplicationUser> signInManager,
        ILogger<LogoutModel> logger)
        {
            _signInManager = signInManager;
            _logger = logger;
        }
/* Code removed for brevity */

    }
}
```

Testing the End-to-End Authentication Flow

In this section, we test the authentication flow by creating a page on the Twitter Bot web application that will act as a secured page and can only be accessed by logged-in users. Create a folder called Tweet in the Pages folder. Right-click the Tweet folder and choose Add ➤ Razor Page. Then call it Index and click Add. For now, keep the default markup, as shown in Listing 6-19.

Listing 6-19. Index.cshtml of the Tweet Folder

```
@page
@model TwitterBot.Web.Pages.Tweet.IndexModel
@{
    ViewData["Title"] = "Index";
}

<h2>Index</h2>
```

To protect the page from unauthorized users, we need to set up the configuration in the ConfigureServices method of the Startup class, as shown in Listing 6-20.

Listing 6-20. Authorization Setup for the Tweet Folder

```
public void ConfigureServices(IServiceCollection services)
{
    /* Code removed for brevity */
        services.AddMvc().SetCompatibilityVersion(CompatibilityVersion.
        Version_2_1)
    .AddRazorPagesOptions(options =>
    {
        options.Conventions.AuthorizeFolder("/Tweet");
    });
}
```

Run the application and click on the Twitter Login button. The application will redirect to the Twitter authorization page, as shown in Figure 6-17.

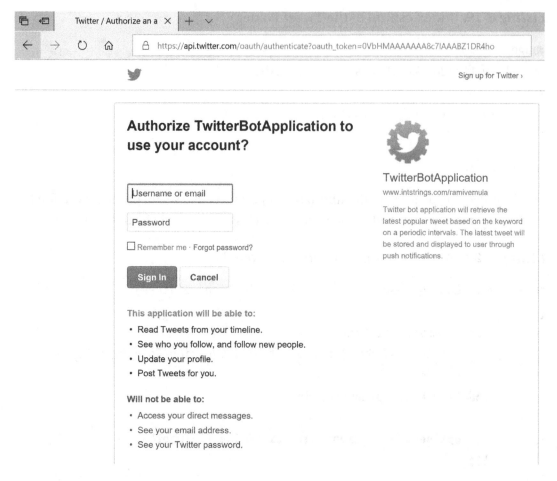

Figure 6-17. *Twitter Authorization page*

Enter your Twitter credentials and click on Sign In. The email registration screen will appear asking you to submit an email to complete the registration, as shown in Figure 6-18.

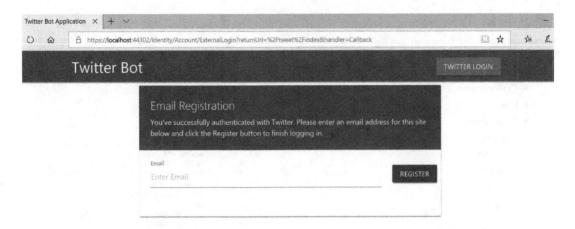

Figure 6-18. *Email registration page*

Enter an email and click on Register. You will be redirected to the /tweet/index page upon successful registration, as shown in Figure 6-19.

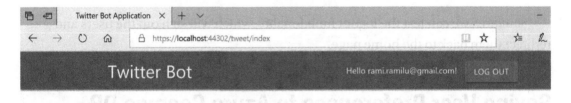

Index

Figure 6-19. *Display the Index page upon successful registration*

Navigate to the TwitterBotDB Cosmos DB and explore the AspNetIdentity collection. You should see the newly created user document, as shown in Figure 6-20.

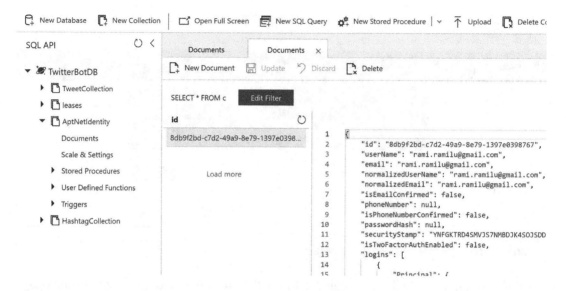

Figure 6-20. *Newly registered user in the AspNetIdentity collection of TwitterBotDB*

Similarly, we can test the logout functionality, which will sign out the users and redirect them back to the home page.

Saving User Preferences to Azure Cosmos DB

In this section, we develop a save preferences functionality so that users can save their Twitter Hashtag preferences to Azure Cosmos DB. As shown in Figure 6-21, we are going to develop a UI component on the Index page. The page will interact with HTTP Trigger-based Azure Functions to perform data operations against Azure Cosmos DB.

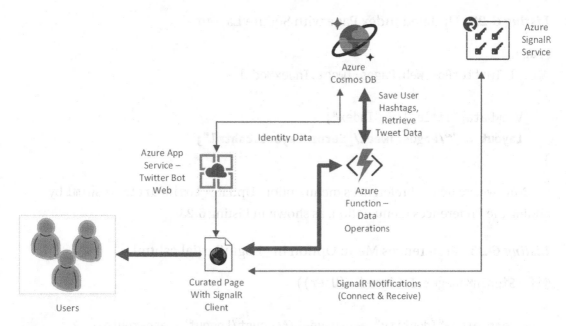

Figure 6-21. *Save and retrieve user preferences to Azure Cosmos DB*

Creating a User Preferences Modal Popup

As the first step, we create a modal popup in the Twitter Bot web application through which users can save their hashtag preferences. We start by creating a secure layout that will inherit from the normal layout. The secure layout is going to have all the common UI components required for secure pages. Create _SecureLayout.cshtml in the Pages/ Tweet folder. The secure layout will use RenderBody to load the content page, as shown in Listing 6-21.

Listing 6-21. *_SecureLayout.cshtml File*

```
@{
    Layout = "~/Pages/Shared/_Layout.cshtml";
}
```

```
@RenderBody()
```

Update Index.cshtml in the Pages/Tweet folder so it uses secure layout as its layout page. Specify the layout, as shown in Listing 6-22.

Listing 6-22. Updated Index Page with Secure Layout

```
@page
@model TwitterBot.Web.Pages.Tweet.IndexModel
@{
    ViewData["Title"] = "Index";
    Layout = "~/Pages/Tweet/_SecureLayout.cshtml";
}
```

Now we create the Preferences menu option. Update _LoginPartial.cshtml by adding the Preferences menu option, as shown in Listing 6-23.

Listing 6-23. Preferences Menu Option in _LoginPartial.cshtml

```
@if (SignInManager.IsSignedIn(User))
{
<form asp-area="Identity" asp-page="/Account/Logout"  asp-route-
returnUrl="@Url.Page("/Index", new { area = "" })" method="post"
id="logoutForm" class="navbar-right">
    <ul class="right hide-on-med-and-down">
        <li>
            <a href="#">Hello @UserManager.GetUserName(User)!</a>
        </li>
        <li>
            <button type="button" class="waves-effect waves-light btn modal-
            trigger orange" href="#preferencesModal">Preferences</button>
            <button type="submit" class="waves-effect waves-light btn
            orange">Log out</button>
        </li>
    </ul>
    <ul id="nav-mobile" class="sidenav">
        <li>
            <a href="#">Hello @UserManager.GetUserName(User)!</a>
        </li>
```

```
    <li>
        <button type="button" class="waves-effect waves-light btn modal-
        trigger orange" href="#preferencesModal">Preferences</button>
        <button type="submit" class="waves-effect waves-light btn
        orange">Log out</button>
    </li>
</ul>
<a href="#" data-target="nav-mobile" class="sidenav-trigger">
<i class="material-icons">menu</i></a>
</form>
}
```

We will display a Materialize CSS modal dialog upon clicking the Preferences menu option. The modal dialog will allow the users to input their hashtag preferences. The input control in modal will be decorated using Materialize CSS's Chips design. We will place the modal dialog in the secure layout, so that it will be available to the users on all secure pages (for now, index is the only secured page).

Update _SecureLayout.cshtml, as shown in Listing 6-24. The div tag with preferenceModal as id is required to tag the modal with the preferences menu option (HREF is pointing to preferenceModal). We need to apply different CSS classes like modal, modal-fixed-footer, modal-content, modal-footer etc., from Materialize CSS to the style preferences modal. We should use the chips class to configure a div tag to display the keywords in the form of Materialize CSS chips.

In the modal footer, we have a Save button and a Close link. The Save button is used to save the user preferences and the Close button is used to close the modal. The jQuery code in the scripts section will configure the respective div tags with Materialize modal and chips functionalities.

Note   In Listing 6-24, we have a hidden field called uid that's required in the future to tie the user preferences to the logged-in user. The value of uid is populated from the logged-in user's nameidentifier claim value.

Listing 6-24. Preferences Modal in _SecureLayout.cshtml

```
@{
    Layout = "~/Pages/Shared/_Layout.cshtml";
}

@RenderBody()

<!-- Modal Structure -->
<div id="preferencesModal" class="modal modal-fixed-footer">
    <div class="modal-content">
        <h4>Preferences</h4>
        <p>Please enter your keywords for which you would like to receive
        notifications.</p>
        <div class="row chips">
        </div>
    </div>
    <div class="modal-footer">
        @Html.Hidden("uid", (User.Identity as System.Security.Claims.
        ClaimsIdentity).Claims.FirstOrDefault(p => p.Type == "http://schemas.
        xmlsoap.org/ws/2005/05/identity/claims/nameidentifier").Value)
        <button type="button" class="waves-effect waves-light btn orange"
        id="btnSave">Save</button>
        <a href="#!" class="modal-close waves-effect waves-green btn-flat"
        id="btnClose">Close</a>
    </div>
</div>

@section Scripts{
    <script>
        $(function () {
            $('.modal').modal();
            $('.chips').chips();
        });
    </script>
@RenderSection("Scripts", required: false)
}
```

Run the Twitter Bot web application and log in to the application. If you do so, you should see the Preferences menu option, as shown in Figure 6-22.

Index

Figure 6-22. *User Preferences option*

Click on the Preferences option. You should see a modal popup, as shown in Figure 6-23. Enter some keywords and press Enter after each keyword. You should then see chips.

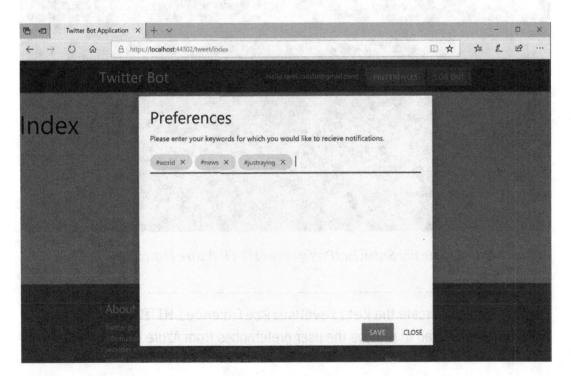

Figure 6-23. *Preferences modal popup and keywords as chips*

Implementing HTTP Azure Functions to Save and Retrieve User Preferences

In this section, we create the backend HTTP Azure Functions, which will save and retrieve user preferences to Azure Cosmos DB. Create a new folder called Http in the TwitterBot.AzureFunctions project. Add a new Azure Function (Right-click the Http folder and choose New Function) called SaveUserPreferences. Select the Http Trigger and click OK, as shown in Figure 6-24.

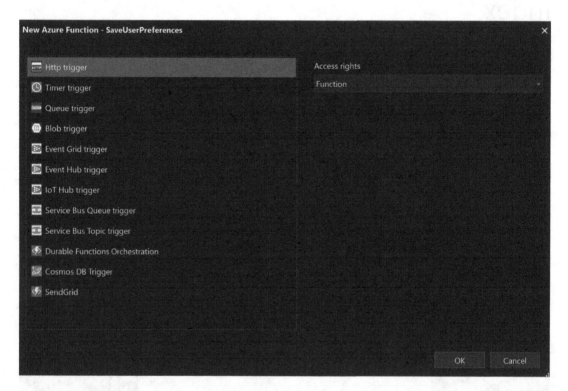

Figure 6-24. Create the SaveUserPreferences HTTP Azure Function

---

Note   Similarly, create the RetrieveUserPreferences HTTP Azure Function. This function is used to retrieve the user preferences from Azure Cosmos DB.

Update SaveUserPreferences as shown in Listing 6-25. SaveUserPreferences supports only the HTTP POST action; currently it supports all requests though anonymous access. We read the incoming User object from the request stream.

The IDocumentDbRepository<Hashtag> repository instance is injected into the function, which is used to check the existence of hashtags at the Cosmos DB HashtagCollection. If the hashtags do not exist, we create them in the HashtagCollection with IsCurrentlyInQueue set to false and LastSyncedDateTime set to 10 minutes less than the current UTC time.

We also inject IDocumentDbRepository<User> into the function that's used to save the User object to Azure Cosmos DB. If the User object already exists, we take the id value and map it to the incoming User object. If the User object doesn't exist, we proceed with the AddOrUpdate operation. Finally, we send OkResult in response.

Listing 6-25. SaveUserPreferences Azure Function

```
using System;
using System.IO;
using System.Threading.Tasks;
using Microsoft.AspNetCore.Mvc;
using Microsoft.Azure.WebJobs;
using Microsoft.Azure.WebJobs.Extensions.Http;
using Microsoft.AspNetCore.Http;
using Microsoft.Extensions.Logging;
using Newtonsoft.Json;
using TwitterBot.Framework.Types;
using TwitterBot.Framework.Contracts.Data;
using TwitterBot.Framework.DependencyInjection;
using System.Linq;
using System.Collections.Generic;

namespace TwitterBot.AzureFunctions.Http
{
    public static class SaveUserPreferences
    {
        [FunctionName("SaveUserPreferences")]
        public static async Task<IActionResult> Run(
            [HttpTrigger(AuthorizationLevel.Anonymous, "post",
            Route = null)] HttpRequest req,
            [Inject]IDocumentDbRepository<User> userRepository,
            [Inject]IDocumentDbRepository<Hashtag> hashtagRepository,
```

```csharp
    ILogger log)
{
    log.LogInformation("SaveUserPreferences started.");

    string requestBody = await new StreamReader(req.Body).
    ReadToEndAsync();
    var user = JsonConvert.DeserializeObject<User>(requestBody);

    // Add/Update Hashtag
    var hashtags = user.Hashtags != null ? user.Hashtags.Select(p
    => p.Text).ToList() : new List<string>();
    var dbHashtagQuery = await hashtagRepository.WhereAsync(p =>
    hashtags.Contains(p.Text));
    var dbHashtags = dbHashtagQuery.ToList();

    foreach (var hashtag in user.Hashtags)
    {
        if (dbHashtags.Any(p => p.Text == hashtag.Text))
        {
            continue;
        }

        hashtag.IsCurrentlyInQueue = false;
        hashtag.LastSyncedDateTime = DateTime.UtcNow.AddMinutes(-10);
        await hashtagRepository.AddOrUpdateAsync(hashtag);
    }

    // Add/Update User
    var dbuserQuery = await userRepository.WhereAsync(p => p.UserId
    == user.UserId);
    var users = dbuserQuery.ToList();

    if (users != null && users.Count() != 0)
    {
        user.Id = users.FirstOrDefault().Id;
    }
    await userRepository.AddOrUpdateAsync(user);
```

```
        log.LogInformation("SaveUserPreferences completed.");

        return new OkResult();
    }
  }
}
```

Update RetrieveUserPreferences as shown in Listing 6-26. RetrieveUserPreferences supports only the HTTP GET action; currently it supports all requests though anonymous access. We inject IDocumentDbRepository<User> into the function, which is used to retrieve the User object from Azure Cosmos DB based on UserId. The UserId is retrieved from the incoming request's query string. Finally, the User object is sent back in the response. If the User object is not available, a null response will be returned.

Listing 6-26. RetrieveUserPreferences Azure Function

```
using System.Threading.Tasks;
using Microsoft.AspNetCore.Mvc;
using Microsoft.Azure.WebJobs;
using Microsoft.Azure.WebJobs.Extensions.Http;
using Microsoft.AspNetCore.Http;
using Microsoft.Extensions.Logging;
using TwitterBot.Framework.Types;
using TwitterBot.Framework.Contracts.Data;
using TwitterBot.Framework.DependencyInjection;
using System.Linq;

namespace TwitterBot.AzureFunctions.Http
{
    public static class RetrieveUserPreferences
    {
        [FunctionName("RetrieveUserPreferences")]
        public static async Task<IActionResult> Run(
            [HttpTrigger(AuthorizationLevel.Anonymous, "get",
            Route = null)] HttpRequest req,
            [Inject]IDocumentDbRepository<User> userRepository,
```

```
        ILogger log)
    {

        log.LogInformation("RetrieveUserPreferences started.");

        string userId = req.Query["uid"];
        var users = await userRepository.TopAsync(p => p.UserId ==
        userId, 1);
        if (users == null || users.Count() == 0)
        {
            return new JsonResult(null);
        }

        var user = users.ToList().FirstOrDefault(p => p.UserId ==
        userId);

        log.LogInformation("RetrieveUserPreferences completed.");

        return new JsonResult(user);
    }
  }
}
```

Note   The HTTP functions are currently not secured through authentication. In next chapter, we will implement an authentication strategy to protect the HTTP functions integration with the Twitter Bot web application.

We can further enhance the two Azure Functions with model validation and sanity checks. There is an exercise at the end of the chapter to achieve model validation.

The SaveUserPreferences and RetrieveUserPreferences Azure Functions run on a domain that's not same as the Twitter Bot web application. To make HTTP calls from the Twitter Bot web application to the TwitterAzureFunctions Function app, we need to enable Cross-Origin Resource Sharing (CORS) in the Azure Functions. In a local environment, we can enable it by setting CORS in the local.settings.json file, as shown in Listing 6-27. The * symbol is used to allow all domains.

Listing 6-27. Enable CORS in the Local Development Environment

```
{
  "IsEncrypted": false,
  "Host": {
    "CORS": "*"
  },
  "Values": {
    "AzureWebJobsStorage": "UseDevelopmentStorage=true",
    "FUNCTIONS_WORKER_RUNTIME": "dotnet"
  }
}
```

In the Azure environment, we can enable CORS from platform features of the TwitterAzureFunctions Function app, as shown in Figure 6-25. Remove all existing origins and Specify https://localhost:44302 and https://twitterbotweb. azurewebsites.net as origins. Then click on Save.

Note https://localhost:44302 is the local domain of the Twitter Bot web application. Later in this chapter, we are going to create a https:// twitterbotweb.azurewebsites.net Azure Web App Service to host the Twitter Bot web application.

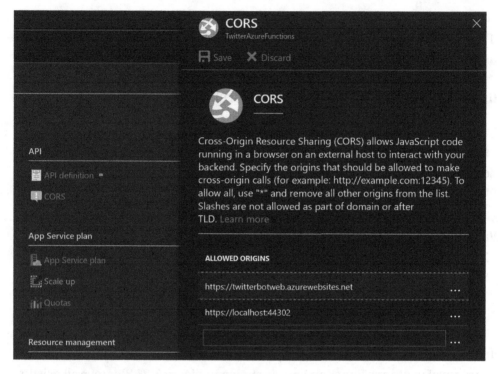

Figure 6-25. *Allow CORS for Azure Functions*

Integrating HTTP Azure Functions with the User Preferences Modal Popup

As the last step of developing the User Preferences functionality, we integrate the Twitter Bot web application with HTTP Azure Functions. We define the Azure Function base URL in the configuration of the web application. To start, we add an AppSetting called ServiceBaseUrl to the appsettings.json file, as shown in Listing 6-28.

Listing 6-28. Azure Function Service Base URL Configuration

```
"AppSettings": {
  "ServiceBaseUrl": "http://localhost:7071"
}
```

Create a folder called Configuration in the TwitterBot.Web project. Create a class called AppSettings, as shown in Listing 6-29. Make sure the class name of the AppSettings matches the appsettings.json configuration section. Similarly, the properties names of the AppSettings class should match the individual application settings names within the AppSettings configuration section, (for example, ServiceBaseUrl within the AppSettings section).

Listing 6-29. AppSettings Class

```
namespace TwitterBot.Web.Configuration
{
    public class AppSettings
    {
        public string ServiceBaseUrl { get; set; }
    }
}
```

Now create a class called AppSettingsConfiguration, as shown in Listing 6-30. AppSettingsConfiguration will hold the AppSettings property.

Listing 6-30. AppSettingsConfiguration Class

```
namespace TwitterBot.Web.Configuration
{
    public class AppSettingsConfiguration
    {
        public AppSettings AppSettings { get; set; }
    }
}
```

Configure the AppSettingsConfiguration class in the ConfigureServices method of the Startup class, as shown in Listing 6-31.

Listing 6-31. Configure AppSettingsConfiguration in the ConfigureServices Method

```
public void ConfigureServices(IServiceCollection services)
{
    services.Configure<TwitterBot.Web.Configuration.
    AppSettingsConfiguration> (Configuration);
    /* Code removed for brevity */
}
```

Update _SecureLayout.cshtml to integrate the HTTP Azure Functions from jQuery, as shown in Listing 6-32. We inject AppSettingsConfiguration into the view and use the Options pattern provided by ASP.NET Core to read the configuration values. The ServiceBaseUrl is used in jQuery to issue HTTP calls to Azure Functions.

We configure Materialize CSS modal to invoke the refreshModal jQuery function at the end of opening of modal popup. The refreshModal function will initialize the chips component and access it using M.Chips.getInstance function, through which we can add/remove chips. Then it makes an HTTP call to the RetrieveUserPreferences Azure Function to retrieve the latest information and uses the response data to add the chips to the modal.

Similarly, the Save button functionality is handled through the jQuery's Click event. We read the current chip information through M.Chips.getInstance function and UserId from the hidden field to formulate the payload, which is sent to the SaveUserPreferences Azure Function. Upon a successful HTTP call, we get the Materialize modal instance and close it.

Listing 6-32. Updated jQuery Code of _SecureLayout.cshtml

```
@inject Microsoft.Extensions.Options.IOptions<TwitterBot.Web.Configuration.
AppSettingsConfiguration> appSettings
@* Code removed for brevity *@
@section Scripts{
    <script>
        $(function () {
            // Modal Configuration
            $('.modal').modal({
                onOpenEnd: function () {
                    refreshModal();
                }
            });

            // Save Button click event
            $('#btnSave').click(function () {
                instance = M.Chips.getInstance($('.chips'));
                var user = {};
                user.uid = $('#uid').val();
                user.hts = [];
```

```
        $.each(instance.chipsData, function (index, chip) {
            user.hts.push({ 'txt': chip.tag });
        });

        $.post("@appSettings.Value.AppSettings.ServiceBaseUrl/api/
        SaveUserPreferences", JSON.stringify(user), function (data) {
            var modal = M.Modal.getInstance($('.modal'));
            modal.close();
        });
    });
    // Refresh the modal with latest information.
    var refreshModal = function () {
        // Initialize chips.
        $('.chips').chips();
        instance = M.Chips.getInstance($('.chips'));

        $.get("@appSettings.Value.AppSettings.ServiceBaseUrl/api/
        RetrieveUserPreferences?uid=" + $('#uid').val(), function
        (data) {
            if (data === null) {
                return;
            }

            $.each(data.hts, function (index, chip) {
                instance.addChip({ tag: chip.txt });
            });
        });
    };
    });
    </script>
@RenderSection("Scripts", required: false)
}
```

Before we start testing the entire flow, we need to make sure UserCollection
is created in the Azure Cosmos DB. Configure UserCollection in the
GetDocumentEntities method of the DocumentDbContext class of the TwitterBot.
Framework project, as shown in Listing 6-33.

Listing 6-33. Configure UserCollection at DocumentDbContext Class

```
private List<IDocumentDbEntity> GetDocumentEntities()
{
    var entityCollection = new List<IDocumentDbEntity>()
    {
/* Code removed for brevity */
        new DocumentDbEntity { EntityType = typeof(TwitterBot.Framework.
        Types.User), Name = "UserCollection" }
    };
    return entityCollection;
}
```

Set the `TwitterBot.AzureFunctions` and `TwitterBot.Web` projects as startup projects, as shown in Figure 6-26.

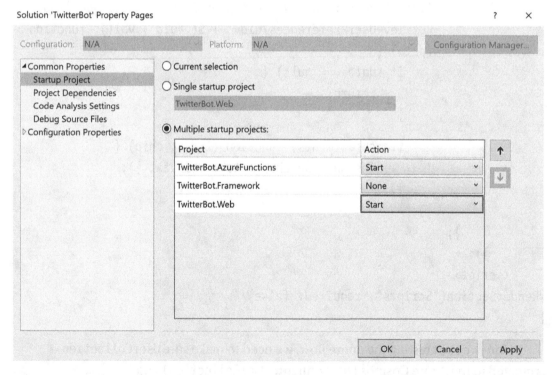

Figure 6-26. *Set TwitterBot.AzureFunctions and TwitterBot.Web projects as Startup projects*

Run the solution in Visual Studio. Log in to the Twitter Bot web application and save the preferences, as shown in Figure 6-27.

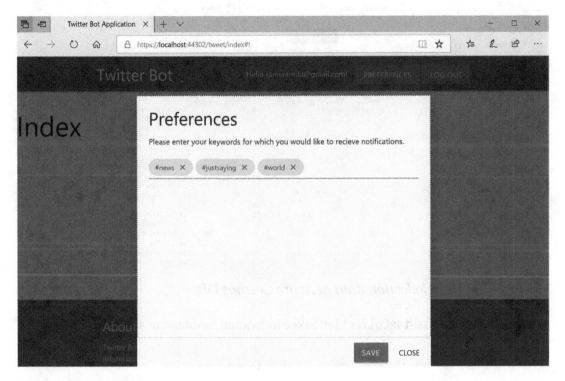

Figure 6-27. *Save user preferences*

We should see user data in the UserCollection of the Azure Cosmos DB Data Explorer, as shown in Figure 6-28.

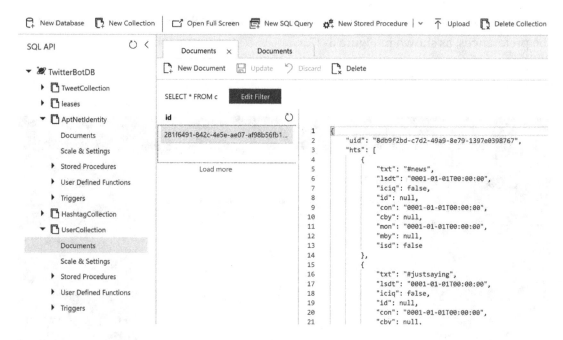

Figure 6-28. *UserCollection data at Azure Cosmos DB*

We can explore `HashtagCollection` to see individual hashtags, as shown in Figure 6-29.

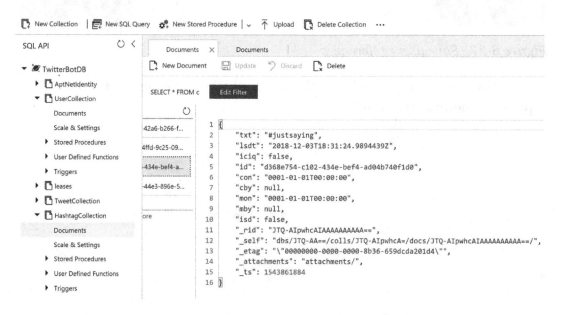

Figure 6-29. *HashtagCollection data at Azure Cosmos DB*

Displaying the Latest Tweets from Azure Cosmos DB

In this section, we display the latest popular tweets from the Azure Cosmos DB on the Index page of the Twitter Bot web application based on user's hashtag subscriptions. We follow the same approach we used to save and retrieve user preferences. We develop an HTTP Azure Function to return all the tweets based on the user's hashtag subscriptions. The HTTP function will be invoked from the Index page using jQuery.

Implementing the HTTP Azure Function to Retrieve the Latest Tweets

As the first step in developing the display tweets functionality, we create an HTTP Azure Function to retrieve the latest tweets from the Azure Cosmos DB based on the user's hashtag subscriptions. Let's get started by updating the IDocumentDbRepository<T> interface of the TwitterBot.Framework project to include the GetTweetsByHashtags method, as shown in Listing 6-34. GetTweetsByHashtags takes an array of hashtags and a notBeforeDate DateTime (to filter the latest tweets) as inputs and returns IEnumerable<T> objects.

Listing 6-34. GetTweetsByHashtags Method In the IDocumentDbRepository<T> Interface

```
/* Code removed for brevity */
using System.Collections.Generic;
public interface IDocumentDbRepository<T> where T : BaseType
{
    /* Code removed for brevity */
    IEnumerable<T> GetTweetsByHashtags(string[] hashtags, DateTime
    notBeforeDate);
}
```

Update the DocumentDbRepository<T> class with the GetTweetsByHashtags implementation, as shown in Listing 6-35. We enclose every hashtag with single quotes and then join them using commas. The concatenated string will serve as a filter in the Where clause of the query. Then we create a document query using the CreateDocumentQuery<T> method of DocumentClient.

303

The document query uses a SQL query to select the Id, Text, FullText, TweetUrl, RetweetCount, FavoriteCount, TweetCreatedBy, TweetCreatedByUrl, and TweetCreatedOn properties of Tweet by joining the Hashtag collection of every tweet document of TweetCollection. The query is filtered for the tweets that have matching hashtags with the input hashtags array and the tweet created on date is not prior to the notBeforeDate. Finally, the results are returned to the calling method.

Listing 6-35. GetTweetsByHashtags Implementation in the DocumentDbRepository<T> Class

```
/* Code removed for brevity */
using System.Collections.Generic;
public IEnumerable<T> GetTweetsByHashtags(string[] hashtags, DateTime
notBeforeDate)
{
    var userHashtagString = string.Join(", ", hashtags.Select(t => "'" +
    t + "'"));
    var query = _context.DocumentClient.CreateDocumentQuery<T>(
                UriFactory.CreateDocumentCollectionUri(_context.DatabaseId,
                _documentCollection.Id),
                string.Format"SELECT Tweets.id, Tweets.txt, Tweets.ftxt,
                Tweets.turl, Tweets.rcnt, Tweets.fcnt, Tweets.tcb, Tweets.
                tcbu, Tweets.tco" +
                " FROM Tweets JOIN Hashtag in Tweets.hts WHERE Hashtag.
                txt in ({0}) AND Tweets.tco >= '{1}'", userHashtagString,
                notBeforeDate.ToString("s")));

    return query.ToList();
}
```

> **Note**   The main reason I am using SQL Query instead of LINQ extensions (in Listing 6-35) is due to the current DocumentDB Core SDK limitation to support all the LINQ extensions, like Any, Where etc., within the query predicate.

Now we create an HTTP Trigger-based Azure Function called GetLatestTweets in the Http folder of the TwitterBot.AzureFunctions project, as shown in Listing 6-36. GetLatestTweets is an anonymous GET function and it is dependent on

IDocumentDbRepository<User> to fetch the user's hashtag subscriptions from
UserCollection. It also uses IDocumentDbRepository<Tweet> to query the tweets from
TweetCollection by using the GetTweetsByHashtags method and passing an array of
user's hashtags along with a DateTime instance to fetch tweets from the last two days.
Finally, the results are placed in descending order based on the TweetCreatedOn date
and returned in JSON format. A null response is returned if neither the user nor the tweet
details are present in the respective collections.

Listing 6-36. GetLatestTweets Azure Function

```
using System.Threading.Tasks;
using Microsoft.AspNetCore.Mvc;
using Microsoft.Azure.WebJobs;
using Microsoft.Azure.WebJobs.Extensions.Http;
using Microsoft.AspNetCore.Http;
using Microsoft.Extensions.Logging;
using TwitterBot.Framework.Contracts.Data;
using TwitterBot.Framework.DependencyInjection;
using TwitterBot.Framework.Types;
using System.Linq;
using System;

namespace TwitterBot.AzureFunctions.Http
{
    public static class GetLatestTweets
    {
        [FunctionName("GetLatestTweets")]
        public static async Task<IActionResult> Run(
            [HttpTrigger(AuthorizationLevel.Anonymous, "get",
            Route = null)] HttpRequest req,
            [Inject]IDocumentDbRepository<User> userRepository,
            [Inject]IDocumentDbRepository<Tweet> tweetRepository,
            ILogger log)
        {
            log.LogInformation("GetLatestTweets started.");

            string userId = req.Query["uid"];
```

```
    var dbUsers = await userRepository.TopAsync(p => p.UserId ==
    userId, 1);
    if (dbUsers == null || dbUsers.Count() == 0)
    {
        return new JsonResult(null);
    }

    var user = dbUsers.ToList().FirstOrDefault(p => p.UserId ==
    userId);
    if (user.Hashtags == null || user.Hashtags.Count == 0)
    {
        return new JsonResult(null);
    }
    var tweets = tweetRepository.GetTweetsByHashtags(user.Hashtags.
    Select(p => p.Text).ToArray(), DateTime.UtcNow.AddDays(-2));
    if(tweets != null)
    {
        tweets = tweets.OrderByDescending(p => p.TweetCreatedOn);
    }

    log.LogInformation("GetLatestTweets completed.");
    return new JsonResult(tweets);
        }
    }
}
```

Integrating an HTTP Azure Function with the Index Page

As the second and last step in developing the display tweets functionality, we update the Index page of the Tweet folder in the TwitterBot.Web project to invoke the GetLatestTweets Azure Function and display tweets on the UI.

The Index page UI will primarily consist of three sections, as shown in Listing 6-37. The No Tweets display section is used to display the No Tweets message to users when no tweet information is available. The Loader section is used conditionally to display a progress loader, which indicates the progress of retrieving tweets from the server. Upon page load, the loader section will be visible on the UI. It will be hidden once the tweet information is available from the HTTP function call.

The last section is the tweet display section and it's used to display the tweets. These sections are mutually exclusive; for example, if tweets are available, no tweets display section will be hidden and the tweets display section will be visible.

Note   The Materialize CSS concepts of Card Panel, Loader, and Cards are used in designing the sections of the Index page. You can find more information at `https://materializecss.com/`.

Listing 6-37. Updated Index Page

```
@page
@model TwitterBot.Web.Pages.Tweet.IndexModel
@{
    ViewData["Title"] = "Index";
    Layout = "~/Pages/Tweet/_SecureLayout.cshtml";
}
<div class="row">
    @* No Tweets display Section - Display no tweets message. *@
    <div class="col s3"></div>
    <div class="col s6">
        <div class="card-panel teal lighten-2 hide">There are no tweets
        available for your subscription!!!</div>
    </div>
    <div class="col s3"></div>
</div>

@* Loader Section - Display loader. *@
<div class="row center loader">
    <div class="preloader-wrapper small active">
        <div class="spinner-layer spinner-green-only">
            <div class="circle-clipper left">
                <div class="circle"></div>
            </div><div class="gap-patch">
                <div class="circle"></div>
            </div><div class="circle-clipper right">
                <div class="circle"></div>
```

```
            </div>
        </div>
    </div>
</div>

@* Tweets display Section - Display tweets. *@
<div class="row">
    <div class="col s2"></div>
    <div class="col s8 dataDiv"></div>
    <div class="col s2"></div>
</div>
```

The jQuery code displays the tweets on the Index page; it's shown in Listing 6-38. We define a global function called getTweets, which will make the HTTP call to the GetLatestTweets Azure Function. Upon the successful callback of the $.get function, the Loader and No Tweets sections will be hidden. The tweet display section will be emptied to populate new tweets. Then, if the data returned from the server is null, we will display the No Tweets display section. If data is not null, then we parse each tweet through the processTweet function and append them to the tweet display section. The getTweets function is invoked when the Index page is loaded.

The processTweet function will construct the HTML of a given tweet and append it to the tweet display section. This function is commonly used to display tweets upon page load along with tweet notifications from SignalR. To differentiate a notification with a normal tweet display, processTweet accepts the isNotification parameter. Based on the isNotification parameter, normal tweets are displayed in chronological order, whereas tweets notified through SignalR are displayed in a different style at the top of the page.

Note   The getTweets function is a global function so that it can be invoked from the secure layout. Especially when users change their preferences, we refresh the tweet information by invoking the getTweets function from _SecureLayout. cshtml.

Listing 6-38. Updated jQuery Code of the Index Page

```
@inject Microsoft.Extensions.Options.IOptions<TwitterBot.Web.Configuration.
AppSettingsConfiguration> appSettings
@section Scripts{
    <script>
        $(function () {
            // Get Tweets for User.
            jQuery.getTweets = function getTweets() {
                $.get("@appSettings.Value.AppSettings.ServiceBaseUrl/api/
                GetLatestTweets?uid=" + $('#uid').val(), function (data) {
                    $('.loader').hide();
                    $('.dataDiv').html('');
                    $('.card-panel').addClass('hide');

                    if (data === null || data.length === 0) {
                        $('.card-panel').removeClass('hide');
                        return;
                    }

                    $.each(data, function (index, tweet) {
                        processTweet(tweet, false);
                    });
                });
            };
            // Update UI with tweet information.
            function processTweet(tweet, isNotification) {
                var displayColor = isNotification ? 'teal lighten-1' :
                'blue-grey darken-1';
                var tweetDate = new Date(tweet.tco);
                var tweetHtml = '<div class="col s12" id="' + tweet.id + '">\
                                <div class="z-depth-3">\
                                    <div class="card ' +
                                    displayColor + ' ">\
```

```
                                          <div class="card-content white-
                                          text">\
                                              <span class="card-title">'
                                              + tweet.tcb + '</span>\
                                              <span>' + tweetDate +
                                              '</span>\
                                              <p>\
                                                  ' + tweet.ftxt + '\
                                              </p>\
                                          </div>\
                                          <div class="card-action">\
                                              <a href="#">' + tweet.fcnt
                                              + ' Favorites</a>\
                                              <a href="#">' + tweet.rcnt
                                              + ' Retweets</a>\
                                              <a href="' + tweet.turl +
                                              '" target="_blank">
                                              <i class="font-size-
                                              point9rem material-icons">
                                              launch</i> Twitter</a>\
                                          </div>\
                                      </div>\
                                  </div>';

                if (isNotification) {
                    $('.dataDiv').prepend(tweetHtml);
                } else {
                    $('.dataDiv').append(tweetHtml);
                }
            }
            $.getTweets();
        });
    </script>
}
```

Update the site.css file with custom styles, as shown in Listing 6-39. The font style is referenced on the Index page to position an external line icon.

Listing 6-39. Custom Styles in site.css

```
.font-size-point9rem {
    font-size: 0.9rem !important;
}
```

Finally, update _SecureLayout.cshtml to invoke the $.getTweets function upon saving the user preferences, as shown in Listing 6-40.

Listing 6-40. Invoke $.getTweets from Secure Layout

```
$.post("@appSettings.Value.AppSettings.ServiceBaseUrl/api/
SaveUserPreferences", JSON.stringify(user), function (data) {
                var modal = M.Modal.getInstance($('.modal'));
                modal.close();
                $.getTweets();
            });
```

Run the application from Visual Studio. If you do so, you should first see a loader, as shown in Figure 6-30.

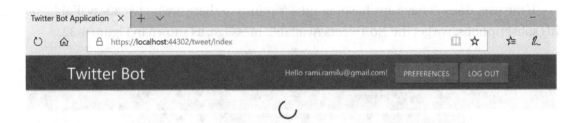

Figure 6-30. *Index page displaying the loader upon retrieving tweets*

The Index page then displays the tweets, as shown in Figure 6-31.

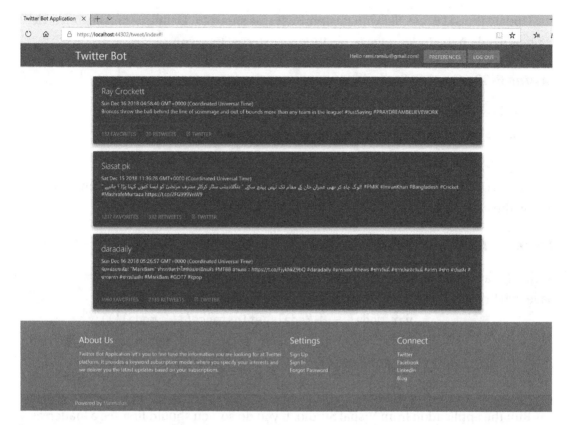

Figure 6-31. *Index page with tweets*

If the user doesn't have any hashtag subscriptions or there are no tweets available for his subscriptions, we get the No Tweets Available message, as shown in Figure 6-32.

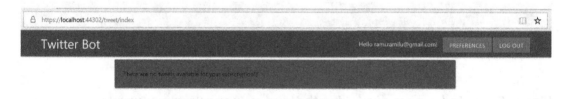

Figure 6-32. *Index page with no tweets message*

Note   The current implementation of the Index page doesn't support pagination while displaying tweets. I personally like the infinite scroll feature, where new content is loaded when you scroll down the page (just like with Twitter). You can take "developer's liberty" and find a nice jQuery Infinite Scroll plugin to extend the Index page to load new content upon page scrolling.

Deploying the Twitter Bot Web Application to the Azure Web App Service

In this section, we deploy the Twitter Bot web application to the Azure App Service and test the entire flow in integration with the `TwitterAzureFunctions` Function app. At Azure portal, navigate to App Services and click on +Add to create a new Azure Web app, as shown in Figure 6-33. Click Create.

Figure 6-33. *New Azure Web App*

Enter the Web App details, as shown in Figure 6-34. Enter TwitterBotWeb as the name. Select TwitterBotApplication as the resource group.

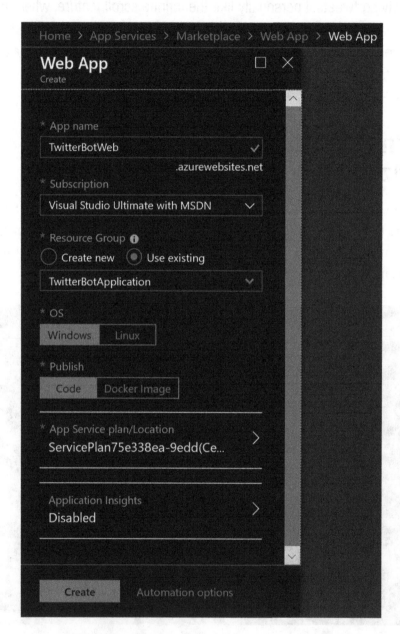

Figure 6-34. *Azure Web App details*

Once the Web app is created, add the `TwitterAzureFunctions` App URL for the `AppSettings:ServiceBaseUrl` Key in the Application settings of the TwitterBotWeb Web app, as shown in Figure 6-35. Click Save.

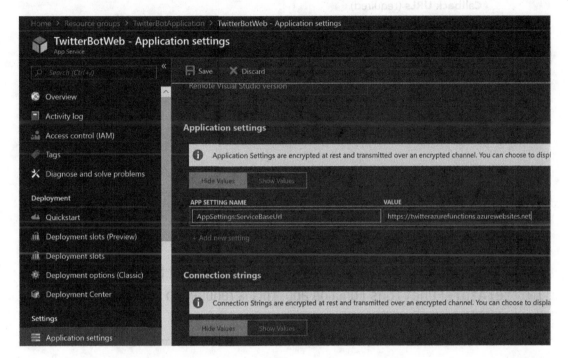

Figure 6-35. *Add the TwitterAzureFunctions app URL as an application setting in the TwitterBot Web app*

Now we need to add the TwitterBotWeb App callback URL to the TwitterBotApplication Twitter app to enable single sign-on with the Twitter platform, as shown in Figure 6-36. Click Save.

Allow this application to be used to sign in with Twitter Learn more

☑ **Enable Sign in with Twitter**

Callback URLs (required) ⓘ

OAuth 1.0a applications should specify their oauth_callback URL on the request token step, which must match the URLs provided here. To restrict your application from using callbacks, leave these blank.

> https://localhost:44302/signin-twitter

> https://twitterbotweb.azurewebsites.net/signin-twitter   ✕

＋Add another

Figure 6-36. *Add the TwitterBotWeb callback URL to the TwitterBotApplication Twitter app*

Note   Publish the `TwitterBot.AzureFunctions` project to the `TwitterAzureFunctions` Function app. This is required to publish the newly created HTTP Azure Functions.

We need to create a Managed Service Identity for the TwitterBotWeb app so we can communicate with Azure Key Vault to retrieve configuration information. Enable the Managed Service Identity, as shown in Figure 6-37. Navigate to the Identity tab of TwitterBotWeb and turn on the status of the system assigned to On. Click Save.

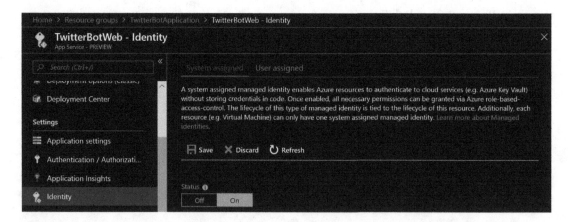

Figure 6-37. *Turn on Managed Service Identity for the TwitterBotWeb app*

Add a new access policy to the `TwitterBotKeyVault` instance, as shown in Figure 6-38. Select the TwitterBotWeb principal and associate the `List` and `Get` permissions for secrets.

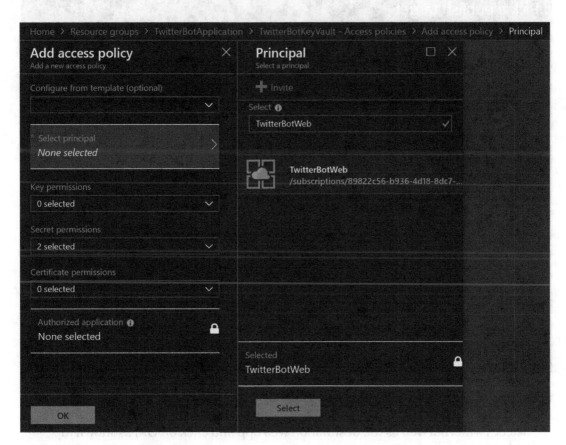

Figure 6-38. *Add a new access policy for TwitterBotWeb in the TwitterBotKeyVault instance*

Now we publish the `TwitterBot.Web` project to the newly created `TwitterBotWeb` app service. Right-click on the `TwitterBot.Web` project in Visual Studio and select the publish option, as shown in Figure 6-39. Select Existing and click Publish.

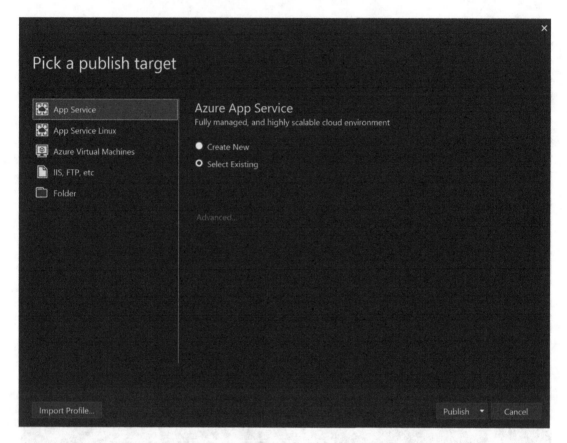

Figure 6-39. *Publish the TwitterBot.Web project from Visual Studio*

Select TwitterBotWeb as the destination web app and click on OK, as shown in Figure 6-40.

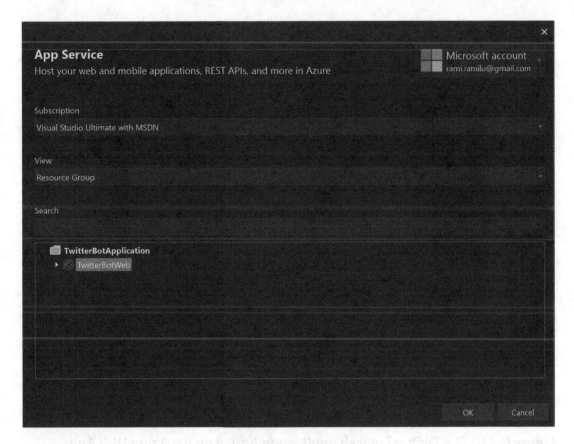

Figure 6-40. *Publish to the TwitterBotWeb app service*

Once the publish activity is completed, we can access the Twitter Bot web application at `https://twitterbotweb.azurewebsites.net`. Log in with the Twitter credentials and subscribe to some hashtags. We can see the Index page displaying the tweet information, as shown in Figure 6-41.

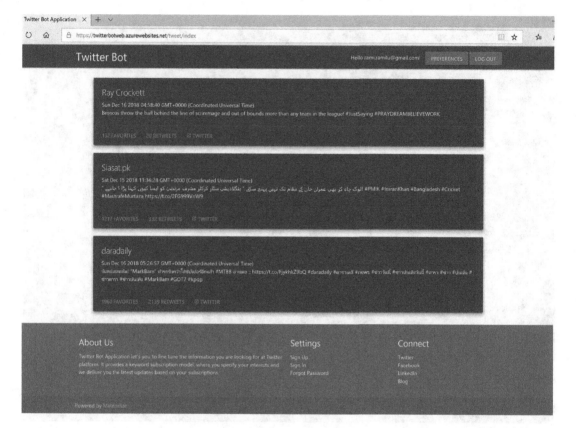

Figure 6-41. *The Twitter bot web application hosted on the Azure Web App Service*

EXERCISE 1

In this chapter, we used the Materialize CSS Starter template to style the home page of the Twitter Bot web application. As part of this exercise, you need to style other pages, such as About, Contact, etc.

All the Materialize CSS styles with samples can be found at `https://materializecss. com/`. Take guidance from the samples and style the pages based on your creative liberties.

EXERCISE 2

In this chapter, we customized `ExternalLogin.cshtml` and `Logout.cshtml` using the ASP.NET Core Scaffolding option in Visual Studio. As part of this exercise, you need to customize Login, Set Password, Forgot Password, and Change Password views. The password operations should be performed on a local account, not on the Twitter account.

Start with the scaffold option and this time add the additional views mentioned in the exercise. Replace the references of `IdentityUser` with `ApplicationUser`. Take the Materialize CSS references from `https://materializecss.com/` and style the views.

EXERCISE 3

In this chapter, we implemented HTTP-based Azure Functions. As part of this exercise, you need to implement model validation in Azure Functions through which the incoming model is validated.

As of today, there is no direct way to achieve model validation in Azure Functions. This active issue is being tracked at `https://github.com/Azure/azure-webjobs-sdk/issues/1848`.

We can achieve model validation in the HTTP Azure Function as suggested by Tsuyoshi Ushio at `https://medium.com/@tsuyoshiushio/how-to-validate-request-for-azure-functions-e6488c028a41`. In short, we can use the code shown here:

```
var results = new List<ValidationResult>();
bool IsValid = Validator.TryValidateObject([Deserialized object from Request
Body], new ValidationContext([Deserialized object from Request Body], null,
null), results, true);
```

Summary

You started this chapter by looking at the importance of web applications in the modern technology ecosystem. Web applications provide affordable, adaptable, reliable, and maintainable business solutions through which we can make mission-critical decisions.

You learned the basics of ASP.NET Core, a new open source and cross-platform framework from Microsoft that builds modern web applications. You explored the main features and different versions of ASP.NET Core. You created an ASP.NET Core Web application and learned about the importance of different project artifacts. You learned the basics of Materialize CSS, a modern, responsive, and frontend CSS framework based on material design concepts. You adopted Materialize CSS's Starter template design for the Twitter Bot web application.

You integrated the Twitter Bot web application with Azure Key Vault to retrieve secret key configuration. You configured the TwitterBotApplication Twitter app to enable sign-in to the Twitter Bot web application using the Twitter Identity Provider. Then you proceeded to override the default ASP.NET Core Identity SQL Database store with the Cosmos DB Collections by leveraging the CodeKoenig.AspNetCore.Identity.DocumentDb nuget. You scaffolded the ASP.NET Core Identity from the default Razor Class library and included ExternalLogin and Logout pages in the TwitterBot.Web project. Finally, you upgraded the styles of Layout, ExternalLogin, and Logout with Materialize CSS and tested the entire authentication flow.

You designed the modal dialog for the Twitter Bot web application by using Materialize CSS to support save and retrieve user preferences functionality. You implemented SaveUserPreferences and RetrieveUserPreferences HTTP Azure Functions and integrated them with the modal using jQuery. You updated Cross Origin Resource Sharing (CORS) configuration in the Azure Function app to allow the Twitter Bot web application to communicate with the TwitterAzureFunctions Function app.

You upgraded the Index page (a secure page) to display lists of tweets from Cosmos DB by using the Cards design of the Materialize CSS. You created a GetLatestTweets HTTP Azure Function to fetch the latest tweets from Azure Cosmos DB. You integrated the HTTP Azure Function with the Index page using jQuery.

Finally, you created TwitterBotWeb, an Azure Web app, and deployed the TwitterBot.Web project to it from Visual Studio. You published the newly created HTTP Azure Functions to the TwitterAzureFunctions function app. You configured Managed Service Identity on the TwitterBotWeb to enable secure connections with Azure Key Vault and updated the TwitterBotApplication Twitter app with the Azure Web app callback URL to support sign-in to the Azure environment. You tested the entire flow, starting from authentication to saving and retrieving user preferences and displaying the latest tweets on the Index page.

In the next chapter, you will integrate the Twitter Bot web application and the Twitter Azure Functions with the Azure SignalR Service to display real-time notifications to users about the latest tweets.

References

1. https://materializecss.com/

2. https://docs.microsoft.com/en-us/aspnet/core/release-
   notes/aspnetcore-2.1?view=aspnetcore-2.1

3. https://docs.microsoft.com/en-us/aspnet/core/razor-
   pages/?view=aspnetcore-2.1&tabs=visual-studio

4. https://docs.microsoft.com/en-us/aspnet/core/security/
   authentication/scaffold-identity?view=aspnetcore-
   2.1&tabs=visual-studio

5. https://docs.microsoft.com/en-us/azure/azure-functions/
   functions-bindings-http-webhook

CHAPTER 7

Getting Started with Azure SignalR Service

The 21st Century has seen some of the greatest innovations in technology. These innovations not only revolutionized business workflow and collaboration, but also changed the traditional ways that businesses and customers communicate. Technology enabled organizations to establish workforces across different geographical locations and still achieve business continuity through powerful and secure communication channels and systems. Effective communication improves the efficiency and productivity of employees as well as their decision-making capabilities through the exchange of critical information.

Real-time communication channels gained significant momentum because of their capability to broadcast critical updates to users and empower them to make better decisions. Software applications, especially mobile applications, offer push notifications through which messages are directly published to users' devices over a network. Real-time communication not only helps in messaging, but also helps support a wide range of automation techniques and robotic processes.

A real-time messaging system can be developed using Azure SignalR Service, which is based on the SignalR library. SignalR is an open source library (under the .NET Foundation) that enables servers to push content to all connected clients instantly, as and when data becomes available. This is more efficient than having the client request new data. SignalR maintains a persistent connection between the server and its clients and subsequently pushes notifications to the clients by using remote procedure calls (RPCs).

© Rami Vemula 2019
R. Vemula, *Integrating Serverless Architecture*, https://doi.org/10.1007/978-1-4842-4489-0_7

In Chapter 6, we created a Twitter Bot web application and integrated it with the Twitter Identity Provider for authentication. We also created a page to capture the users' hashtag preferences and display the latest popular tweets based on user preferences. In this chapter, we:

- Learn about the basics of the Azure SignalR Service.

- Create a new instance of the SignalR Service for the Twitter Bot application.

- Integrate the `TweetNotifierFunction` with the SignalR Service to broadcast the latest tweets to users based on their hashtag subscriptions.

- Integrate the Twitter Bot web application with SignalR Service using a JavaScript client to display tweet notifications on an Index page.

Introducing Azure SignalR Service

Azure SignalR Service is a fully managed service from Azure through which content notifications are published to the connected clients over HTTP by leveraging the SignalR library. Azure SignalR Service is useful in many applications where the content on the server changes frequently and the changes need to be published to the users instantly. It is especially helpful in applications involving instant messaging, collaboration, stock market information, dashboards, IoT, gaming, monitoring, medical information, diagnostics, etc.

Prior to SignalR, developers designed real-time notifications by using polling methods such as long/short polling in which a client polled the server for new information on specific time intervals. This approach is always performance intense, network offensive, and requires more hardware. SignalR solves this problem by establishing a persistent connection between the client and the server. It uses the Hubs API to push notifications from the server to the client, and it supports multiple channels such as WebSockets, server-sent events, and long polling. SignalR supports different clients, ranging from C#/C++ to JavaScript. SignalR has built-in compatibility for SQL Server, Redis, Azure Service Bus etc., to achieve scalability. The Azure SignalR Service offers 99.9% SLA for features like performance, scalability, and availability.

There are currently two versions of SignalR—SignalR for ASP.NET and ASP.NET Core SignalR. ASP.NET Core SignalR is the latest version and it supports the .NET Standard and multiple platforms. Every SignalR application includes server and client components. Azure SignalR Service is the server component managed by Azure and it is based on ASP.NET Core SignalR.

The Azure SignalR Service is available in free and standard pricing modes. Compared to the free mode, you get more units, connections, and messages per day using the standard mode. The standard mode also offers SSL transport.

Creating an Azure SignalR Service Instance

In this section, we create a new instance of Azure SignalR Service. Search for SignalR in the Azure Marketplace, as shown in Figure 7-1. Select SignalR Service and click Create.

Figure 7-1. *SignalR Service in the Azure Marketplace*

Enter the name `TwitterBotSignalR` and select `TwitterBotApplication` as the Resource Group, as shown in Figure 7-2. Select Free Pricing Tier (we will use the free tier for development; for production, we configure the standard tier) and East US as the location. Click Create.

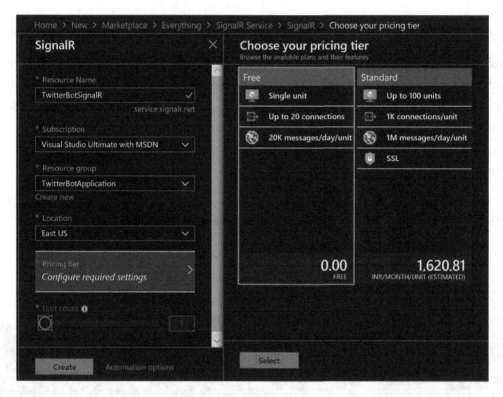

Figure 7-2.   *Create the TwitterBotSignalR Service*

Once the SignalR Service is created, navigate to the Keys section to find the hostname, keys, and ConnectionString configuration, as shown in Figure 7-3. We need the ConnectionString to connect to the SignalR Service from `TweetNotifierFunction`.

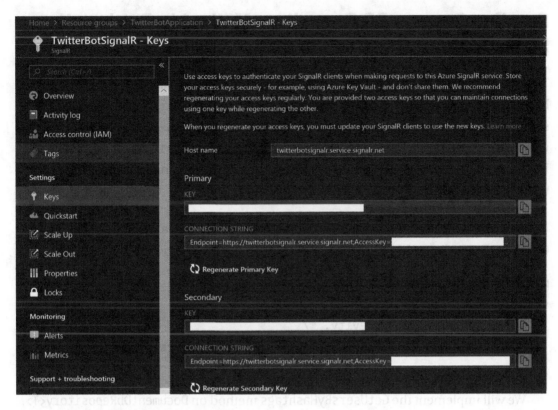

Figure 7-3. *TwitterBotSignalR service keys*

Integrating Tweet Notifier Function with the Twitter Bot SignalR Service

In this section, we integrate TweetNotifierFunction with the TwitterBotSignalR Service. TweetNotifierFunction will send the messages to the TwitterBotSignalR service based on the change feed notifications it receives from TwitterBotDB Cosmos DB. The TwitterBotSignalR service will then broadcast the messages to all the connected clients on the Twitter Bot web application.

Creating Cosmos DB Repository Method to Retrieve Users by Hashtags

TweetNotifierFunction should support SignalR notifications based on the user's hashtag subscriptions, i.e., if a new tweet is available for a hashtag, the notification should be sent to users who subscribed to that hashtag. To achieve this requirement, we will create a GetUsersByHashtags method at IDocumentDbRepository<T>, as shown in Listing 7-1. GetUsersByHashtags takes an array of hashtags as an input parameter and returns IEnumerable of the user objects.

Listing 7-1. Updated IDocumentDbRepository<T> Interface with GetUsersByHashtags Method

```
public interface IDocumentDbRepository<T> where T : BaseType
{
    /* Code removed for brevity. */
    IEnumerable<T> GetUsersByHashtags(string[] hashtags);
}
```

We will implement the GetUsersByHashtags method on DocumentDbRepository<T>, as shown in Listing 7-2. We enclose every hashtag with single quotes and then join them using commas. The concatenated string of hashtags will serve as a filter in the Where clause of the Cosmos DB query. Then we create a document query using a CreateDocumentQuery<T> method of DocumentClient.

The document query uses a SQL query to select the uid property of User. It does so by joining with the hashtag collection of every user document of UserCollection. The query is filtered for the users who have matching hashtags with the input hashtags array. Finally, the user list will be returned.

Listing 7-2. Updated DocumentDbRepository<T> with GetUsersByHashtags Method Implementation

```
public IEnumerable<T> GetUsersByHashtags(string[] hashtags)
{
    var userHashtagString = string.Join(", ", hashtags.Select(t => "'" + t
    + "'"));
```

```
var query = _context.DocumentClient.CreateDocumentQuery<T>(
        UriFactory.CreateDocumentCollectionUri(_context.DatabaseId,
        _documentCollection.Id),
        string.Format("SELECT Users.uid" +
        " FROM Users JOIN Hashtag in Users.hts WHERE Hashtag.txt in
        ({0})", userHashtagString));

    return query.ToList();
}
```

> **Note**   The main reason I am using the SQL query instead of LINQ extensions (in
> Listing 7-2) is due to the current DocumentDB Core SDK limitation to support all
> the LINQ extensions like Any, Where etc., within the query predicate.

Sending SignalR Notifications from the Tweet Notifier Function

In this section, we update TweetNotifierFunction to send SignalR notifications
by using the GetUsersByHashtags method of the Cosmos DB Repository. Let's get
started by adding the TwitterBotSignalR ConnectionString with a key called
AzureSignalRConnectionString at the Azure Key Vault Secrets, as shown in Figure 7-4.

> **Note**   AzureSignalRConnectionString is the default name of the
> ConnectionString setting for the SignalR Output binding, which we are going to
> use in just a moment.
>
> As we are using the Azure Key Vault, if you are not signed in to Visual Studio
> with the same Azure account that's holding Key Vault, you need to add the
> AzureSignalRConnectionString setting to the local.settings.json file
> as well.

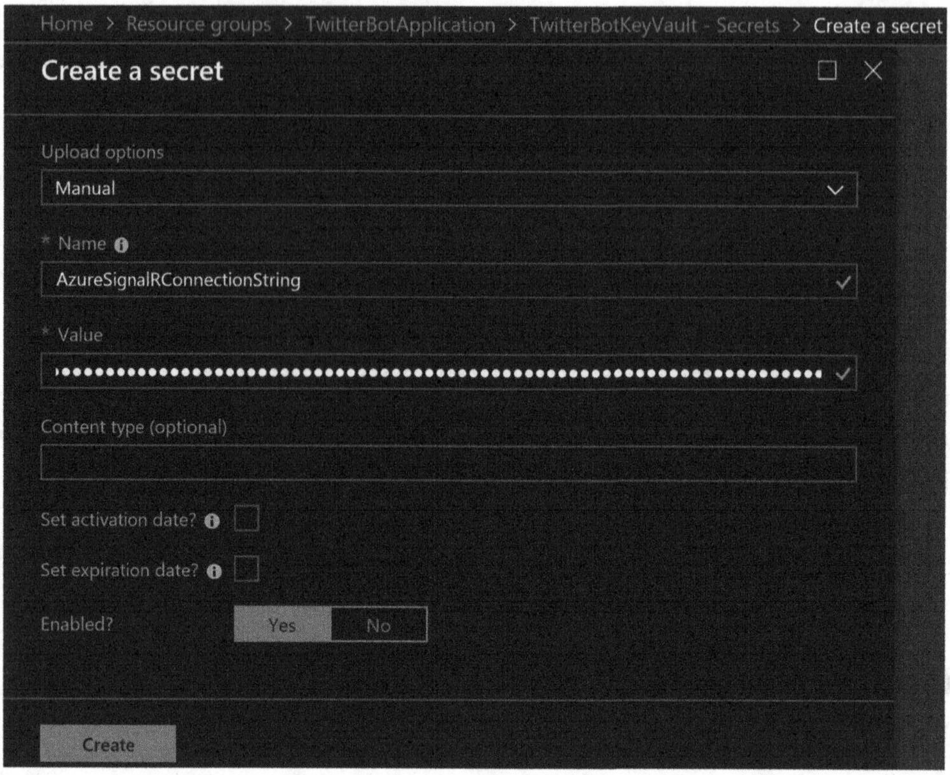

Figure 7-4. *Adding the TwitterBotSignalR ConnectionString to Azure Key Vault secrets*

Now we install the `Microsoft.Azure.WebJobs.Extensions.SignalRService` Nuget in the `TwitterBot.AzureFunctions` project, as shown in Figure 7-5.

Note   SignalR Service bindings for Azure Functions are currently in preview.

Figure 7-5. *Install the Microsoft.Azure.WebJobs.Extensions.SignalRService nuget on the TwitterBot.AzureFunctions project*

Now update `TweetNotifierFunction`, as shown in Listing 7-3. Add the SignalR output binding parameter to the `Run` method. The SignalR binding accepts `HubName` as input, which is configured to `TweetNotificationsHub` (later in this chapter, we will use the same hub name from the Twitter Bot web application to connect to the Azure SignalR Service). The SignalR binding will also publish a collection (`IAsyncCollector`) of messages of type `SignalRMessage` to the `TwitterBotSignalR` Service. We will also inject `IDocumentDbRepository<User>` and `IDocumentDbRepository<Tweet>` instances into the `Run` method.

Within the `Run` method, we can access the modified Cosmos DB documents from the `IReadOnlyList<Document>` input parameter. We iterate the `IReadOnlyList<Document>` collection and retrieve the tweet information from every document from the `TweetCollection` by using an `IDocumentDbRepository<Tweet>` instance. Using the hashtags associated with the tweet, we retrieve all the users who are subscribed to the hashtags from the `UserCollection` by using the `IDocumentDbRepository<User>` instance.

We create a new `SignalRMessage` instance by specifying `UserId`, `Target`, and `Arguments` properties and adding the instance to the `IAsyncCollector<T>` SignalR messages collection using the `AddAsync` method. The `UserId` property is populated from the user (who subscribed to the hashtags), which will ensure that the SignalR notification is sent only to the relevant users.

The Target property should be set with the name (the updateTweets method will also be present in the web application) of the function on the SignalR client that needs to be invoked on receiving the notification. Arguments is set to the Tweet object, which is communicated in the SignalR notification. Finally, the FlushAsync method of IAsyncCollector is used to send the notifications to the clients.

Note   The updateTweets JavaScript function is developed in the next section.

Listing 7-3. Updated TweetNotifierFunction Class

```csharp
using System.Collections.Generic;
using System.Linq;
using System.Threading.Tasks;
using Microsoft.Azure.Documents;
using Microsoft.Azure.WebJobs;
using Microsoft.Azure.WebJobs.Extensions.SignalRService;
using Microsoft.Extensions.Logging;
using TwitterBot.Framework.Contracts.Data;
using TwitterBot.Framework.DependencyInjection;
using TwitterBot.Framework.Types;

namespace TwitterBot.AzureFunctions
{
    public static class TweetNotifierFunction
    {
        [FunctionName("TweetNotifierFunction")]
        public static async Task Run([CosmosDBTrigger(
            databaseName: "TwitterBotDB",
            collectionName: "TweetCollection",
            ConnectionStringSetting = "TwitterBotDbConnectionString",
            LeaseCollectionName = "leases",
            CreateLeaseCollectionIfNotExists = true)]
            IReadOnlyList<Document> documents,
```

```
    [SignalR(HubName = " TweetNotificationsHub")]
    IAsyncCollector<SignalRMessage> messages,
    [Inject]IDocumentDbRepository<Framework.Types.User>
    userRepository,
    [Inject]IDocumentDbRepository<Framework.Types.Tweet>
    tweetRepository,
    ILogger log)
{
    log.LogInformation("Documents modified " + documents.Count);
    foreach (var document in documents)
    {
        var tweet = await tweetRepository.GetByIdAsync(document.Id);
        var users = userRepository.GetUsersByHashtags(tweet.
        Hashtags.Select(p => p.Text).ToArray());
        foreach (var user in users)
        {
            await messages.AddAsync(new SignalRMessage
            {
                UserId = user.Id,
                Target = "updateTweets",
                Arguments = new[] { tweet }
            });
        }
    }

    await messages.FlushAsync();
}
}
}
```

Note   The current implementation of TweetNotifierFunction will send multiple notifications to the same user when there are multiple input documents under the same Cosmos DB notification.

The current logic can be further optimized by creating a group of unique hashtags across all input documents. Then we need only one Cosmos DB query to find all subscribed users. With the query result, we can create a mapping among user/hashtag/tweet based on the query result and input the tweet documents.

Finally, SignalRMessage can be formed per user with a specific payload based on the user/hashtag/tweet map and added to the IAsyncCollector<T> collection.

Integrating the Twitter Bot Web App and the Twitter Bot SignalR Service

In this section, we create an HTTP Azure Function that will return the connection information of the TwitterBotSignalR Service for a specific authenticated user. Then we will create a SignalR JavaScript client at the Twitter Bot web application that will establish a connection with the TwitterBotSignalR Service using the connection information retrieved from the HTTP Azure Function. The client also holds the callback function that will be invoked upon SignalR notifications.

Creating an HTTP Azure Function to Fetch SignalR Service Connection Information

In this section, we create an HTTP Azure Function to retrieve the SignalR Service connection information. Let's get started by creating an HTTP Get Azure Function called SignalRConnection in the HTTP folder of the TwitterBot.AzureFunctions project, as shown in Listing 7-4. The SignalRConnection Azure Function will use SignalRConnectionInfo binding to retrieve the SignalR connection details of the TwitterBotSignalR Service. SignalRConnectionInfo uses the x-userid header from the HTTP request as a unique identifier for the connection and TweetNotificationsHub as the hub name.

Finally, this function returns a `SignalRConnectionInfo` object containing the AccessToken and URL of the Azure SignalR Service. The client uses those settings to establish a connection.

Note   `SignalRConnectionInfo` uses the default connection string called `AzureSignalRConnectionString`. This connection string is added to Azure Key Vault pointing to the `TwitterBotSignalR` Service instance.

Listing 7-4. SignalRConnection Azure Function

```
using Microsoft.AspNetCore.Mvc;
using Microsoft.Azure.WebJobs;
using Microsoft.Azure.WebJobs.Extensions.Http;
using Microsoft.AspNetCore.Http;
using Microsoft.Azure.WebJobs.Extensions.SignalRService;

namespace TwitterBot.AzureFunctions.Http
{
    public static class SignalRConnection
    {
        [FunctionName("SignalRConnection")]
        public static IActionResult GetSignalRInfo(
            [HttpTrigger(AuthorizationLevel.Anonymous, "get", Route =
            null)]HttpRequest req,
            [SignalRConnectionInfo(HubName = "TweetNotificationsHub",
            UserId = "{headers.x-userid}")]SignalRConnectionInfo
            connectionInfo)
        {
            return new OkObjectResult(connectionInfo);
        }
    }
}
```

Implementing SignalR JavaScript Client at the Twitter Bot Web Application

In this section, we create a JavaScript SignalR client at the Twitter Bot web application. Let's get started by adding the SignalR client library to the TwitterBot.Web project. Right-click the TwitterBot.Web project and choose Add ➤ Client-Side Library. Select unpkg as the provider and search for the @aspnet/signalr@1.1.0 package, as shown in Figure 7-6. Select signalr.js and its minified version. Click Install.

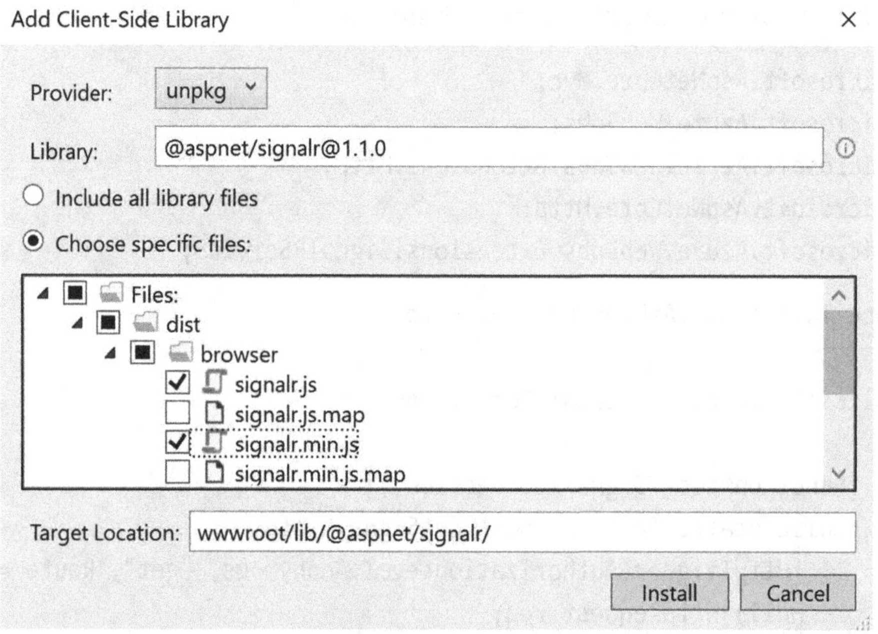

Figure 7-6. *Install @aspnet/signalr@1.1.0 on the Twitter Bot web application*

The installed SignalR client library is located at wwwroot/lib/@aspnet/signalr. Update _Layout.cshtml with the SignalR client library references, as shown in Listing 7-5.

Listing 7-5. Update Layout with SignalR Library Reference

```
<!-- Scripts-->
<environment exclude="Development">
    <script type="text/javascript" src="https://code.jquery.com/jquery
    -2.1.1.min.js"></script>
```

```
<script src="~/js/materialize.min.js"></script>
<script src="~/lib/@@aspnet/signalr/dist/browser/signalr.min.js">
</script>
</environment>
<environment include="Development">
    <script src="~/lib/jquery/dist/jquery.js"></script>
    <script src="~/js/materialize.js"></script>
    <script src="~/lib/@@aspnet/signalr/dist/browser/signalr.js"></script>
</environment>
    <script src="~/js/site.js"></script>
```

Now we will update the Index page with a SignalR JavaScript client, as shown in Listing 7-6. We define a function called `signalRInfo` which will make an HTTP call to the `SignalRConnection` Azure Function. Once URL and `AccessToken` are retrieved, `signalRInfo` will create an instance of a hub connection using the `build` method of `signalR.HubConnectionBuilder`. It does this by passing URL and `AccessToken` to its `WithUrl` extension method.

We start the connection and configure the `updateTweets` event with a handler. The `updateTweets` event handler will process the tweet using the `processTweet` method, by passing the `isNotification` parameter as `true`. If the tweet is already present on the UI, `updateTweets` will remove it and add it back to the UI to make sure the latest tweet is displayed. Finally, the `signalRInfo` method is invoked upon loading the index page.

Note   In the current implementation, the JavaScript client directly connects to Azure SignalR Service with the help of URL and `AccessToken`. We must make sure that `AccessToken` is accessible only to the authenticated users of the Twitter Bot web application, which will eventually secure the connection to the SignalR Service. In the next chapter, we will secure all the HTTP trigger-based Azure Functions using Azure App Service Authentication.

Another way to achieve a SignalR connection is to create a SignalR Hub at the Twitter Bot web application and configure it to connect to the `TwitterBotSignalR` Service. The JavaScript client will then connect to the hub of the Twitter Bot web application, which is secured using App Service Authentication.

Listing 7-6. Update Index Page with a SignalR Connection

```
section Scripts{
    <script>
        $(function () {
            var signalRInfo = function () {
                $.get("@appSettings.Value.AppSettings.ServiceBaseUrl/api/
                SignalRConnection", function (data) {
                    const connection = new signalR.HubConnectionBuilder()
                    .withUrl(data.url, {
                        accessTokenFactory: () => data.accessToken
                    })
                    .build();

                    connection.start().catch(err => console.error(err.
                    toString()));

                    connection.on("updateTweets", (tweet) => {
                    $('.card-panel').addClass('hide');

                        var existingTweet = $('#' + tweet.id);
                        if (existingTweet.length > 0) {
                            $('#' + tweet.id).remove();
                        }

                        processTweet(tweet, true);
                    });
                });
            };

            signalRInfo();

            @* Code removed for brevity. *@
        });
    </script>
}
```

We need to set up the Ajax configuration to include an x-userid header in every HTTP call. It will be populated from the hidden field called uid, which is present upon secure layout. Update _SecureLayout.cshtml, as shown in Listing 7-7. By having the setup in a secure layout, we can include this functionality on every page inherited from a secure layout.

Listing 7-7. Ajax Setup in _SecureLayout.cshtml

```
@section Scripts{
    <script>
        $(function () {

            $.ajaxSetup({
                headers: { 'x-userid': $('#uid').val() }
            });

            @* Code removed for brevity. *@

        });
    </script>
    @RenderSection("Scripts", required: false)
}
```

If you run the application from Visual Studio, you should see the notifications in Figure 7-7.

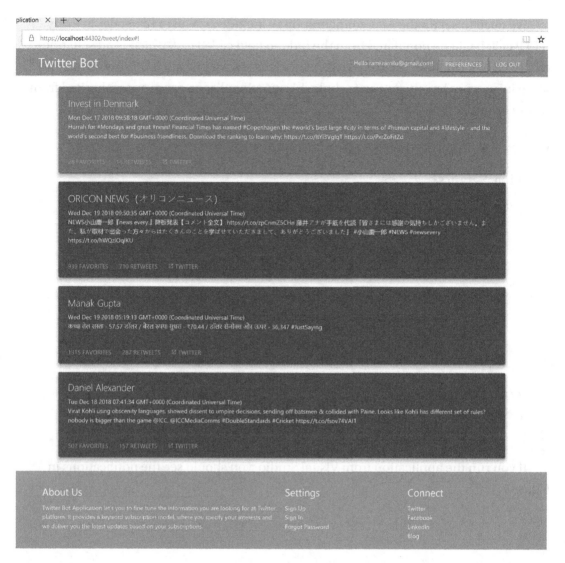

Figure 7-7. *The Twitter Bot web application Index page with SignalR notifications*

At this point, we can publish the `TwitterBot.AzureFunctions` and `TwitterBot.Web` projects to the Azure environment and test the entire flow. It will work seamlessly.

Summary

In this chapter, you learned about the importance of real-time communication in achieving greater productivity and responsiveness in business workflows. Real-time communication not only helps organizations make critical business decisions, but also helps them serve their customers and partners in a better way.

Azure SignalR Service is a fully managed service from Azure that allows you to push content updates to connected clients by leveraging the SignalR library. You learned the basics of the Azure SignalR Service and created an instance of a SignalR Service for the Twitter Bot application. You also configured the SignalR Service `ConnectionString` at the Azure Key Vault.

You integrated the Azure SignalR Service with `TweetNotifierFunction` using the `Microsoft.Azure.WebJobs.Extensions.SignalRService` Nuget package. `TweetNotifierFunction` will send messages to SignalR Service, which will in turn broadcast the messages to the connected SignalR clients.

You created the `SignalRConnection` Azure Function, which is used by the Twitter Bot web application to retrieve the connection information of the `TwitterBotSignalR` Service. Then you proceeded to install the `@aspnet/signalr@1.1.0` SignalR JavaScript library and created a JavaScript client at the Twitter Bot web application on an Index page. Using the JavaScript client, the Twitter Bot web application established a connection with the `TwitterBotSignalR` Service and registered the `updateTweets` function callback, which will be invoked on SignalR notifications.

You published the `TwitterBot.AzureFunctions` and `TwitterBot.Web` projects to the Azure environment and tested the entire flow.

In the next chapter, you will see how to manage application settings in Azure Functions. You will also learn how to secure the Azure Function app using the App Service Authentication feature.

References

1. https://docs.microsoft.com/en-us/azure/azure-signalr/
   signalr-overview

2. https://docs.microsoft.com/en-us/azure/azure-signalr/
   signalr-overview-scale-aspnet-core

3. https://docs.microsoft.com/en-us/azure/azure-functions/
   functions-bindings-signalr-service

CHAPTER 8

Managing App Settings and Implementing Authentication in Azure Functions

Modern-day technologies and innovations have created platforms and tools for individuals and organizations to explore new opportunities and solve complex problems. On the other hand, hackers and malicious groups continuously explore the vulnerabilities in these software solutions through which they can breach these systems for fraudulent activities. These security lapses not only cost millions in loss, but the reputation and trust of the software solutions are also affected. Hence, the need for strong data protection and application security patterns and practices has gained momentum to safeguard the integrity, privacy, and trust of the users.

As we learned in Chapter 5, securing the application and infrastructure data can be achieved in many ways, including managing user identities through authentication and authorization protocols, enhancing server security through strong firewalls, securing configuration information at centralized vaults, etc. We leveraged Azure Key Vault to securely store sensitive infrastructure keys along with external providers configuration. While Azure Key Vault provides security for application secrets, we still need to work on the normal application settings that usually do not qualify as sensitive information. In the first part of this chapter, we:

- Inject application settings configuration into Azure Functions by using dependency injection principles.

- Configure application settings at the Azure Functions app.

345

© Rami Vemula 2019
R. Vemula, *Integrating Serverless Architecture*, https://doi.org/10.1007/978-1-4842-4489-0_8

Managing user identities through authentication and authorization strategies is considered the most prominent way of securing software applications. User identity provides the context of the user who is interacting with the application using which fine-grained access can be provided to his information. Fortunately, ASP.NET Core and Azure Functions come with default support for authentication using different identity providers like Twitter, Google, and so on.

In Chapter 6, we secured the Twitter Bot web application by implementing authentication using the ASP.NET Core Identity with the Twitter Identity Provider and the OAuth 2.0 protocol. In Chapter 7, we integrated the Azure SignalR Service with the Twitter Bot web app through the HTTP Azure Function by passing the logged-in user's identifier. Securing HTTP Azure Functions is the last step in achieving overall security for the Twitter Bot application. In the second part of this chapter, we:

- Secure the `TwitterAzureFunctions` Function app by leveraging the Azure App Service Authentication feature.

- Authenticate the connection between the Twitter Bot web application and `TwitterAzureFunctions` with the help of the user's authentication token.

Managing Application Settings Configuration in Azure Functions

In this section, we develop a mechanism to load application settings configuration of the `TwitterBot.AzureFunctions` project from a centralized location and inject it into the functions using Dependency Injection. We also create the configuration values at the Application Settings option of the `TwitterAzureFunctions` Function app and test the functions in an Azure environment.

Note   To support local debugging, we need to add configuration to the `local. settings.json` file. For Azure environment deployment, we should add the values at the Application Settings of the Azure Function app.

Let's get started by updating the local.settings.json file configuration, as shown in Listing 8-1. Add the AppSettings section, which will hold the TweetsFilterIntervalInDays, HashtagSyncIntervalInMinutes, and HashtagQueueThresholdIntervalInHours settings. These settings will be used in the GetLatestTweets, TweetSchedulerFunction, and SaveUserPreferences functions.

Listing 8-1. Updated local.settings.json Configuration File

```
{
  "IsEncrypted": false,
  "Host": {
    "CORS": "*"
  },
  "Values": {
    "AzureWebJobsStorage": "UseDevelopmentStorage=true",
    "FUNCTIONS_WORKER_RUNTIME": "dotnet"
  },
  "AppSettings": {
    "TweetsFilterIntervalInDays": -2,
    "HashtagSyncIntervalInMinutes": -10,
    "HashtagQueueThresholdIntervalInHours":  -1
  }
}
```

Create a folder called Configuration in the TwitterBot.Framework project. Create two new classes called AppSettingsConfiguration and AppSettings within the configuration folder, as shown in Listings 8-2 and 8-3. Make sure the class name of AppSettings matches the appsettings section of the local.settings.json file. Similarly, the property names of the AppSettings class should match the individual application settings names within the AppSettings configuration section.

Listing 8-2. AppSettingsConfiguration Class

```
namespace TwitterBot.Framework.Configuration
{
    public class AppSettingsConfiguration
    {
```

```
        public AppSettings AppSettings { get; set; }
    }
}
```

Listing 8-3. AppSettings Class

```
namespace TwitterBot.Framework.Configuration
{
    public class AppSettings
    {
        public int TweetsFilterIntervalInDays { get; set; }
        public int HashtagSyncIntervalInMinutes { get; set; }
        public int HashtagQueueThresholdIntervalInHours { get; set; }
    }
}
```

Now we update WebJobsExtensionStartup in the TwitterBot.AzureFunctions
project, as shown in Listing 8-4. We add Environment.CurrentDirectory as the base
path to the ConfigurationBuilder using the SetBasePath extension method. Then we
add the local.settings.json file to the configuration using the AddJsonFile extension
and build the configuration using the Build method. AppSettingsConfiguration
is configured with the config instance using the Configure extension method of
IServiceCollection.

Listing 8-4. Updated WebJobsExtensionStartup Class

```
/* Code removed for brevity. */
using TwitterBot.Framework.Configuration;

[assembly: WebJobsStartup(typeof(WebJobsExtensionStartup), "TwitterBot
Extensions Startup")]
namespace TwitterBot.AzureFunctions
{
    public class WebJobsExtensionStartup : IWebJobsStartup
    {
        public void Configure(IWebJobsBuilder builder)
        {
            /* Code removed for brevity. */
```

```
        // Create a new config by merging default with Azure Key Vault
            configuration.
        string keyvaultName = "TwitterBotKeyVault";
        var config = new ConfigurationBuilder()
            .AddConfiguration(defaultConfig)
            .SetBasePath(Environment.CurrentDirectory)
            .AddJsonFile("local.settings.json", optional: true,
            reloadOnChange: true)
            .AddAzureKeyVault($"https://{keyvaultName} .vault.azure.
            net/").Build();

        // Replace the existing config
        builder.Services.AddSingleton<IConfiguration>(config);
        builder.Services.Configure<AppSettingsConfiguration>(config);

        /* Code removed for brevity. */
        }
    }
}
```

Finally, we can use the configuration in any of the Azure Functions, for example the GetLatestTweets function, as shown in Listing 8-5. Inject an IOptions<AppSettingsC onfiguration> instance using the Inject attribute. Update the GetTweetsByHashtags method parameter to config.Value.AppSettings.TweetsFilterIntervalInDays.

Listing 8-5. Updated GetLatestTweets Function Class

```
/* Code removed for brevity. */
using Microsoft.Extensions.Options;
using TwitterBot.Framework.Configuration;

namespace TwitterBot.AzureFunctions.Http
{
    public static class GetLatestTweets
    {
        [FunctionName("GetLatestTweets")]
```

```
public static async Task<IActionResult> Run(
    [HttpTrigger(AuthorizationLevel.Anonymous, "get", Route =
    null)] HttpRequest req,
    [Inject]IDocumentDbRepository<User> userRepository,
    [Inject]IDocumentDbRepository<Tweet> tweetRepository,
    [Inject]IOptions<AppSettingsConfiguration> config,
    ILogger log)
{
    log.LogInformation("GetLatestTweets started.");

    /* Code removed for brevity. */
    var tweets = tweetRepository.GetTweetsByHashtags(user.Hashtags.
    Select(p => p.Text).ToArray(), DateTime.UtcNow.AddDays(config.
    Value.AppSettings.TweetsFilterIntervalInDays));

    /* Code removed for brevity. */
    }
  }
}
```

Note   Similarly update `TweetSchedulerFunction` to use the
`HashtagSyncIntervalInMinutes` and
`HashtagQueueThresholdIntervalInHours` configuration values.
Update the `SaveUserPreferences` function with a
`HashtagSyncIntervalInMinutes` configuration value.

Run the solution from Visual Studio. All the Azure functions and the web portal
will work seamlessly with these new configuration values. We can now publish the
`TwitterBot.AzureFunctions` project to the Azure environment. Add the `AppSettings`
at the `TwitterAzureFunctions` Function app, as shown in Figure 8-1. The format of the
application setting should be in the `AppSettings:{Key Name}` format. Click Save. Restart
the `TwitterAzureFunctions` Function app. All functions and the web application should
work with the new configuration values; we can test the entire flow.

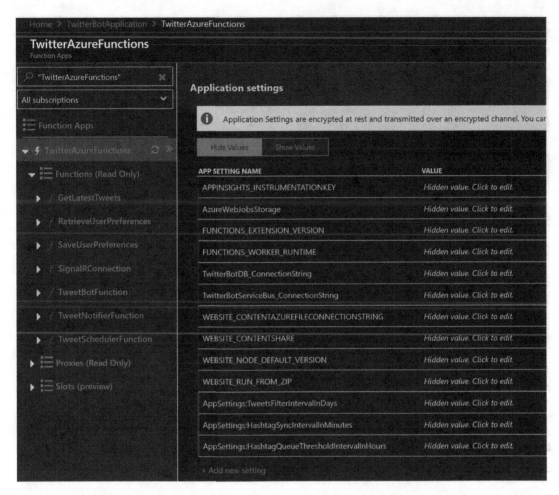

Figure 8-1.   Add AppSettings at TwitterAzureFunctions Function app

Enabling App Service Authentication at the Azure Function App

In this section, we enable the App Service Authentication feature at the TwitterAzureFunctions Function app. App Service Authentication allows users to access the Azure resources in a secured way by integrating with different identity providers with minimal custom code. We can enable authentication and authorization on TwitterAzureFunctions from the Platform Features area, as shown in Figure 8-2. Click on the Authentication/Authorization option.

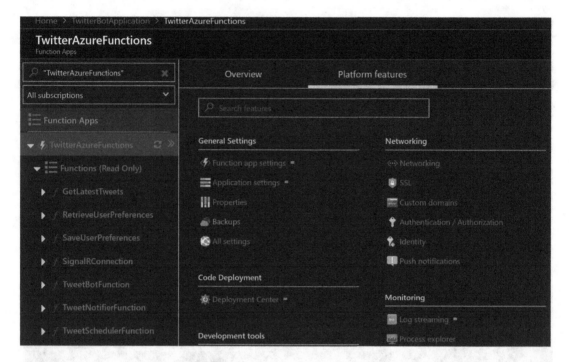

Figure 8-2. *Authentication and Authorization option in the Platform Features area*

Turn on App Service Authentication and select the Log In with Twitter option for the action to take when the request is not authenticated, as shown in Figure 8-3. Turn on Token Store and click the Twitter Authentication Provider to configure the settings.

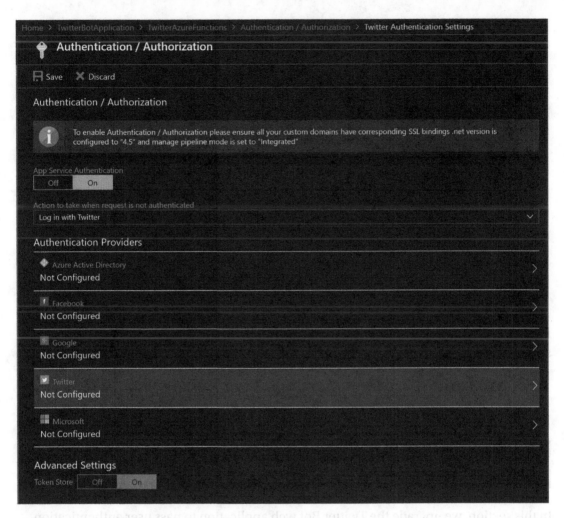

Figure 8-3. *Turn on app service authentication*

Enter the Twitter API key and the secret of the Twitter Bot app, as shown in Figure 8-4. Click OK.

Note   There is an open question at GitHub about how to configure the Twitter Authentication Settings from the Azure Key Vault settings. See `https://github.com/Azure/Azure-Functions/issues/1085`.

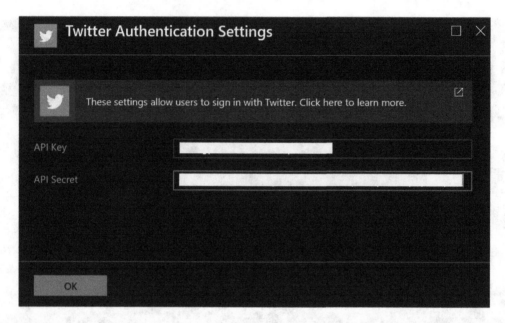

Figure 8-4. *Configure authentication settings from the Twitter Bot app's key and secret*

Finally, click Save to update the authentication configuration of TwitterAzureFunctions.

Integrating the Authentication Flow Between the Web App and the Azure Functions

In this section, we upgrade the Twitter Bot web application to pass user authentication token to the TwitterAzureFunctions Function app. The token will be validated at TwitterAzureFunctions and the resulting ClaimsPrincipal will be injected into the individual functions. The complete authentication flow is depicted in Figure 8-5.

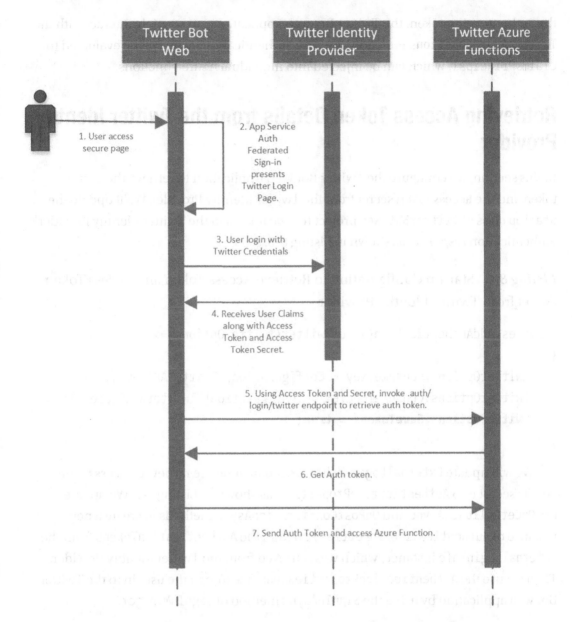

Figure 8-5. *Twitter Bot web and Azure Functions authentication flow*

When users log in to the Twitter Bot web application with valid credentials, the Twitter Identity Provider will send user claims along with the access token and access token secret in the authentication response. The Twitter Bot web application uses the access token and its secret to make a request to the `/.auth/login/twitter` endpoint of the `TwitterAzureFunctions` Function app to retrieve the authentication token. Using the authentication token, the Twitter Bot web application can securely interact with the `TwitterAzureFunctions` Function app. The authentication token will be evaluated to `ClaimsPrincipal`, which can be injected into individual Azure Functions.

Retrieving Access Token Details from the Twitter Identity Provider

In this section, we configure the Twitter Bot Web Application to retrieve the access token and the access token secret from the Twitter Identity Provider. We'll update the `Startup` class of `TwitterBot.Web` project to save tokens in the Twitter Identity Provider's authentication response, as shown in Listing 8-6.

Listing 8-6. Startup Configuration to Retrieve Access Token and Access Token Secret from Twitter Identity Provider

```
services.AddAuthentication().AddTwitter(twitterOptions =>
{
    twitterOptions.ConsumerKey = Configuration["TwitterAPIKey"];
    twitterOptions.ConsumerSecret = Configuration["TwitterAPISecret"];
    twitterOptions.SaveTokens = true;
});
```

We will update `ExternalLogin.cshtml.cs` to include the retrieved access token and its secret into `AuthenticationProperties`, as shown in Listing 8-7. We update the `OnGetCallbackAsync` and `OnPostConfirmationAsync` methods to create a new instance of `AuthenticationProperties` and hold the `AuthenticationTokens` from the `ExternalLoginInfo` instance, which was retrieved from the Twitter Identity Provider. Then we use the `AuthenticationProperties` instance to sign the user in to the Twitter Bot web application by using the `SignInAsync` method of `SignInManager`.

Listing 8-7. Updated ExternalLogin.cshtml.cs Class

```
/* Code removed for brevity. */
using Microsoft.AspNetCore.Authentication;

namespace TwitterBot.Web.Areas.Identity.Pages.Account
{
    [AllowAnonymous]
```

```csharp
public class ExternalLoginModel : PageModel
{
    /* Code removed for brevity. */

    public async Task<IActionResult> OnGetCallbackAsync(string
    returnUrl = null, string remoteError = null)
    {
        /* Code removed for brevity. */

        var result = await _signInManager.
        ExternalLoginSignInAsync(info.LoginProvider, info.ProviderKey,
        isPersistent: false, bypassTwoFactor : true);
        if (result.Succeeded)
        {
            _logger.LogInformation("{Name} logged in with
            {LoginProvider} provider.", info.Principal.Identity.Name,
            info.LoginProvider);
            var user = await _userManager.FindByLoginAsync(info.
            LoginProvider, info.ProviderKey);

            var props = new AuthenticationProperties();
            props.StoreTokens(info.AuthenticationTokens);

            await _signInManager.SignInAsync(user, props, info.
            LoginProvider);
            return LocalRedirect(returnUrl);
        }

        /* Code removed for brevity. */
    }

    public async Task<IActionResult> OnPostConfirmationAsync(string
    returnUrl = null)
    {
        /* Code removed for brevity. */

        if (ModelState.IsValid)
        {
```

```
        var user = new ApplicationUser { UserName = Input.Email,
        Email = Input.Email };
        var result = await _userManager.CreateAsync(user);
        if (result.Succeeded)
        {
            result = await _userManager.AddLoginAsync(user, info);
            if (result.Succeeded)
            {
                var props = new AuthenticationProperties();
                props.StoreTokens(info.AuthenticationTokens);

                await _signInManager.SignInAsync(user, props,
                authenticationMethod: info.LoginProvider);
                _logger.LogInformation("User created an account
                using {Name} provider.", info.LoginProvider);
                return LocalRedirect(returnUrl);
            }
        }
        foreach (var error in result.Errors)
        {
            ModelState.AddModelError(string.Empty, error.Description);
        }
    }

    /* Code removed for brevity. */
    }
  }
}
```

As we are making HTTP calls to TwitterAzureFunctions from the client-side JavaScript of the Twitter Bot web application, we need to hold the access token and access token secret in client-side hidden fields. We therefore update _SecureLayout.cshtml to hold the access token and secret, as shown in Listing 8-8. We use the AuthenticateAsync method of the HttpContext to retrieve the AuthenticateResult, through which we get the access token and secret values. The access token and secret values are stored in hidden fields, which are used later to retrieve an authentication token from TwitterAzureFunctions. Authentication token is stored in the auth_token hidden field.

Listing 8-8. Updated _SecureLayout.cshtml

```
@using Microsoft.AspNetCore.Authentication;
@{
    Layout = "~/Pages/Shared/_Layout.cshtml";
    var authenticateInfo = await this.Context.AuthenticateAsync();
}

@RenderBody()

<!-- Modal Structure -->
<div id="preferencesModal" class="modal modal-fixed-footer">
    @* Code removed for brevity. *@
    <div class="modal-footer">
        @Html.Hidden("uid", (User.Identity as System.Security.Claims.
        ClaimsIdentity).Claims.FirstOrDefault(p => p.Type == "http://schemas.
        xmlsoap.org/ws/2005/05/identity/claims/nameidentifier").Value)
        @Html.Hidden("access_token", authenticateInfo.Properties.Items[".
        Token.access_token"])
        @Html.Hidden("access_token_secret", authenticateInfo.Properties.
        Items[".Token.access_token_secret"])
        @Html.Hidden("auth_token", "")
        <button type="button" class="waves-effect waves-light btn orange"
        id="btnSave">Save</button>
        <a href="#!" class="modal-close waves-effect waves-green btn-flat"
        id="btnClose">Close</a>
    </div>
</div>
```

Obtaining an Authentication Token and Securely Accessing HTTP Azure Functions

In this section, we obtain the authentication token, populate the auth_token hidden field value, and pass it in all the TwitterAzureFunctions Function app HTTP calls. We create a JavaScript global function in _SecureLayout.cshtml called getAuthToken, as shown in Listing 8-9. The getAuthToken function creates an object with the access_token and access_token_secret properties populated from the respective hidden fields. The Ajax call is made to the /.auth/login/twitter endpoint of TwitterAzureFunctions to retrieve the authentication token and it is stored in the auth_token hidden field. The getAuthToken function is invoked upon loading the secure layout.

The Ajax setup is updated to include the X-ZUMO-AUTH header with the auth_token hidden field value in every HTTP Azure Function call to the TwitterAzureFunctions Function app.

Note   The Ajax call is synchronous to ensure the authentication token is available before the Twitter Bot web application interacts with TwitterAzureFunctions.

Listing 8-9. Updated _SecureLayout.cshtml JavaScript Code

```
@section Scripts{
    <script>
        $(function () {
            // Get auth token for User.
            jQuery.getAuthToken = function getAuthToken() {
                var authObject = {};
                authObject.access_token = $('#access_token').val();
                authObject.access_token_secret = $('#access_token_secret').
                val();
                $.ajax({
                    type: 'POST',
                    url: "@appSettings.Value.AppSettings.ServiceBaseUrl/.
                    auth/login/twitter",
                    data: JSON.stringify(authObject),
                    success: function (data) {
                        $('#auth_token').val(data.authenticationToken);
                    },
                    error: function (xhr, textStatus, errorThrown) {
                        alert('Something went wrong! Please try again
                        later!');
                    },
```

```
            async: false
        });
    };

    jQuery.getAuthToken();

    $.ajaxSetup({
        headers: { 'x-userid': $('#uid').val(), 'X-ZUMO-AUTH':
        $('#auth_token').val() }
    });

    // Modal Configuration
    $('.modal').modal({
        onOpenEnd: function () {
            refreshModal();
        }
    });

    @* Code removed for brevity. *@

    });
    </script>
    @RenderSection("Scripts", required: false)
}
```

We can now publish the TwitterBot.Web project to the Azure environment
and test the entire flow. If we inspect the request headers in the browser's Network
tab, we find x-userid and X-ZUMO-AUTH headers being sent in every request to the
TwitterAzureFunctions Function app, as shown in Figure 8-6.

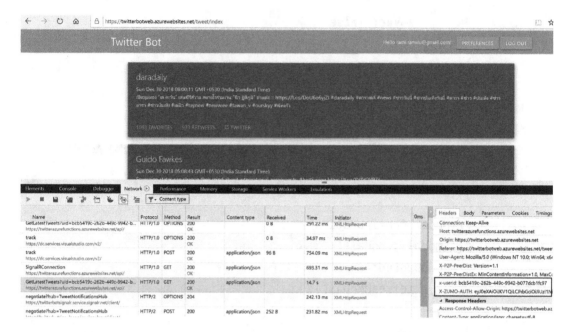

Figure 8-6. *HTTP headers inspection in the browser network tab*

If we use a free web debugging proxy tool like postman, we can test the
TwitterAzureFunctions endpoints by not passing the X-ZUMO-AUTH header. We will get a
401 Unauthorized response, as shown in Figure 8-7.

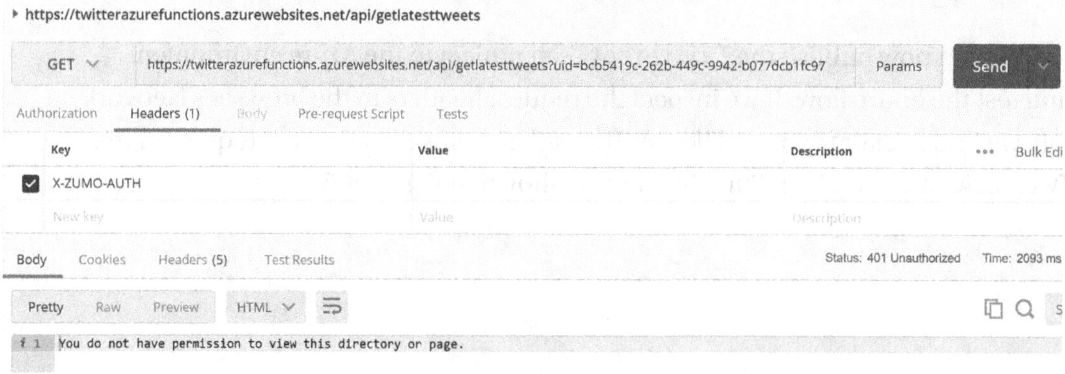

Figure 8-7. *Request testing by not passing the X-ZUMO-AUTH header*

If we pass a valid X-ZUMO-AUTH header, we should see the output in Figure 8-8.

Figure 8-8. *Request testing by passing a valid X-ZUMO-AUTH header*

HTTP Azure Functions of the Twitter Bot application are now secured with App Service authentication. If we want to find the user who invoked the Azure Function, we can inject ClaimsPrincipal into the Azure Function, as shown in Listing 8-10.

Note   Injecting ClaimsPrincipal into the Azure Function should ideally be enough to retrieve the user claims data. But in the current version of Azure Functions, ClaimsPrincipal is not auto populated from the authentication token of the request. The current workaround to populate the ClaimsPrincipal is mentioned on GitHub at https://github.com/Azure/azure-functions-host/issues/33#issuecomment-444366166.

We must first set the AuthorizationLevel of Azure Functions to Anonymous or Function.

Then we must implement API Key Authorization, as mentioned at https://docs.microsoft.com/en-us/azure/azure-functions/functions-bindings-http-webhook#api-key-authorization.

We must pass the master key or default key from the Host Keys section of the Function App settings in a query string parameter and call it code. We do this on every Azure Function HTTP call. For example, when making an HTTP call to the GetLatestTweets function, we would use the https://twitterazurefunctions.azurewebsites. net/api/getlatesttweets?uid=bcb5419c-262b-449c-9942-b077dcb1fc97&code= [Master or Default Key from Host Keys section of Function App Settings] URL.

Hopefully, the next versions of Azure Function will address this issue.

For now, I am not upgrading TwitterAzureFunctions to include a code query string with the master or default key in every HTTP call. You can take this as an exercise and implement it.

Listing 8-10. Updated GetLatestTweets Function Class

```
// Code removed for brevity.
using System.Security.Claims;

namespace TwitterBot.AzureFunctions.Http
{
    public static class GetLatestTweets
    {
        [FunctionName("GetLatestTweets")]
        public static async Task<IActionResult> Run(
            [HttpTrigger(AuthorizationLevel.Anonymous, "get", Route =
            null)] HttpRequest req,
            [Inject]IDocumentDbRepository<User> userRepository,
            [Inject]IDocumentDbRepository<Tweet> tweetRepository,
            [Inject]IOptions<AppSettingsConfiguration> config,
            ClaimsPrincipal principal,
            ILogger log)
        {
            // Use principal to get the user claims.
```

```
        // We can query AspNetIdentity Cosmos DB collection based on
        the claims and retrieve full user details.
        // We can use principal.Identity.IsAuthenticated to check for
        authenticated user.

        // Code removed for brevity.

    }

  }

}
```

Note   Similarly, we can upgrade other functions of the `TwitterAzureFunctions` project. For now, I am not upgrading them.

EXERCISE 1

In this chapter, we have implemented authentication for Azure Functions using the Twitter Identity Provider. As part of this exercise, implement authentication using any other identity provider (such as Google, Azure Active Directory, etc.).

Solution: Using Google Identity Provider, we need to first create a Google project at the Google Console API, as described in `https://docs.microsoft.com/en-us/aspnet/core/security/authentication/social/google-logins?view=aspnetcore-2.2`.

At the time of configuring Google Identity at the ASP.NET Core Web application, we can handle an `OnCreatingTicket` event, as shown in Listing 8-11, which will fetch the `id_token` value. Using `id_token` as the payload, we can call the `/.auth/login/google` endpoint of the Azure Functions to retrieve the authentication token, as described in `https://docs.microsoft.com/en-us/azure/app-service/app-service-authentication-how-to`.

The retrieved authentication token can be passed in the `X-ZUMO-AUTH` header while invoking Azure Functions, which will authenticate the request.

Listing 8-11. Google Identity Provider Configuration at ASP.NET Core Web Application

```
services.AddAuthentication().AddGoogle(googleOptions =>
{
    googleOptions.ClientId = "Client Id";
    googleOptions.ClientSecret = "Client Secret";
    googleOptions.SaveTokens = true;
    googleOptions.Events.OnCreatingTicket = context =>
    {
        var content = context.TokenResponse.Response.ToString();

        // We get id_token in content which we can serialize to strong type.
        // We can make a call to Azure Function's /.auth/login/google
            endpoint using id_token to get authentication token.
        // Store the authentication token in the context.
        // We can use authentication token in X-ZUMO-AUTH header to
            interact with Azure Functions.
         return Task.CompletedTask;
    };
});
```

EXERCISE 2

In this chapter, we integrated the Twitter Bot web application with the TwitterAzureFunctions Function app by passing the X-ZUMO-AUTH header with an authentication token. Sometimes the authentication token can expire and might result in failed HTTP calls. As part of this exercise, develop a JavaScript error callback for Ajax Setup, which will be invoked for failed HTTP calls and renew the authentication token.

Solution: Handle error callback for $.ajaxSetup on _SecureLayout.cshtml.

Summary

You started off this chapter by learning about the importance of securing software applications. Designing software solutions by adhering to security principles not only protects applications from threats, but also improves the overall reputation and trust of these applications. The Twitter Bot application leverages Azure Key Vault to store infrastructure and application secrets. To securely store application settings, the Twitter Bot application relies on the Application Settings configuration of the Azure Function app.

You defined the `AppSettings` configuration section in the `local.settings.json` file of the `TwitterBot.AzureFunctions` project and moved all the configuration values residing in the code to this section. You created the `AppSettingsConfiguration` and `AppSettings` classes and configured the `WebJobsExtensionStartup` class to load the configuration. Then, you injected an `IOptions<AppSettingsConfiguration>` instance into the respective Azure Functions and started using the config values in the code. Finally, you configured the application settings at the `TwitterAzureFunctions` Function app and tested the configuration changes in the Azure environment.

Later in the chapter, you configured App Service Authentication at the `TwitterAzureFunctions` Function app with the Twitter Identity Provider. In the Twitter Bot web application, you configured the Twitter Identity Provider to include an access token and an access token secret in the authentication response, which are later preserved in the `AuthenticationProperties` of the ASP.NET Core Identity.

You updated `_SecureLayout.cshtml` to hold the access token and its secret in hidden fields from `AuthenticationProperties`. You created a JavaScript function to invoke `TwitterAzureFunctions` Function app's `/.auth/login/twitter` endpoint to retrieve an authentication token by passing the access token and its secret. The retrieved auth token is saved in the hidden field and is passed in every HTTP call to `TwitterAzureFunctions` by including it in the `X-ZUMO-AUTH` header. You implemented a known workaround from GitHub to read the user identity claims by injecting `ClaimsPrincipal` into Azure Functions.

Finally, you tested the entire flow by deploying the Azure Functions and web projects to the Azure environment. In the next chapter, you will create unit test cases for Twitter Bot Azure Functions. You will design and implement a Continuous Integration and Continuous Delivery pipeline for the Twitter Bot application by leveraging Azure DevOps.

References

1. https://blog.jongallant.com/2018/01/azure-function-
    config/.

2. https://docs.microsoft.com/en-us/azure/app-service/
    overview-authentication-authorization.

3. https://blogs.msdn.microsoft.com/stuartleeks/2018/02/19/
    azure-functions-and-app-service-authentication/.

CHAPTER 9

Setting Up a Continuous Integration and Continuous Delivery Pipeline for Azure Functions

As we enter a new era of software development, the complexity of business requirements is growing exponentially because of the need to meet the expectations of global audience, which requires collaboration and integration among different systems. With increasing demand for automation and connectivity between business processes, managing and maintaining source code has become increasingly complex. Version control systems play a crucial role in managing and tracking source code artifacts. The technical advancements in code version control systems and tools not only made software development more resilient and effective, but also opened new global opportunities for people across the world to collaborate without worrying about source code dependencies.

Many modern platforms and tools provide Continuous Integration (CI) with various version control repositories, through which we can configure and execute automatic build and test cycles on the source code. *Build* is the process of compiling the source code into an executable package, which can then be used to run the application on a server or a client. *Test* is the automated process of executing unit test cases (for example, xUnit tests) as part of the build to make sure that the source code is properly aligned with its business and technical objectives. *Continuous Integration* ensures good code quality, minimizes the impact of build errors, and automates repetitive tasks.

369

© Rami Vemula 2019
R. Vemula, *Integrating Serverless Architecture*, https://doi.org/10.1007/978-1-4842-4489-0_9

Deployment is another crucial phase of the software development lifecycle, which is almost considered the last step in the process of making software available to end customers and stakeholders. The process of deployment has evolved and matured over the last decade with the invention of sophisticated tools and platforms. Today's deployment pipelines not only provide reliable automation techniques but also improve the overall system performance by reducing build/deployment time with minimal resource consumption. *Continuous Delivery* (CD) is the process of propagating a successful build output to different environments such as test, staging, and production.

Continuous Integration and Continuous Delivery together formulate a strong pipeline that's required to deliver software solutions with less operational effort and minimal errors. So far in this book, we have designed and developed the Twitter Bot application by leveraging Azure Functions with the Azure Web App Service as the frontend. As the last step in making the application available to end customers, we cover the following topics in this chapter:

- Create unit test cases for Azure Functions with the xUnit.Net framework.

- Manage the source code of the Twitter Bot solution using Azure DevOps (previously known as Visual Studio Team Services).

- Design and build an end-to-end CI/CD pipeline for the Twitter Bot solution.

Creating Unit Tests for Twitter Azure Functions

In this section, we create unit test cases for the `TwitterBot.AzureFunctions` project using xUnit.Net. Unit test cases not only help developers identify design mishaps and edge cases at early stages of development, but also provide better control on code quality. xUnit.Net is a free, open source, community-based, unit-testing framework for solutions built using .NET Framework and .NET Core. Developed by James Newkirk and Brad Wilson, xUnit is the latest framework for unit testing in C#, F#, VB.NET, and other .NET languages. It is part of the .NET Foundation and provides an exhaustive API for writing unit test cases. Its test runner can be easily integrated with Visual Studio and automated build systems. We will use Moq as the mocking framework through which we will mock the function dependencies.

Note   We can always follow Test Driven Development (TDD) for Azure Functions,
which is a widely accepted model for identifying design and technical gaps much
before the development of a function. TDD is out of the scope of this book, but
this chapter will familiarize you with the basic concepts of unit tests for Azure
Functions.

Let's get started by creating a new xUnit test project (.NET Core) called
TwitterBot.Tests in the TwitterBot solution, as shown in Figure 9-1.

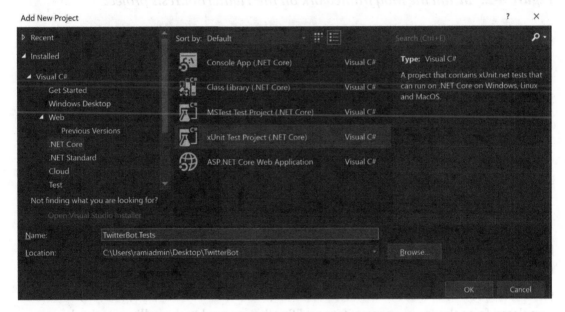

Figure 9-1. *New xUnit test project in the TwitterBot solution*

Install the Moq framework on the `TwitterBot.Tests` project, as shown in Figure 9-2.

Figure 9-2. *Install the Moq framework on the TwitterBot.Tests project*

Add the `TwitterBot.AzureFunctions` and `TwitterBot.Framework` project references to the `TwitterBot.Tests` project. Delete the default `UnitTest1` class.

Note   In this section, we write unit tests for the `GetLatestTweets` Azure Function. You can follow the same approach and write unit test cases for other functions.

Add a new folder called `Helpers` and create a class called `HttpTestHelper`. We are going to hold all the helper classes related to tests in the `Helpers` folder. `HttpTestHelper` will have a `CreateHttpRequest` method, as shown in Listing 9-1. The `CreateHttpRequest` method will take `url`, `method`, `headers`, and `body` as parameters and create an `HttpRequest` object from `DefaultHttpContext`. The `HttpRequest` object is populated from the inputs parameters and finally returned to the calling method.

Listing 9-1. HttpTestHelper Class

```
using Microsoft.AspNetCore.Http;
using Microsoft.AspNetCore.Http.Features;
using System;
using System.Text;
using System.IO;

namespace TwitterBot.Tests.Helpers
{
    public class HttpTestHelper
```

```
{
    public static HttpRequest CreateHttpRequest(string url, string
    method, IHeaderDictionary headers = null, string body = null)
    {
        var uri = new Uri(url);
        var request = new DefaultHttpContext().Request;
        var requestFeature = request.HttpContext.Features.
        Get<IHttpRequestFeature>();
        requestFeature.Method = method;
        requestFeature.Scheme = uri.Scheme;
        requestFeature.Path = uri.GetComponents(UriComponents.
        KeepDelimiter | UriComponents.Path, UriFormat.Unescaped);
        requestFeature.PathBase = string.Empty;
        requestFeature.QueryString = uri.GetComponents(UriComponents.
        KeepDelimiter | UriComponents.Query, UriFormat.Unescaped);

        headers = headers ?? new HeaderDictionary();

        if (!string.IsNullOrEmpty(uri.Host))
        {
            headers.Add("Host", uri.Host);
        }

        if (body != null)
        {
            byte[] bytes = Encoding.UTF8.GetBytes(body);
            requestFeature.Body = new MemoryStream(bytes);
            request.ContentLength = request.Body.Length;
            headers.Add("Content-Length", request.Body.Length.ToString());
        }

        requestFeature.Headers = headers;

        return request;
    }
}
}
```

Create a class called GetLatestTweetsFunctionTests. It is going to hold the test cases of the GetLatestTweets function, as shown in Listing 9-2. We create the mock instances of IDocumentDbRepository<User>, IDocumentDbRepository<Tweet>, IOptions<AppSettingsConfiguration>, and ILogger and instantiate them in the constructor. We also create the ClaimsPrincipal instance and set it to null (as we are not using it in the GetLatestTweets function).

Create two test cases called GetLatestTweets_Null_User_Test and GetLatestTweets_Null_Hashtags_Test. Both methods are decorated with the Fact attribute from the xUnit framework to get identified as test cases. These tests will execute the GetLatestTweets function for a null response when the user or his hashtags are not available. We set up the IDocumentDbRepository<User>'s TopAsync method using the Moq framework to return the appropriate test data, i.e., in the first test, we return an empty user list, and in the second test, we return a single user with empty hashtags. We invoke the Run method of the GetLatestTweets function with all the dependent objects and assert the function's result with a null object.

Listing 9-2. GetLatestTweetsFunctionTests Class

```
using Microsoft.AspNetCore.Mvc;
using Microsoft.Extensions.Logging;
using Microsoft.Extensions.Options;
using Moq;
using System;
using System.Collections.Generic;
using System.Linq;
using System.Linq.Expressions;
using System.Security.Claims;
using System.Threading.Tasks;
using TwitterBot.AzureFunctions.Http;
using TwitterBot.Framework.Configuration;
using TwitterBot.Framework.Contracts.Data;
using TwitterBot.Framework.Types;
using TwitterBot.Tests.Helpers;
using Xunit;
```

```
namespace TwitterBot.Tests
{
    public class GetLatestTweetsFunctionTests
    {
        private readonly Mock<IDocumentDbRepository<User>> mockUserRepository;
        private readonly Mock<IDocumentDbRepository<Tweet>> mockTweetRepository;
        private readonly Mock<IOptions<AppSettingsConfiguration>> mockConfig;
        private readonly ClaimsPrincipal principal;
        private readonly Mock<ILogger> mockLogger;
        private readonly string UserId;
        public GetLatestTweetsFunctionTests()
        {
            mockUserRepository = new Mock<IDocumentDbRepository<User>>();
            mockTweetRepository = new Mock<IDocumentDbRepository<Tweet>>();
            mockConfig = new Mock<IOptions<AppSettingsConfiguration>>();
            principal = null;
            mockLogger = new Mock<ILogger>();
            UserId = "bcb5419c-262b-449c-9942-b077dcb1fc97";

            mockConfig.Setup(p => p.Value).Returns(new AppSettingsConfiguration
            {
                AppSettings = new AppSettings { TweetsFilterIntervalInDays = 1 }
            });
        }

        [Fact]
        public async Task GetLatestTweets_Null_User_Test()
        {
            var users = new List<User>();
            mockUserRepository.Setup(p => p.TopAsync(It.IsAny<Expression
            <Func<User, bool>>>(), It.IsAny<int>())).ReturnsAsync(users.
            AsQueryable());

            var result = await GetLatestTweets.Run(
                HttpTestHelper.CreateHttpRequest(string.Format("https://
                localhost/api/getlatesttweets?uid={0}", UserId), "GET"),
                mockUserRepository.Object,
```

```
            mockTweetRepository.Object,
            mockConfig.Object,
            principal,
            mockLogger.Object
            );

        var jsonObject = (JsonResult) result;
        Assert.Null(jsonObject.Value);
    }

    [Fact]
    public async Task GetLatestTweets_Null_Hashtags_Test()
    {
        var users = new List<User> { new User { UserId = UserId } };
        mockUserRepository.Setup(p => p.TopAsync(It.IsAny
        <Expression<Func<User, bool>>>(), It.IsAny<int>())).
        ReturnsAsync(users.AsQueryable());

        var result = await GetLatestTweets.Run(
            HttpTestHelper.CreateHttpRequest(string.Format("https://
            localhost/api/getlatesttweets?uid={0}", UserId), "GET"),
            mockUserRepository.Object,
            mockTweetRepository.Object,
            mockConfig.Object,
            principal,
            mockLogger.Object
            );

        var jsonObject = (JsonResult)result;
        Assert.Null(jsonObject.Value);
    }
    }
}
```

Now we build the entire solution and run the tests from Visual Studio Test Explorer
(Test Menu ➤ Windows ➤ Test Explorer), as shown in Figure 9-3.

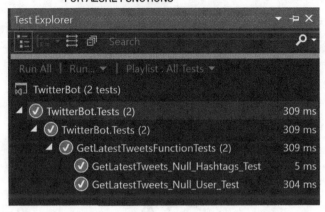

Figure 9-3. *Test cases executed in Visual Studio*

Note   In a similar way, we can cover all the possible test cases for the
GetLatestTweets function. We can also continue writing unit test cases for other
functions using a similar approach.

Designing a Continuous Integration and Continuous Delivery Pipeline

Continuous Integration (CI) and Continuous Delivery (CD) are the key DevOps practices
in the modern-day application deployment strategy. These operations prevent manual
effort and repetitive tasks on every build, and thereby reduce the possibility of human
errors, improve the build quality, and improve the overall efficiency of the software
development lifecycle.

The Continuous Integration and Continuous Delivery (CI/CD) pipeline for the
Twitter Bot application is depicted in Figure 9-4. Upon successful completion of a
feature, the developer checks the code in to the Azure DevOps source code repository.
As part of the check-in, Azure DevOps triggers a build to validate the source code and
executes the xUnit test cases. If the build fails, the check-in will be rejected, and the
developer should fix the build/test issues and retrigger the check-in. Upon a successful
build, a deployment package will be created and stored in the build staging directory for
further processing by release management.

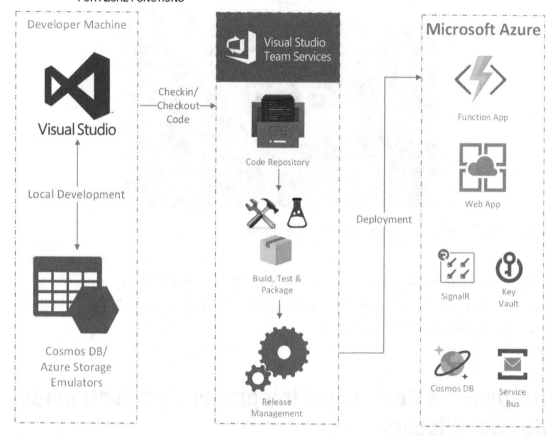

Figure 9-4. *Continuous Integration and Continuous Delivery pipeline for the Twitter Bot application*

At this point, authorized personnel can manually trigger the release pipeline, which picks up the build packages and deploys them to the Azure Function app and Azure Web app. We can also control the behavior of the release pipeline between the manual and automatic triggers.

- Automatic deployments are useful for lower environments like development, staging etc., where the latest code should be packaged, deployed, and tested quickly by dev and test teams.

- Manual deployments are useful for production workloads where the selective build should be deployed to a live environment after thorough testing.

Note   Creating and configuring build and release definitions are important steps
for a successful CI/CD pipeline. We create definitions in the coming sections of this
chapter.

Managing Source Code Using Azure DevOps

In this section, we create an Azure DevOps account and manage the Twitter Bot
application's source code using an Azure Repo. Azure DevOps is a collection of services
from Microsoft through which developers can collaborate and develop solutions. The
following are the important features of Azure DevOps:

- Support for Git-based and Team Foundation Version Control (TFVC)
  repositories for versioning source code.

- Build and release pipelines for Continuous Integration and
  Continuous Delivery.

- Agile tools to support planning and tracking tasks, code defects, and
  issues using Kanban and Scrum methods.

- Testing tools for manual/exploratory testing, load testing, and
  continuous testing.

- Dashboards, boards, and wikis.

Creating a New Azure DevOps Project

In this section, we create a new Azure DevOps project for the Twitter Bot
application source code. Let's get started by creating a new Azure DevOps account.
Visit https://azure.microsoft.com/en-in/services/devops/ and click on Start Free.
Log in with your Microsoft account.

Note   If you don't have a Microsoft account, you can create one
at https://signup.live.com.

Upon successful login, you need to accept the Azure DevOps terms and conditions
shown in Figure 9-5. Click Continue to create the account.

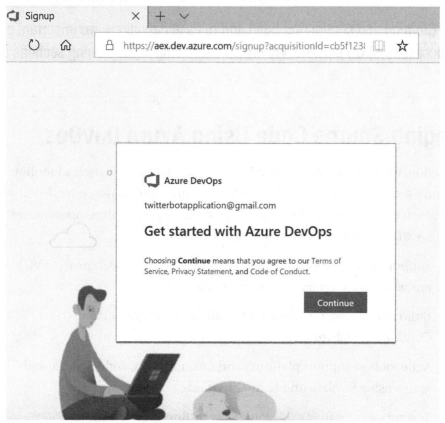

Figure 9-5. *Azure DevOps terms and conditions*

Now we can create a new project by visiting `https://dev.azure.com/`, as shown
in Figure 9-6. Enter the project name as `TwitterBotApplication` and add a suitable
description. Set the visibility status of the project to `Private` to prevent unauthorized
access. Select `Team Foundation Version Control` as the version control mechanism
and `Agile` as the Work Item process. Click on Create Project.

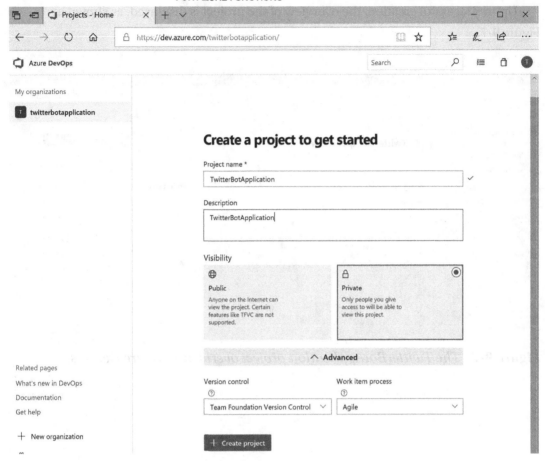

Figure 9-6. *Create a new project at Azure DevOps*

Note You can also choose Git over Team Foundation Version Control as the
version control mechanism. Similarly, you can opt for Scrum or Capability
Maturity Model Integration (CMMI) configuration for the Work Item process. These
options should be carefully selected by evaluating the business and operational
requirements.

I like both TFVC and GIT for their own features. There are no specific reasons for
not using Git.

Upon successful creation, the overview of the project is displayed, as shown in Figure 9-7.

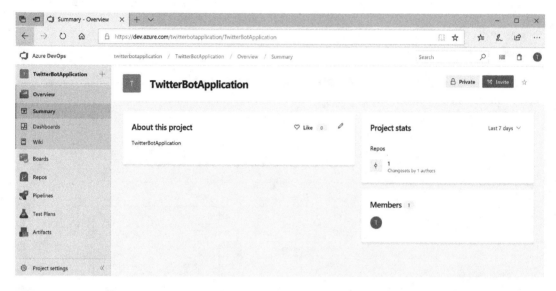

Figure 9-7. *The TwitterBotApplication project overview at Azure DevOps*

Configuring Visual Studio with an Azure DevOps Project

In this section, we configure Visual Studio to connect with the Azure DevOps project and map the project to a local directory. Open Visual Studio and navigate to the Team Explorer (View Menu ➤ Team Explorer), as shown in Figure 9-8.

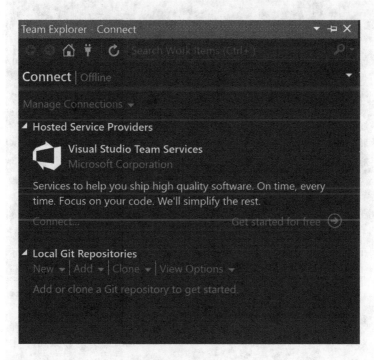

Figure 9-8. Team Explorer in Visual Studio

Click on the Connect option of the Visual Studio Team Services section (under Hosted Service Providers). The Connect to a Project popup will be displayed. From the hosted repositories options, select Add an Account… to log in to the Azure DevOps account, as shown in Figure 9-9.

Figure 9-9. *Add an Azure DevOps account from Visual Studio*

Upon successful login to the Azure DevOps account, we should see the
TwitterBotApplication project, as shown in Figure 9-10. Click on Connect.

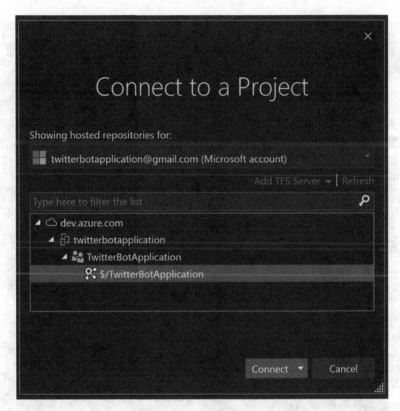

Figure 9-10. *The TwitterBotApplication project under the Azure DevOps account*

Upon successful connection with the TwitterBotApplication project, Visual Studio
Team Explorer will display the project, as shown in Figure 9-11.

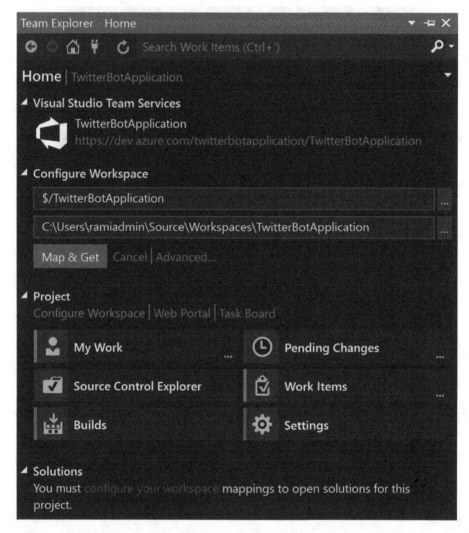

Figure 9-11. *TwitterBotApplication project under Team Explorer*

Click the Map & Get button under the Configure Workspace section to configure
the TwitterBotApplication project with a specific local path. Navigate to the mapped
location and create the Source folder and then the Main folder (under the Source folder).
Place the TwitterBot folder (with all projects) under the Main folder, as shown in
Figure 9-12.

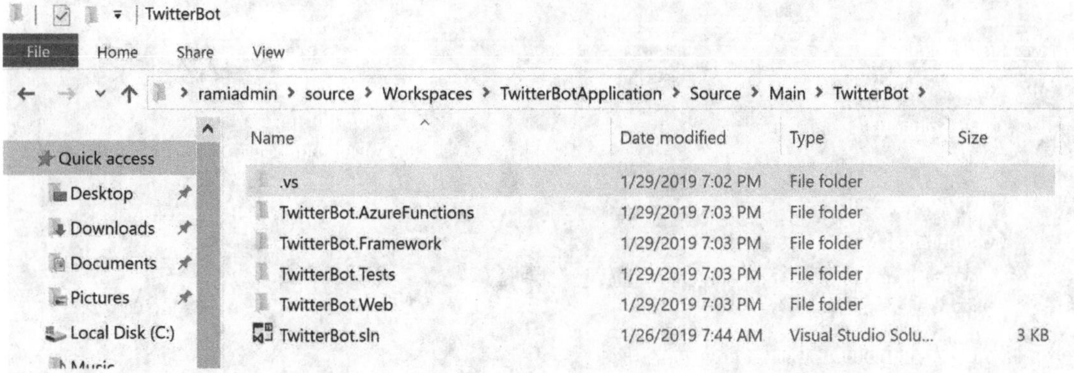

Figure 9-12. *TwitterBotApplication project source code folder structure*

The Source folder will be the parent for all code artifacts. The Main folder will hold
the source code version currently in production. Soon we will convert the Main folder
to a branch and all the production builds will be taken from the main branch. We can
create any number of branches from the main branch to support different phases of
testing, such as System Integration Testing, User Acceptance Testing, etc. Finally, the
verified and certified code versions from all the branches will be merged to the main
branch, which will eventually make it to production deployment.

Note   Branches are extremely useful to support development and testing
activities in parallel. When different teams are working on different releases of
the same application in parallel, branches serve as a logical boundary for code
segregation.

Checking In Source Code to the Azure Repository

In this section, we check in the source code of the Twitter Bot application to the Azure
DevOps project. Open the TwitterBot solution in Visual Studio from the Source/Main/
TwitterBot folder location. Right-click the solution and select the Add Solution to
Source Control... option, as shown in Figure 9-13.

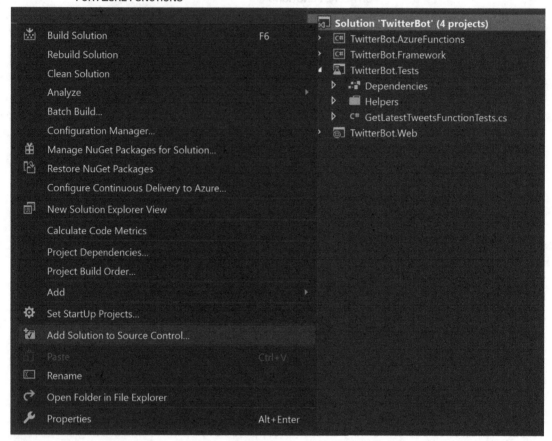

Figure 9-13. *Add the TwitterBot Visual Studio solution to the source control*

Note   While adding the solution to the source control, Visual Studio might prompt you with warnings about xUnit DLLs not getting added to the source control. Click Ignore on each prompt.

Now we can see the TwitterBot solution being tracked by source control, as shown in Figure 9-14.

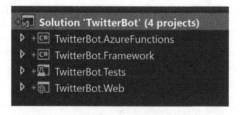

Figure 9-14. *The TwitterBot solution being tracked by source control*

Right-click on the solution and select the check-in option, which will navigate to the
Pending Changes tab of the Team Explorer, as shown in Figure 9-15. Enter a comment
for the check-in and click on the Check In button. You will be prompted for a check-in
confirmation. Upon confirmation, all the files displayed under the Included Changes
section will be committed to the `TwitterBotApplication` Azure DevOps repository.

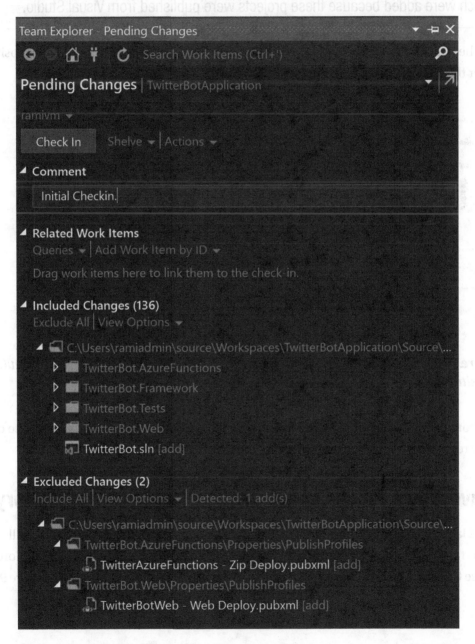

Figure 9-15. *Pending Changes tab of Team Explorer*

Note   We can exclude the files and folders that we don't want to check in to source control. Under the Included Changes section, right-click on the file/folder that you want to exclude and select the Exclude option. I excluded the publish profile folders of the `TwitterBot.AzureFunctions` and `TwitterBot.Web` projects, which were added because these projects were published from Visual Studio.

The checked-in source code can be found in the `TwitterBotApplication` repository, under the Files section of the Repos tab, as shown in Figure 9-16.

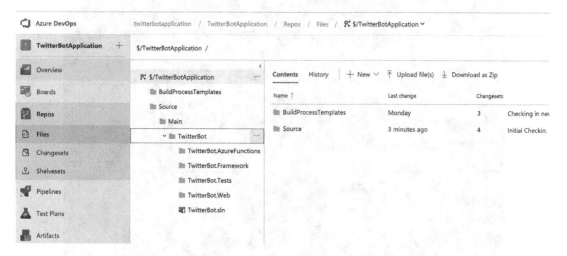

Figure 9-16. *Checked-in source code in the TwitterBotApplication Azure DevOps repository*

From now on, we can start making changes to the source code and check in the code to the repository by following the process mentioned so far in this section.

Converting a Folder to a Branch in the Azure Repository

As the last step in managing source code with the Azure DevOps repository, we will convert the Main folder to a branch. Open the Source Control Explorer (Team Explorer ➤ Source Control Explorer), and you should see the project structure shown in Figure 9-17.

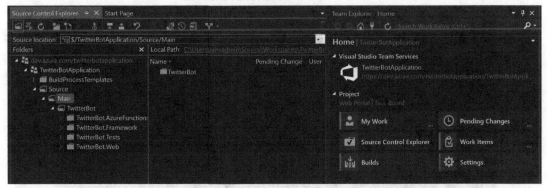

Figure 9-17. *The TwitterBot solution structure under the Source Control Explorer*

Note   Converting the `Main` folder to a branch is a completely optional step.
If you do not want to convert the `Main` folder to a branch, you can skip the rest
of this section.

Right-click the `Main` folder and select the Branching and Merging option. Click on
Convert to Branch, as shown in Figure 9-18.

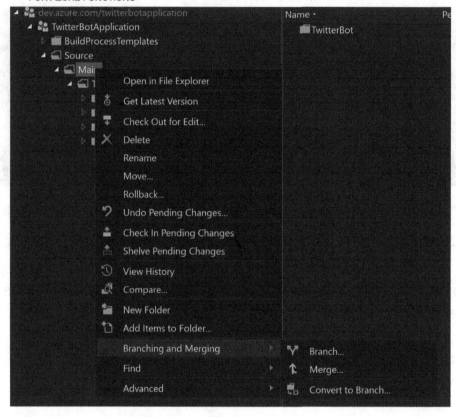

Figure 9-18. *The Convert to Branch option in the Source Control Explorer*

A Convert Folder to Branch popup will be prompted to capture the Owner and
Description of the branch. Leave the default values and click on Convert, as shown in
Figure 9-19.

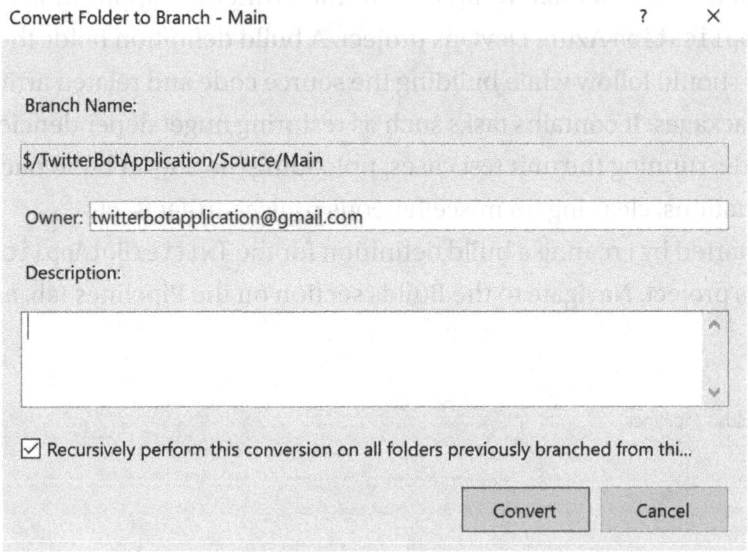

Convert Folder to Branch - Main   ?   ×

Branch Name:

$/TwitterBotApplication/Source/Main

Owner: twitterbotapplication@gmail.com

Description:

☑ Recursively perform this conversion on all folders previously branched from thi...

Convert   Cancel

Figure 9-19. *Convert Folder to Branch popup*

Finally, the Main folder will be converted to a branch (identified with a different
icon), as shown in Figure 9-20.

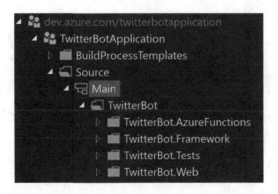

Figure 9-20. *Main branch of the TwitterBot solution*

Creating a Build Definition for the Twitter Bot Solution

In this section, we create a Build Definition for the Twitter Bot application in the
TwitterBotApplication Azure DevOps project. A build definition holds the tasks that
a build server should follow while building the source code and related artifacts into
meaningful packages. It contains tasks such as restoring nuget dependencies, building
the source code, running the unit test cases, uploading the output build packages to
specific destinations, cleaning up miscellaneous project artifacts, etc.

Let's get started by creating a build definition for the TwitterBotApplication
Azure DevOps project. Navigate to the Builds section on the Pipelines tab, as shown in
Figure 9-21.

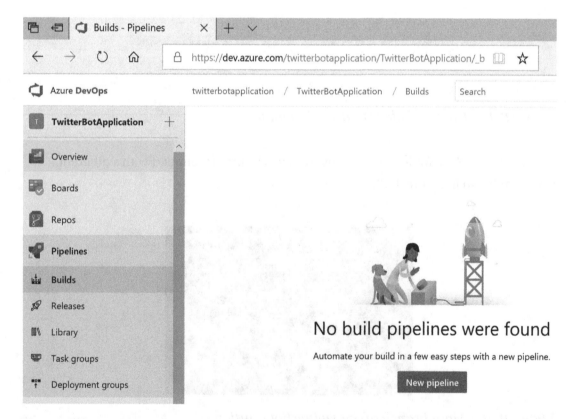

Figure 9-21. *The Builds section under the Pipelines tab of the
TwitterBotApplication DevOps project*

Click on the New Pipeline button, which will take us to the Source Code repository
selection page, as shown in Figure 9-22.

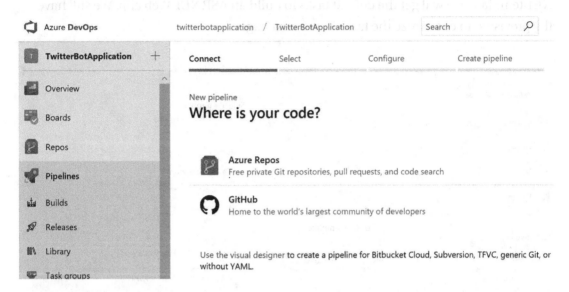

Figure 9-22.   *Source Code Repository selection*

As we are using Team Foundation Version Control (TFVC), click on the Use the
Visual Designer link, which will navigate to the Select a Source screen. Select TFVC as
the source and make sure the server path is set to $/TwitterBotApplication under the
Workspace mappings section, as shown in Figure 9-23. Click Continue.

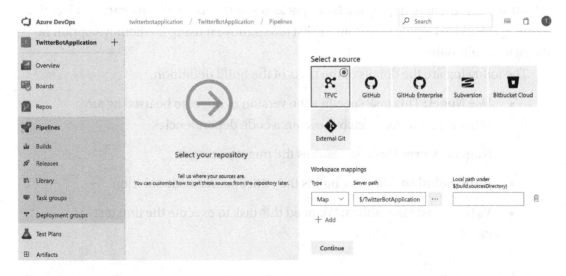

Figure 9-23.   *Source code repository selection and configuring workspace mappings*

On the Select a Template screen, select the Azure Web App for ASP.NET template and click the Apply button, as shown in Figure 9-24. By selecting Azure Web App for ASP. NET template, we will get the default tasks to build an ASP.NET Web app. We still have the provision to customize the tasks in the next page.

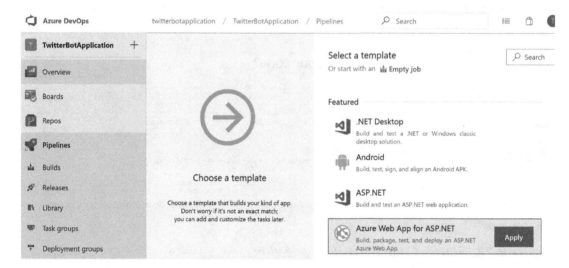

Figure 9-24. *Selecting the Azure Web App for ASP.NET template for the build definition*

On the next page, we can see all the tasks of the build definition, as shown in Figure 9-25. We do not require the Azure App Service Deploy task, as we are going to use release management to deploy the build packages to the Azure environment. Select the Azure App Service Deploy task from the list and remove it using the Remove option in the right details pane.

The following are the details of the tasks of the build definition.

- **Use Nuget:** This task specifies the version of nuget to be used by any other Nuget tasks to fetch the source code dependencies.

- **Nuget restore:** This task restores the nuget packages.

- **Build Solution:** This task builds the entire source code solution.

- **VsTest – testAssemblies:** We need this task to execute the unit test cases.

- **Publish symbols path:** This task enables us to use the .PDB symbol
  files to debug an app on a machine other than the one you used to
  build the app.

- **Publish Artifact: drop:** This task is useful to drop the build packages
  to a specific location.

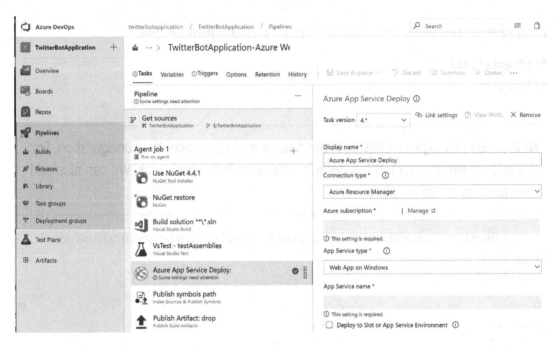

Figure 9-25. *Default tasks in the build definition*

Update the Build Solution task's MSBuild Arguments, as shown in Listing 9-3. The
GenerateProjectSpecificOutputFolder attribute is used to generate project-specific
build packages, which can be independently deployed to respective Azure services. In
the Twitter Bot application, we will get separate packages for Web and Azure functions
projects.

Listing 9-3. MSBuild Arguments of the Build Solution Task

```
/p:DeployOnBuild=true /p:WebPublishMethod=Package
/p:PackageAsSingleFile=true /p:SkipInvalidConfigurations=true
/p:PackageLocation="$(build.artifactstagingdirectory)\\"
/p:GenerateProjectSpecificOutputFolder=true
```

Under the VsTest – testAssemblies task, update the Test Files location, as shown in Listing 9-4. The new path - ***tests*.dll will make the test runner execute all the tests from all the DLLs that have tests in their name. Unit test cases for the Twitter Bot application are written under the TwitterBot.Tests project, which will be compiled to the TwitterBot.Tests.dll file and therefore will be picked up by the test runner to execute tests.

Listing 9-4. Test Files Location of VsTest - testAssemblies Task

***tests*.dll
!**\obj**

Note   You can explore individual build tasks and customize the configuration. For the sake of simplicity, I left the default options as is for each task. We can also add new tasks with the + option.

The final list of tasks used for the TwitterBotApplication project are shown in Figure 9-26.

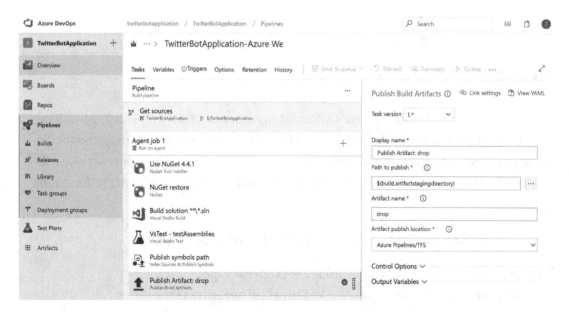

Figure 9-26. *Tasks in the build definition*

Now navigate to the Triggers tab and add a path filter, as shown in Figure 9-27.
A path filter is required to enable Continuous Integration. Specify the Type as Include
and the Path specification as $/TwitterBotApplication, which is used to trigger a
build when files in the specified path are modified. Make sure to enable the Continuous
Integration option.

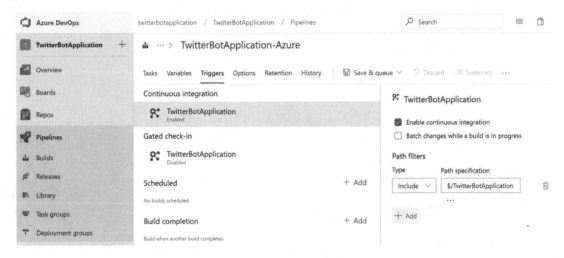

Figure 9-27. *Path filter for Continuous Integration*

We can enable the Gated Check-in option, which will trigger a build on every
check-in. Figure 9-28 shows this option.

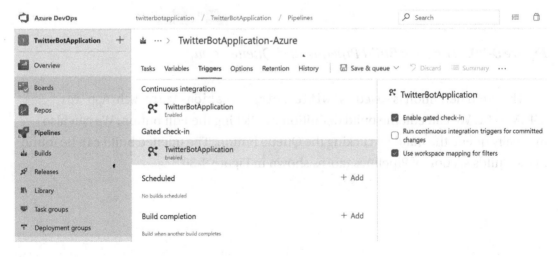

Figure 9-28. *Enable Gated Check-in*

Click on Save & Queue to save the build definition and immediately trigger a build on the source code. Leave the default values on the Save Build Pipeline and Queue Popup and then click Save & Queue, as shown in Figure 9-29.

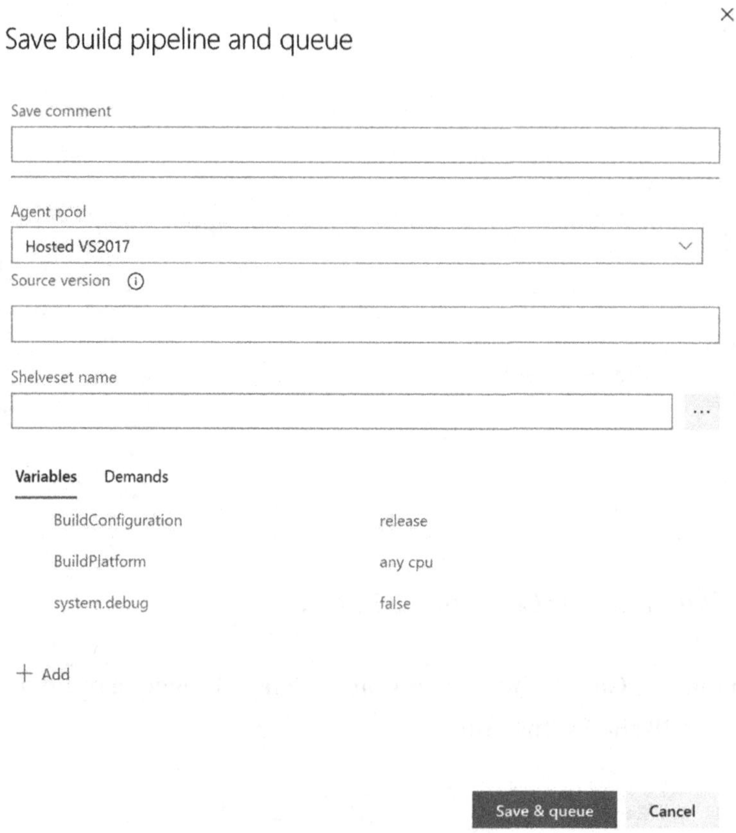

Save build pipeline and queue   ×

Save comment

Agent pool

Hosted VS2017   ∨

Source version   ⓘ

Shelveset name

                                                                      ...

Variables   Demands

        BuildConfiguration   release

        BuildPlatform   any cpu

        system.debug   false

    + Add

                                        Save & queue   Cancel

Figure 9-29. *The Save Build Pipeline and Queue popup*

The build definition is saved as `TwitterBotApplication-Azure Web App for ASP.NET-CI`. We can edit the build definition by clicking the Edit button. We can also manually queue the build by clicking the Queue button. The queued build can be found in the Builds section of Pipelines tab, as shown in Figure 9-30.

Figure 9-30. *Queued build in the Builds section*

We can view the build details by clicking on the build, as shown in Figure 9-31. We
can see that the build got succeeded with all tasks marked as succeeded.

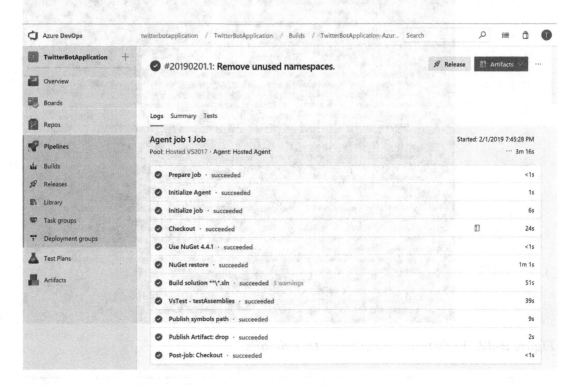

Figure 9-31. *Build details in the Builds section*

The individual task details can be explored by clicking on the specific task. For example, we can see the VsTest – testAssemblies task details, as shown in Figure 9-32. We can see two tests were executed and that there are no failed test cases (line 59).

Figure 9-32. *VsTest – testAssemblies task details*

Note   If we check Build Solution task details, we can see the build process created the `TwitterBot.Web.zip` and `TwitterBot.AzureFunctions.zip` packages as build output. In the next section, we create a release pipeline, which will pick up these packages and deploy them to the Azure Web app and the Azure Functions app.

Release Management for the Twitter Bot Solution

In this section, we create a release pipeline for the Twitter Bot application in the TwitterBotApplication Azure DevOps project. Using the release pipeline, we can either manually or automatically deploy the build packages to a target environment. For the Twitter Bot application, we will deploy the build packages created by the build definition to the TwitterBotWeb Azure Web app and the TwitterAzureFunctions Azure Function app.

Creating a Service Connection Between Azure DevOps and Cloud Accounts

Before we start creating a release pipeline for the Twitter Bot application, we need to establish a connection between the Azure DevOps account to the Azure Cloud Subscription. Navigate to Project Settings (bottom-left option) and click on Service Connections under the Pipelines section, as shown in Figure 9-33.

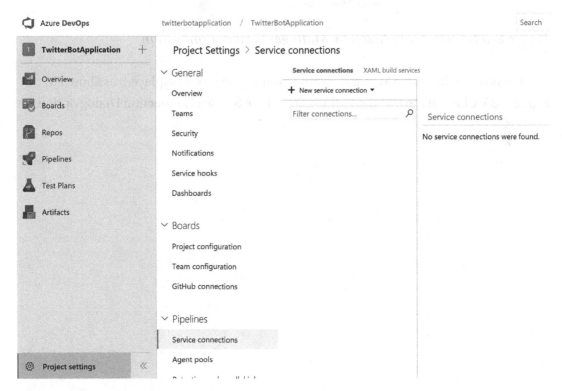

Figure 9-33. *Azure DevOps Service Connections*

Note   If the Azure DevOps account has its own Azure Cloud Subscription, we can
skip the following tasks and directly navigate to creating the release pipeline. If the
Azure DevOps account doesn't have its own Azure Cloud subscription, we need to
add a Service Connection using a Service Principal.

Click on the New Service Connection option. Select the Azure Resource Manager
option, as shown in Figure 9-34.

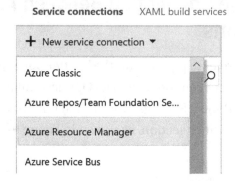

Figure 9-34. *New Azure Resource Manager Service Connection*

A new Azure Resource Manager Connection dialog box is displayed, as shown in
Figure 9-35. Click on the Use the Full Version of the Service Connection Dialog option.

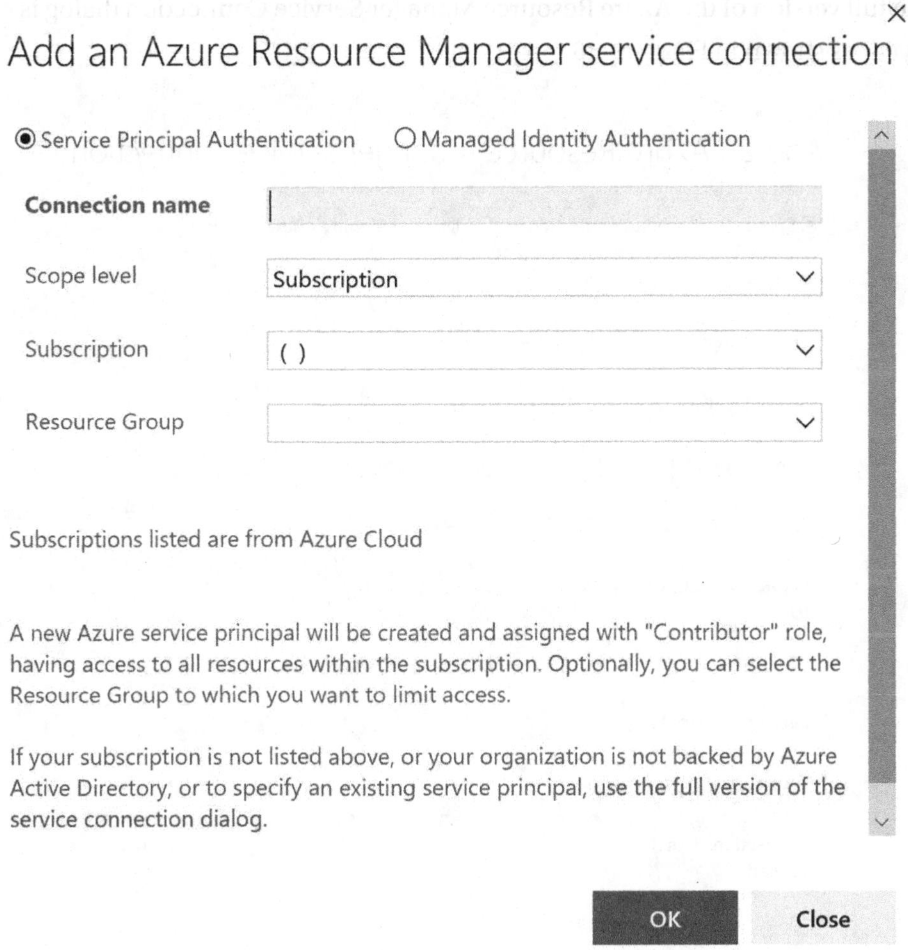

Add an Azure Resource Manager service connection

◉ Service Principal Authentication   ○ Managed Identity Authentication

Connection name

| Scope level | Subscription ⌄ |

| Subscription | ( ) ⌄ |

| Resource Group | ⌄ |

Subscriptions listed are from Azure Cloud

A new Azure service principal will be created and assigned with "Contributor" role, having access to all resources within the subscription. Optionally, you can select the Resource Group to which you want to limit access.

If your subscription is not listed above, or your organization is not backed by Azure Active Directory, or to specify an existing service principal, use the full version of the service connection dialog.

OK   Close

Figure 9-35. *New Azure Resource Manager Service Connection dialog*

The full version of the Azure Resource Manager Service Connection dialog is
displayed, as shown in Figure 9-36.

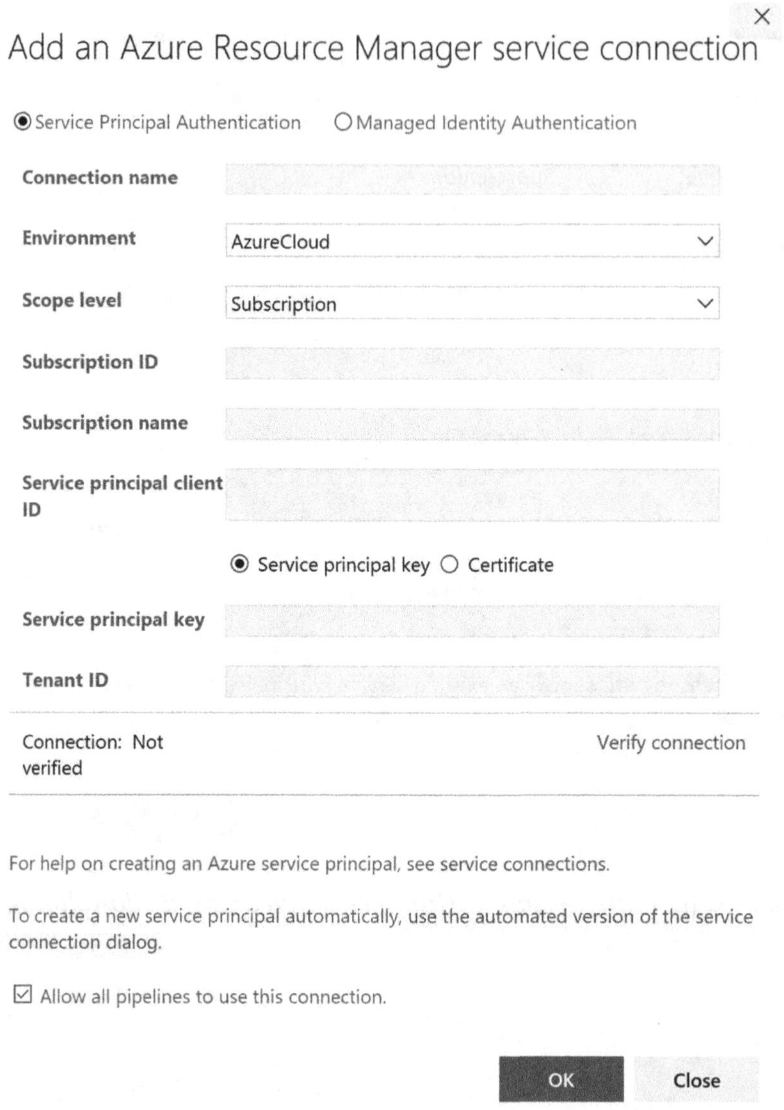

Figure 9-36. *Full version of Azure Resource Manager Service Connection
dialog*

We need to name the connection. Fill in the Subscription ID and Subscription
Name fields with the details of the Azure subscription. We need to create a new Azure
Application Registration in the Azure Subscription to get the Service Principal Client ID

and Service Principal Key. The Tenant ID can be populated with the Directory ID of the
Azure Active Directory.

To fetch the subscription ID and name, navigate to the Azure portal and log in to the
subscription. Under the All Services ➤ General ➤ Subscriptions section, we can find the
Subscription name and ID, as shown in Figure 9-37.

Figure 9-37. *Azure subscription ID and name*

To get the Tenant ID, navigate to the All Services ➤ Identity ➤ Azure Active Directory
section. Select the Properties tab. You can then see the Directory ID, as shown in
Figure 9-38.

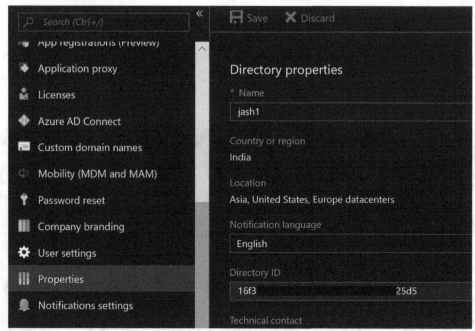

Figure 9-38. *Azure Active Directory ID*

To create a new application registration, click on the App Registrations tab of the Azure Active Directory, as shown in Figure 9-39.

Figure 9-39. *App Registrations in the Azure Active Directory*

Click on the New Application Registration option. Enter TwitterBotDevOps as the name, http://VisualStudio/SPN as the sign-on URL (can be an arbitrary value), and Web App/API as the application type, as shown in Figure 9-40. Click on Create.

Figure 9-40. *New App Registration in the Azure Active Directory*

The Service Principal Client ID is the Application ID of the `TwitterBotDevOps` app registration, as shown in Figure 9-41.

Figure 9-41. *Application ID of TwitterBotDevOps app registration*

To retrieve the Service Principal Key, click on the Settings of the TwitterBotDevOps app registration and navigate to the Keys section. Under the Passwords section, enter DevOps as the description and a valid expiry date. Click on Save. You will get the key value, which will serve as the Service Principal Key, as shown in Figure 9-42.

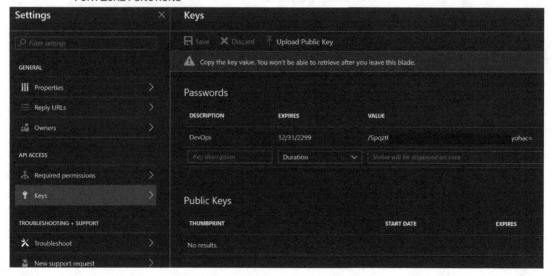

Figure 9-42. *Service Principal Key of the TwitterBotDevOps app registration*

As the last step, we need to give the appropriate permissions for the
TwitterBotDevOps app in the the Azure subscription. Navigate to the All Services ➤
Subscriptions ➤ Access Control (IAM) tab, as shown in Figure 9-43.

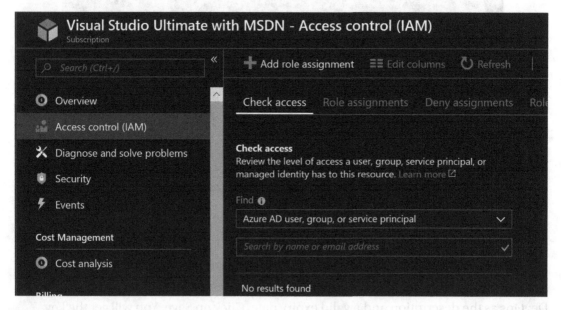

Figure 9-43. *Access Control tab of the Azure Subscription*

Click on the + Add Role Assignment option. Enter `Contributor` as the role, `Azure
AD User, Group, Or Service Principal` for the Assign Access To option, and
`TwitterBotDevOps` as the member, as shown in Figure 9-44. Click on Save.

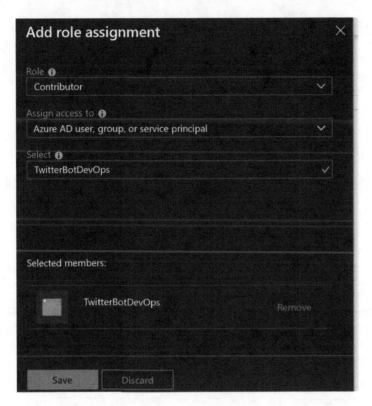

Figure 9-44. *Role assignment for TwitterBotDevOps app registration*

Now we will complete the Azure Resource Manager Service Connection in the
Azure DevOps project. Enter all the details and click on Verify Connection, as shown in
Figure 9-45. With all the correct details, the connection should be verified successfully.
Click OK.

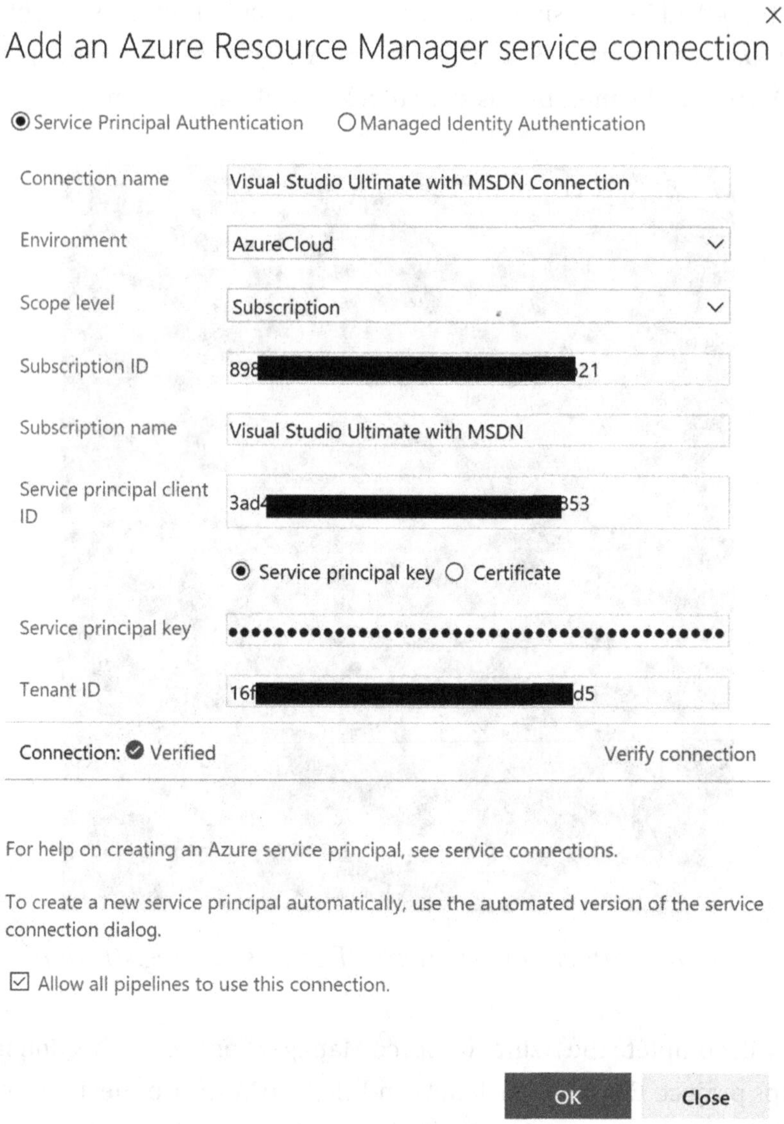

Figure 9-45. *New Azure Resource Manager Service Connection*

We should see the new service connection in the Service Connections section, as shown in Figure 9-46.

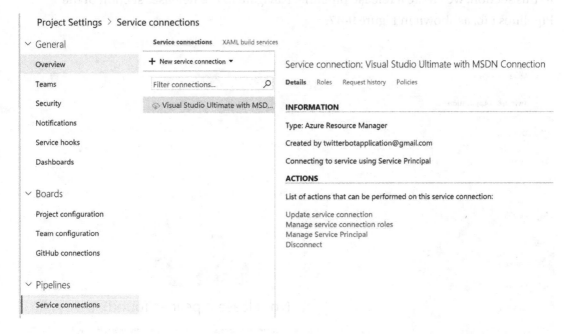

Figure 9-46. *Created Azure Resource Manager Service Connection*

Creating a Release Pipeline at Azure DevOps

In this section, we create a release pipeline. Navigate to the Releases section of the Pipelines tab, as shown in Figure 9-47.

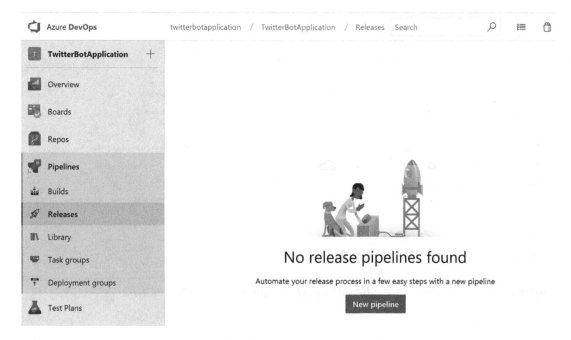

Figure 9-47. *Releases section of the Pipelines tab*

Click on New Pipeline. Select the Azure App Service Deployment template for Stage 1, as shown in Figure 9-48.

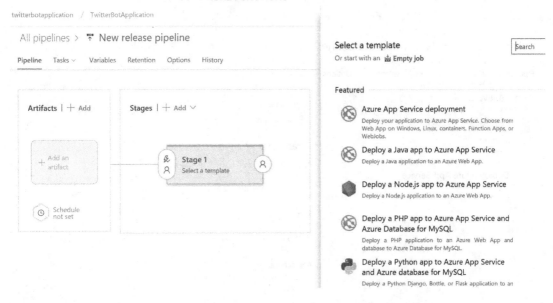

Figure 9-48.   *Selecting Azure App Service Deployment for Stage 1*

Provide `Twitter Bot Web` as the name for Stage 1, as shown in Figure 9-49.

Figure 9-49.   *Set Twitter Bot Web as the name for Stage 1*

Click on 1 job, 1 task to configure the `TwitterBotWeb` Azure web app settings. Under
the Twitter Bot Web Deployment process, select Visual Studio Ultimate with MSDN
Connection as the Azure Subscription, Web App on Windows as the App Type, and
TwitterBotWeb as the App Service name, as shown in Figure 9-50.

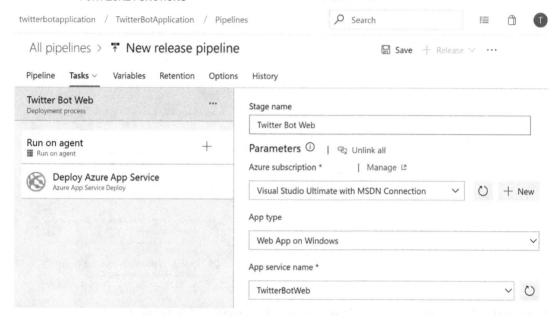

Figure 9-50. *Configure the Azure subscription and app service for the Twitter Bot web stage*

Select the Deploy Azure App Service task and change the package or folder to point to `TwitterBot.Web.zip`, as shown in Figure 9-51.

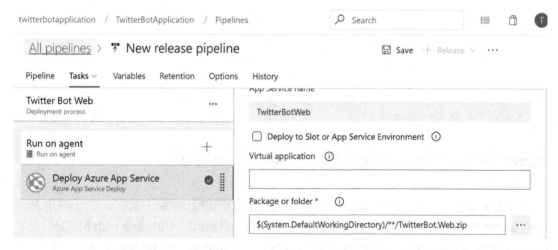

Figure 9-51. *Configure the package source for the Twitter Bot web stage*

Now create a new stage in the release pipeline using the Add option. Enter the name
`Twitter Bot Functions.` Select the pre-deployment conditions (trigger icon) of the
Twitter Bot functions stage, as shown in Figure 9-52. Select the After Release option to
execute the release process in parallel with the Twitter Bot web stage.

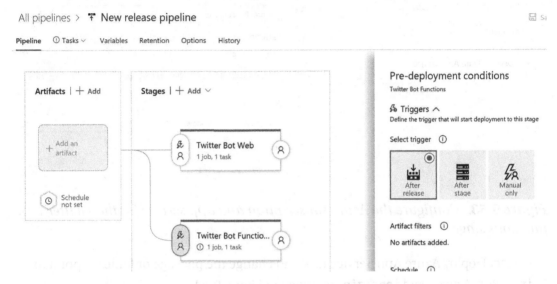

Figure 9-52. *Parallel execution of Twitter Bot web and functions stages*

Click on 1 job, 1 task to configure the TwitterAzureFunctions Azure function app
settings. For the Twitter Bot functions deployment process, select Visual Studio Ultimate
with MSDN Connection as the Azure Subscription, Function App on Windows as the
App Type, and TwitterAzureFunctions as the app service name, as shown in Figure 9-53.

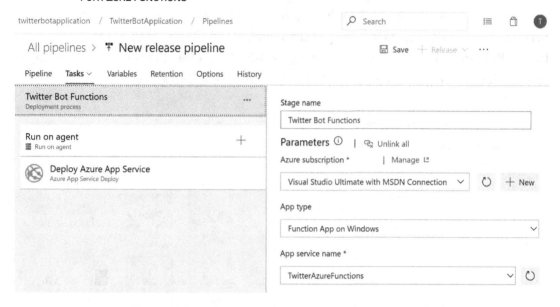

Figure 9-53. *Configure the Azure subscription and app service for the Twitter Bot functions stage*

Select Deploy Azure App Service task and change the package or folder to point to `TwitterBot.AzureFunctions.zip`, as shown in Figure 9-54.

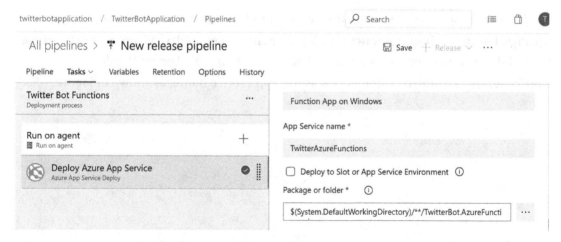

Figure 9-54. *Configure the package source for the Twitter Bot functions stage*

Now we will configure the artifacts. Click on Add an Artifact, as shown in Figure 9-55.

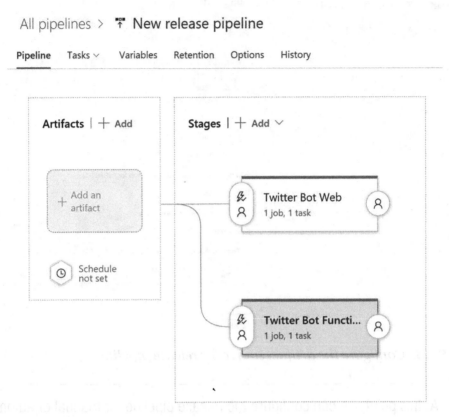

Figure 9-55. *Artifacts at release pipeline*

Select TwitterBotApplication-Azure Web App for ASP.NET-CI as the source (build pipeline), as shown in Figure 9-56. Click on Add.

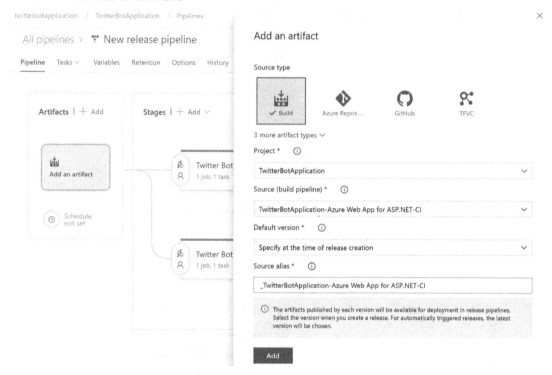

Figure 9-56. *Configure the artifact source for release pipeline*

Note   At this point, we can configure the release pipeline for manual or automatic deployments. Continuous Delivery encourages manual deployments to production workloads, whereas Continuous Deployment is used to automatically deploy builds to dev and test environments.

Configuring Continuous Deployment is an optional step for the Twitter Bot release pipeline.

To configure Continuous Deployment, click on the Triggers icon, as shown in Figure 9-57. Enable the Continuous Deployment trigger.

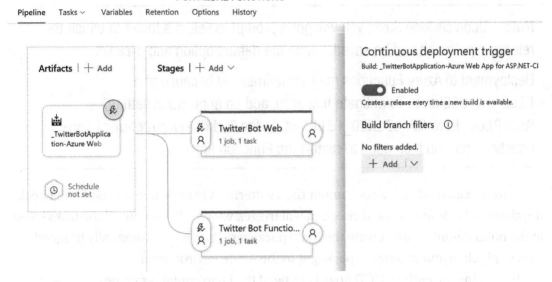

Figure 9-57. Configure the Continuous Deployment trigger

Finally, enter TwitterBotApplication-Azure-CD as the name of the release pipeline
and click on Save, as shown in Figure 9-58.

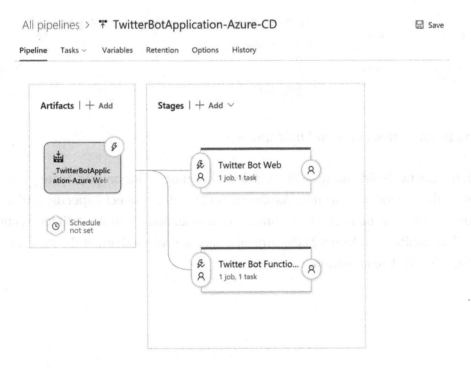

Figure 9-58. The Twitter Bot application release pipeline

Note   Upon clicking Save, you will get a prompt to select a folder to which the release pipeline should be saved. Leave the default option and click OK.

Deployment to Azure Functions may sometimes fail because of a `FILE_IN_USE` error. To mitigate this error, add an application setting, `MSDEPLOY_RENAME_LOCKED_FILES=1`, to the `TwitterAzureFunctions` Function app. You then need to restart the Function app.

Now we can modify the code under the TwitterBot Visual Studio solution and check the changes in. At first, a gated check-in will trigger, which will execute all the tasks listed in the build definition and create the build packages. Then we can manually trigger the release pipeline and deploy the packages to the Azure environment.

For testing the entire CI/CD flow, I changed the Logo container name (`_Layout.cshtml`) from `Twitter Bot` to `Twitter Bot App` of the `TwitterBot.Web` project and triggered a check-in. We can see that the build succeeded, as shown in Figure 9-59.

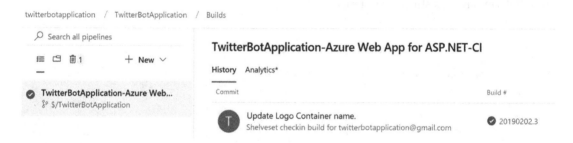

Figure 9-59. *Gated check-in build success*

To release the build output to the Azure environment, click on the Create a Release button under the Releases section. As shown in Figure 9-60, select a specific artifact version (which is the build number from the Builds section) from the Artifacts section that will be deployed to Azure. Make sure all stages are selected under the Pipeline section. Click the Create button.

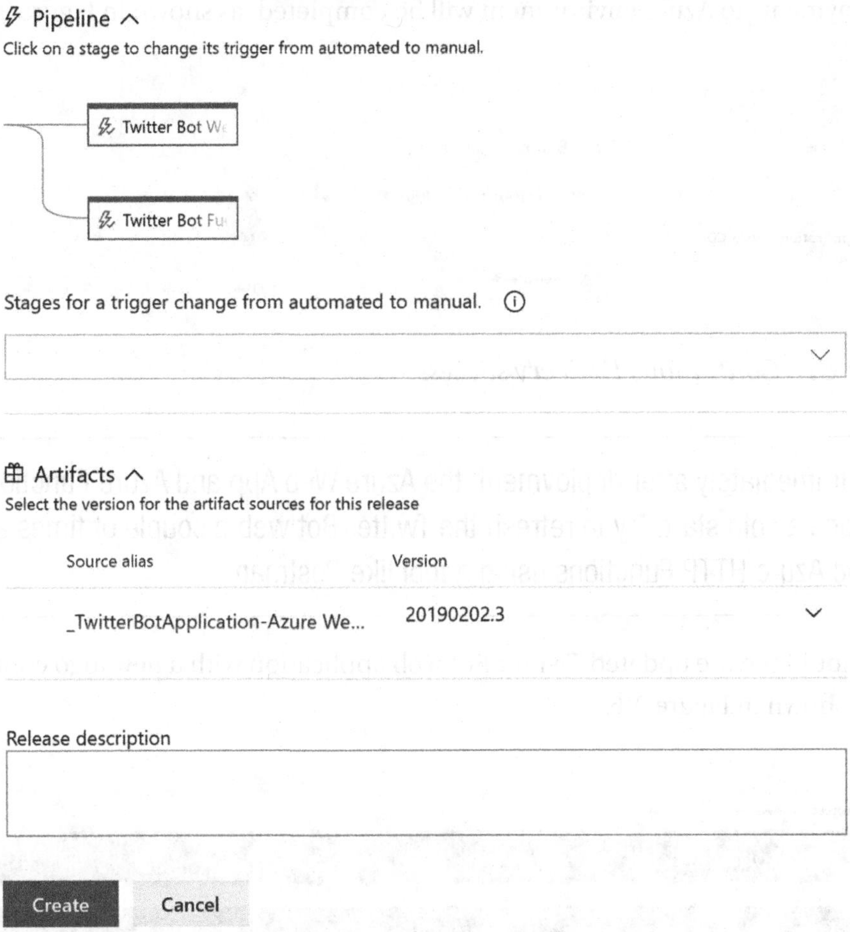

⚡ Pipeline ⌃

Click on a stage to change its trigger from automated to manual.

⚡ Twitter Bot W

⚡ Twitter Bot Fu

Stages for a trigger change from automated to manual.   ⓘ

⌄

🎁 Artifacts ⌃

Select the version for the artifact sources for this release

Source alias	Version
_TwitterBotApplication-Azure We...	20190202.3 ⌄

Release description

Create   Cancel

Figure 9-60. *Create a release for the Twitter Bot web application*

Deployments to Azure environment will be completed, as shown in Figure 9-61.

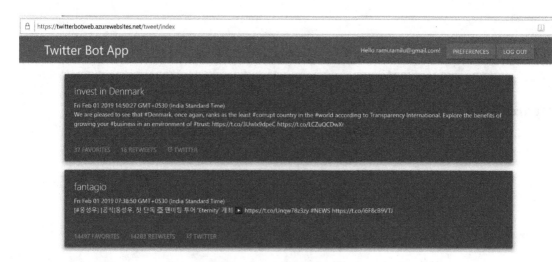

Figure 9-61. *Continuous Delivery success*

Note   Immediately after deployment, the Azure Web App and Azure Functions app might face a cold start. Try to refresh the Twitter Bot web a couple of times and try to hit the Azure HTTP Functions using a tool like Postman.

We should see the updated Twitter Bot web application with a new logo container name, as shown in Figure 9-62.

Figure 9-62. *Updated Twitter Bot web application*

Recommended Exercises

I propose the following exercises to extend the Twitter Bot application, which will give
you more technical exposure:

1. Simulate a large test data of users with hashtags and evaluate
   performance and load metrics of Azure Functions.

2. Implement hashtag subscriptions based on a language filter to
   deliver content in regional languages.

3. Create an alternative implementation of
   TweetSchedulerFunction, TweetBotFunction, and
   TweetNotifierFunction with durable Azure Functions concepts.

4. We learned in Chapter 8 that to get the ClaimsPrincipal
   populated with user's claims, we need to pass a master key or a
   default key in the code query string parameter on every Azure
   Function HTTP call. As part of this exercise, implement Azure
   Function proxies through which the query string can be hidden
   from external applications.

Summary

In this chapter, you learned the importance of version control systems in managing
source code and making software development more productive through effective
developer collaboration. The latest tools and platforms enable software organizations
to implement crucial DevOps strategies like Continuous Integration and Continuous
Delivery (CI/CD) in conjunction with robust version control systems. CI/CD not only
reduce build and deployment time, but also improve the overall system reliability by
ensuring high code quality and minimal manual effort by automating repetitive tasks.
Azure DevOps is a collection of services from Microsoft that provide developers with a
version control system to collaborate, develop, and effectively manage the end-to-end
DevOps cycle for software solutions.

You created unit test cases for Twitter Bot Azure Functions by using xUnit.Net,
a free, open source, community-based, unit-testing framework for the .NET Framework
and .NET Core-based solutions. The Moq framework is used to mock the function
dependencies. You executed the test cases using Visual Studio's Test Explorer.

You designed an Azure DevOps-based CI/CD pipeline for the Twitter Bot application. The CI/CD process triggers when a developer checks in the code to the Azure DevOps project, which will trigger a build to validate the source code for errors and execute the xUnit test cases. On a successful build, a deployment package will be created and stored in a staging directory. The release pipeline picks up the build artifacts and deploys the packages to Azure services.

As part of CI/CD implementation, you signed up for an Azure DevOps account and created the `TwitterBotApplication` project. You configured the project in Visual Studio through Team Explorer and checked in the TwitterBot solution source code. Later, you created a build definition in the `TwitterBotApplication` project with the default Azure Web App for ASP.NET template. You explored individual tasks of the build definition and configured build and unit tests tasks to align with the Twitter Bot application code. You enabled gated check-in at the build definition and tested it by triggering a manual build.

You proceeded to create an Azure Resource Manager service connection to establish a connection between the Azure DevOps account and Azure Subscription. Using the service connection, you created a release pipeline by configuring the Azure App Service Deployment template for web and function stages. Finally, the entire CI/CD pipeline is tested in integration with Azure Web and Function Apps.

The Final Word

The key mantra for the success of any business lies in providing the right solutions to the right problems with a customer-centric approach. The software industry is no exception. The exceptional pace of innovations in the software industry not only creates different business opportunities but also provides exceptional solutions to complicated technical challenges. Understanding and implementing the right technologies to deliver a business solution and building eminence around the latest technologies have been the most common problems faced by organizations in the recent past. This book builds eminence around some of the modern technologies by demonstrating an end-to-end application design through the latest serverless architecture paradigm.

Throughout the journey of this book, you have seen various technologies used for different purposes, which cater to the overall business workflow. The technical solution narrated in this book is one of the many ways to achieve the end business result.

The same result can be achieved with altogether different technologies, including open source and other cloud variants. The main intention behind this book is to introduce the concepts of serverless architecture through the Microsoft Azure cloud.

I sincerely thank the developers at Microsoft and the open source communities for providing great platforms and toolkits that are continuously used in this book. I hope you enjoyed the content and have learned something new and interesting. I hope to see you soon in another interesting venture.

Reference

1. `https://www.wintellect.com/devops-connect-vsts-azure/`

Index

429

© Rami Vemula 2019
R. Vemula, *Integrating Serverless Architecture*, https://doi.org/10.1007/978-1-4842-4489-0

U, V

W, X, Y, Z

Printed in the United States
By Bookmasters